Contents

CONSUMPTION, FOOD AND TASTE

Culinary Antinomies and Commodity Culture

Alan Warde

SAGE Publications
London • Thousand Oaks • New Delhi

This edition first published 1997

 SAGE Publications Ltd
6 Bonhill Street
London EC2A 4PU

SAGE Publications Inc.
2455 Teller Road
Thousand Oaks, California 91320

SAGE Publications India Pvt Ltd
32, M-Block Market
Greater Kailash – I
New Delhi 110 048

British Library Cataloguing in Publication data

A catalogue record for this book is available from the British Library.

ISBN 0 8039 7972–X
ISBN 0 8039 7973–8 (pbk)

Library of Congress catalog record available

Typeset by Mayhew Typesetting, Rhayader, Powys
Printed in Great Britain by Redwood Books, Trowbridge, Wiltshire

Acknowledgements

Much of the empirical data collection and analysis was conducted in 1991–2 at the University of Manchester, which awarded me a Hallsworth Fellowship for which I am extremely grateful. During that year I was fortunate to be associated with an inter-disciplinary group exploring food choice. This permitted interesting discussions with Mike Burton, David Morgan, Sue Scott, Mark Tomlinson and Trevor Young. I am particularly indebted to Mark, who was responsible for much of the computation and advice on the interpretation of data about household food expenditure.

That data, from the Family Expenditure Survey, was made available by the Department of Employment through the Economic and Social Research Council's Data Archive and has been used by permission of the Controller of HM Stationery Office. Neither the Department of Employment nor the ESRC Data Archive bears any responsibility for the analysis or interpretation of the data reported here.

Keith Soothill and Dan Shapiro gave advice and help in organizing household surveys in the North-West. I am also very grateful to the teachers, lecturers and students in schools and colleges who gave up their precious time to administer the questionnaires. Special thanks are due to Kevin Hetherington who worked on data preparation, analysis and presentation of the survey results.

I very gratefully acknowledge extensive help given in the coding of recipes and food advertisements by Hilary Arksey.

I would also like to thank numerous people who have shared with me their ideas on the sociologies of food and consumption and especially those who have read and commented on parts of the manuscript: Nick Abercrombie, Hilary Arksey, Jukka Gronow, Deborah Lupton, Celia Lury, Lydia Martens, Stephen Mennell, Mike Savage, Sue Scott, Dale Southerton and John Urry.

More generally I thank my colleagues in the Sociology Department at Lancaster for providing a congenial, stimulating and supportive environment for conducting sociological research. I am also grateful to Lancaster University which granted me study leave and a small grant to work on this project.

Alan Warde, Lancaster
June 1996

Abbreviations for Popular Magazines

FC   *Family Circle*
GH   *Good Housekeeping*
IH   *Ideal Home*
MW *My Weekly*
PF   *People's Friend*
WH *Woman and Home*
WO *Woman's Own*
WR *Woman's Realm*
WW *Woman's Weekly*

Introduction

This book arose from dismay about shifting fashions in sociology. A decade or more of analysis, founded in political economy and developing a materialist perspective on social life, seemed suddenly to be abandoned for a mode of studying culture which operated with wholly antithetical assumptions, according signs, discourses and mental constructs an exclusive role in understanding social activity. This shift entailed a radical change of substantive focus from the shop floor to the theme park, from labouring to shopping, from class to lifestyle, from resources to images, from practice to interpretation, from production to consumption. From this has emerged a large corpus of often interesting and suggestive work on consumption and consumer behaviour, a field previously dominated almost exclusively by practical concerns with marketing commodities. These shifts in intellectual focus were justified in different ways. Sometimes methodological and epistemological reasons were foremost. Sometimes political considerations were primary. On other occasions it was maintained that rapid social change required the reorientation of sociology: general material security, the declining importance of work, the fading of class divisions, final recognition of the impossibility of modernist social and political projects, and enhanced cultural complexity and differentiation were all cited. Doubts about the adequacy of this third set of, ultimately empirical, claims inspired the research reported in this book.

My ultimate theoretical concern is to reconcile the achievements of materialist and cultural analysis, which here takes the form of seeking to understand systematically the interrelationship between processes of economic production and patterns of consumption. Currently the main barrier to this endeavour is the inadequacy and inconsistency of accounts of consumption. Because it is a comparatively new area of investigation it is inevitably underdeveloped and remains in a condition where each discipline in the social sciences tends to operate with different premises and in the light of a limited and restrictive set of examples. There remains a shortage of systematic and focused analyses of consumption practices. Too often simplification results from using illustrations chosen arbitrarily to confer credibility on a preferred thesis. Also, there is a tendency to generate general theory from the study of the more glamorous aspects of a field of behaviour, particularly those most subject to fashion. Perhaps different impressions will arise from examination of a mundane field like food consumption which, while having highlights of display and symbolic distinction, is more characteristically a routine, practical and private matter.

The research reported in this study was structured around doubts about the adequacy and accuracy of theories of radical social transformation prominent in the late 1980s – especially postmodernism and post-Fordism. The first is primarily a theory about cultural trends, the other a thesis about industrial production. Both entailed that there was a turning point in economic and cultural production after the 1960s the consequences of which had become well established and entrenched by the end of the 1980s. An example might be David Harvey's analysis in *The Condition of Postmodernity* (1989), where he seeks to 'represent all the shifting and churning that has gone on since the first major post-war recession of 1973' as evidence of a turning point following which there was both an intensification of a postmodern structure of feeling and the replacement of a Fordist system of mass production by flexible accumulation. Concerned with such debates, the research was designed to explore change in the period identified as critical by such theories, thereby in some sense to 'test' them. The ambition to adjudicate rigorously and decisively between competing theories remains unfulfilled, but empirical examination of particular social practices provides much evidence to challenge current accounts of the transformation of the field of consumption.

The elaboration of these theories, for neither any longer constitutes a single unified position, generated a series of new claims about contemporary social and cultural processes relating to consumption. Particularly important was an idea of enhanced individual freedom, the notion that people are increasingly empowered, through their own choices exercised in the market-place, and by virtue of their personal tastes, to determine the form and direction of their own lives. This proposition was based on a number of ideas: that membership of a social group or category was less decisive in determining consumption decisions, as lifestyle became elective rather than prescriptive; that self-identity was increasingly bound up with lifestyle, itself ever more a function of consumer behaviour; that individuals now continuously monitor their own consumption behaviour with a view to estimating the impression that they present to others; that cultural preferences became increasingly important in the presentation of self in the context of a process described as the aestheticization of everyday life. Projections such as these have major implications not only for understanding social change but also for theoretical explanations of consumption itself. The identity-value conferred by commodities, the way they constitute the self and communicate it to others, replaces use or exchange value as the central mechanism driving consumption decisions. Personal taste and aesthetic judgment become critical assets in the project of self-development.

Ultimately I argue that such positions exaggerate the degree of change in consumer behaviour. While accepting that selection among the ever-expanding range of commodities is a complex and skilled task, I find it a less individualized process. Strategies for dealing with the diversity of goods include drawing upon deeply seated social dispositions and the advice of experts.

The book explores the expression of taste through consumption. I use food as a case study and seek to estimate the effects of social and cultural change on British food habits between 1968 and 1992. I collected and analysed data on what people are advised to do and on how they spend their money and their time.

The advice offered to people about what to eat comes from many sources which are, on the surface, incoherent. However, I argue that there is a systematic basis to these contradictory messages which can be found in what I describe as four 'antinomies of taste'. These oppositions – novelty and tradition, health and indulgence, economy and extravagance, care and convenience – are criteria for making legitimate choices between foodstuffs. They permeate the food and recipe columns in the mass media and provide guidance in the face of the diversity of alternatives. I interpret systematically the changes and continuities apparent in popular media representations of taste.

As regards practice, I examined food expenditure patterns and aspects of household organization for the provision of meals. The influence of social group is examined by analysing the food budgets of different types of individuals and households. Persistent and shared patterns of spending are taken as some indication of the power of the 'habitus', a set of deeply seated dispositions that act as practical and aesthetic criteria in the activities of consumption. I argue that contemporary consumption is best viewed as a process of continual selection from an unprecedented range of generally accessible items which are made available both commercially and informally. In response to the enormous variety of mass- and batch-produced commercial foodstuffs and food services for sale, consumers select an array of products which is in one sense, but only a trivial sense, personally unique. No two people will exhibit identical behaviour. However, and this is an empirical matter, there may remain considerable similarities between some individuals, and systematic differences between one group and another. This arises because consumers draw on many but shared sources of guidance in order to make their selections, including their own experience as children and adults, the recommendations and practices of networks of friends and kin, expert advice, official propaganda, and commercial advertisements. My conclusion is that tastes are still collectively shared to a very significant extent.

These themes are introduced through some general theories of change in the late 20th century which bear upon consumer behaviour. I outline those theories in Part I and show that they generate parallel applications in accounts of changing food behaviour. Part II reports in detail empirical evidence about food practice and representation and how this has changed since the late 1960s. This might be read as an extended critical footnote to the major sociological history of British food habits, Mennell's *All Manners of Food* (1985). Part III summarizes changes in both the representation and the purchase of food and argues that they can be understood structurally, their contradictory aspects reflecting the dilemmas of practical life in late modernity. From this are drawn the implications of the case study of food for theoretical accounts of changing patterns of consumption.

PART I

Issues of Taste

Part I contains three chapters. The first gives an overview of general competing theoretical explanations of the way that consumption is changing. The second shows that similar theoretical positions have generated contrasting accounts of changing food habits. The third chapter describes the empirical research carried out in order to estimate the origins and extent of change in British food habits between 1968 and 1992.

1

Consumption, Taste
and Social Change

1.1 Sociology and consumption

After decades of comparative neglect, there has been an explosion of interest in the topic of consumption. Some sociologists have made strong claims for the new structural role of consumption practice as a central focus of everyday life, a focus in earlier times provided by occupation. In such a view, *lifestyle* increasingly becomes a basis of *social identity*, displacing class as the central organizing principle of social life:

> The crucial effect of 'affluence' in post-war capitalism has surely been to justify the ideology and allow the practice of individualism and to link the acquisition and use of consumer goods to values which emphasize the importance of the search for personal identity and authenticity. (Moorhouse, 1983: 422)

Concomitantly, attention has shifted from seeking producer-centred explanations of social change to interpretive analysis of cultural meaning and communication. The portrayal of consumer culture, or the consumer society, as a world of signs and images challenges fundamentally previously dominant materialist approaches which concentrate on labour and production.

Most sociological accounts of consumption, until very recently, implicitly began from a set of materialist premises, considering consumption a matter of survival in the face of unequally distributed resources. The classical sociology of Marx, Weber and Simmel considered consumption a function of production, and consumption patterns a corollary of class position. Consumption was an expression of a central social hierarchy, inequalities of resource being turned into tools of class and status group struggle. Max Weber offered an understanding of the *nouveaux riches* and Thorstein Veblen dissected the social practices of the leisure class. In similar vein, at the opposite end of the social scale, the experience and culture of ordinary working people were deemed the effect of household class position, which exerted material constraint upon possessions, adequacy of diet, level of health, educational opportunities, and so forth.

Such theories revolve around unequal distribution of resources in both spheres of production and consumption. They isolate distinctive classes, with particular property or occupational bases, behaving or expressing themselves in particular ways through their consumption practices. Hierarchical inequalities, derived from a collective role in production, are reinforced in consumption and create a social identity for a producer group. Thus differential consumption practices were explained in terms of the location of social classes in the system of production.

It is widely accepted, and is a starting point of my analysis, that class used to be the dominant social division with respect to consumption. For example, there are many characterizations of British class cultures: consumption behaviour characterizes class position in Hobsbawm's (1978) description of British proletarian culture in the first half of the 20th century, in Cronin's (1984: 70–92) persuasive account of a homogeneous working-class culture in inter-war Britain, and in Martin's (1981) depiction of traditional respectable working-class life in northern cities in the 1950s. The aristocracy and the middle class in the 19th and for much of the 20th centuries had their own distinctiveness, with stereotypical routines, pastimes and tastes. But many argue this is no longer so, though exactly when the demise of class cultures began is much contested (compare Moorhouse, 1983; Bauman, 1983; Benson, 1994). The decline of class is in many respects an empirical question and I deal with it as an historical claim about the dominant trends in consumption.

While some analysts, like Bourdieu, continue to move within the ambit of the classical sociological accounts of distribution, display and class expression, class-based accounts of consumption have been increasingly criticized. Much contemporary social theory posits new social forces and a reorientation of personal motivations which underpin modern, or post-modern, culture. Consumption is very important to such accounts, 'consumer culture' being one prevalent term denoting the present condition. The next section examines the debate by contrasting the contributions of Bourdieu and Bauman. Section 3 examines the nature of some general social trends and counter-tendencies with implications for consumption which might suggest that the determinants of consumption practices have changed. Section 4 locates some competing theories of consumption in terms of these trends. Section 5 identifies some conceptual and methodological difficulties involved in evaluating alternative theories. Section 6 summarizes the position, i.e. what is at stake in current debates about the nature of contemporary consumption.

1.2 Consumption: from habitus to freedom

To the extent that class cultures were once homogeneous, then mechanisms of socialization were sufficient to explain consumption behaviour; the social group determined norms of consumption and the individual learned appropriate tastes and consumer behaviour occurred within the parameters of such cultures. The concept of habitus, popularized by Pierre Bourdieu, is often used to explain the mechanism.

Habitus and distinction

The most sophisticated exponent of the theoretical view that consumption behaviour is an *expression* of class position is Pierre Bourdieu (1984). Taste, knowledge and the desire for particular commodities are necessary elements in the process of class formation and class reproduction. Classes can be identified by their consumption patterns; and consumer behaviour can be explained in terms of the role of display and social judgment in the formation of class identities.

Bourdieu (1984) offers a complex and nuanced account of everyday practice. He is primarily concerned to map the differences between social groups in terms of their distinctive social practices and their capacities, reflexively, to appreciate those differences. Habitus links a person's social and economic position with corresponding position in 'the universe of lifestyles' and 'makes it possible to account both for classifiable practices and products and for the judgments, themselves classified, which make these practices and works into a system of distinctive signs' (1984: 170). This suggests that people's own practices, their capacity to appreciate and judge (i.e. classify) their own practices, and also to be able to do the same about others' practices, are indissolubly linked. Moreover, classifying and passing judgment are simultaneous. Such capacities for reflection and judgment are automatic and in many ways subconscious, and represent deeply embedded dispositions to thought and action.

'The habitus is necessity internalised and converted into a disposition that generates meaningful practices and meaning-giving perceptions; it is a general, transposable disposition' and hence can be applied to unknown and unanticipated situations. In other words, agents possess 'systems of generative schemes applicable, by simple transfer, to the most varied areas of practice' (ibid.).

Bourdieu argues that from these capacities emerge unified and distinctive lifestyles. 'That is why an agent's whole set of practices (or those of a whole set of agents produced by similar conditions) are both systematic . . . and systematically distinct from the practices constituting another life-style' (1984: 170). He continues:

> Systematicity . . . is found in all the properties – and property – with which individuals and groups surround themselves, houses, furniture, paintings, books, cars, spirits, cigarettes, perfume, clothes, and in the practices in which they manifest their distinction, sports, games, entertainments, only because it is the synthetic unity of the habitus, the unifying generative principle of all practices. Taste, the propensity and capacity to appropriate (materially or symbolically) a given class of classified, classifying objects or practices, is the generative formula of life-style, a unitary set of distinctive preferences which express the same expressive intention in the specific logic of each of the symbolic sub-spaces, furniture, clothing, language or body hexis. (1984: 173)

Thus Bourdieu is unequivocal about the coherence of lifestyles and the unity of the habitus, which he attributes primarily to different social classes.

Arguably, Bourdieu offers the most coherent set of propositions about taste and its social uses. He claims:

> Taste is the practical operator of the transmutation of things into distinct and distinctive signs, of continuous distributions into discontinuous oppositions; it raises the differences inscribed in the physical order of bodies to the symbolic order of significant distinctions. . . . Taste is thus the source of the system of distinctive features which cannot fail to be perceived as a systematic expression of a particular class of conditions of existence, i.e., as distinctive life-style, by anyone who possesses the practical knowledge of the relationships between distinctive signs and positions in the distributions. (ibid.: 174–5)

Thus, overall, Bourdieu maintains that consumption behaviour, broadly conceived, is a means whereby social classes display their 'cultural capital' and their place in a hierarchical system of social distinction. Consumption practices are generated by the habitus, a learned set of dispositions that underpin and generate social and cultural judgments in both familiar and novel social situations. Taste is deeply socially embedded in affective class cultures and is normatively highly regulated.[1]

Identity and freedom

In the world described by Bourdieu there could be only a minimal role for 'choice'. However, consumption, especially in its most glamorous and visible aspect, shopping, is increasingly conceptualized in terms of choice. Usually, it is assumed that the consumer makes real choices because no severe penalties can ever be invoked to ensure a particular mode of conduct. In the workplace, autonomy is limited by the threat of dismissal; one obeys laws for fear of sanctions; but when shopping, although subject to certain enforceable constraints (one cannot allow one's children to starve, nor can one freely lay down one's bed in a department store) there are few formal sanctions to require the purchase of particular items, engagement in particular leisure pursuits, or the eating of particular kinds of food. As Bauman (1988) says, most people are less restricted in the field of consumption than in any other part of their lives. Consumption appears to be a realm of freedom.

In this context, one of Bauman's remarkable insights was his stress on the individual responsibility incurred when faced with consumer choice. He was one of many social theorists to connect consumption with the predominance of a specific social psychology of the self, a self which is defined by the effort of creating and sustaining a 'self-identity'. The predicament, a problem of modernity and postmodernity, is the requirement that individuals construct their own selves. No longer are people placed in society by way of their lineage, caste or class, but each must invent and consciously create a personal identity. In this process, consumption is considered central, for commodities are principal channels for the communication of self-identity. People define themselves through the messages they transmit to others by the goods and practices they possess and display. Thus, whether they have personally exercised choice or not, they will be judged to have done so. Actors are deemed to have chosen their self-images and can thus be held to account for a wrong decision. As with all situations in which real decisions are made, there is the possibility of anxiety being provoked.

Although there can be no doubt that some people some of the time adopt consumption strategies that are primarily oriented towards presentation of self as distinctive individuals, there are many reasons for believing that the extent of such practices has been exaggerated. I have criticized this notion in some depth elsewhere because it suggests a too highly individualized sense of consumer decision-making: in general, consumer behaviour is more socially disciplined, less anxiety-provoking and less concerned with self-identity than implied by Bauman (see Warde, 1994b). There exists a set of social mechanisms that allay personal anxiety. Nevertheless in contemporary society the options available in the field of consumption are truly enormous and continue to expand. Among the reasons for this are the imperative for capitalist companies to design and deliver ever more differentiated goods and services, higher levels of real personal income for the majority of the population, and a wider knowledge, transmitted by global mass media, of alternatives. This magnifies the problem of selection, as people are compelled to make more choices from more possibilities. Moreover, to the extent that individuals become disembedded from the protective shield of a habitus, and to the extent that the objective of consumption has become expression of self-identity, then selection indeed becomes a risky, unregulated and uncertain exercise of freedom.

1.3 Social forces and the transformation of distinction

Estimating social constraints

The differences between the positions of Bourdieu and Bauman are in part the result of the way they have estimated the strength of certain social forces operating in the contemporary world. For Bourdieu there remain powerful group regulatory and normative constraints on the behaviour of individuals. Bauman, by contrast, believes that these have seriously attenuated as people become more detached from social collectivities and less subject to authoritative regulation of their social standards and judgments. Their disagreement appears to revolve around their estimations of current levels of social attachment and moral regulation.

Figure 1.1 illustrates the issue in terms derived from Durkheim's *Suicide*, first published in 1895, which remains the classic sociological exploration of the connection between individual acts and social regulation. To commit suicide, Durkheim reasoned, is the ultimate individual act, a personal exercise of will that demonstrates control over one's own destiny. It might be deemed the extreme and limiting example of pure personal choice. Yet Durkheim shows that the incidence of suicide is patterned in such a way as

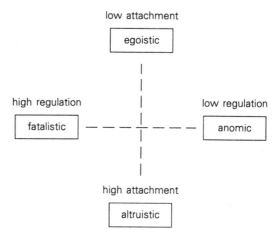

Figure 1.1   *Types of suicide (based on Durkheim, 1970)*

to suggest that isolable social forces underpin the propensity to suicide. It is less personal a decision than might be imagined; social circumstances as well as individual inclinations determine its incidence. So, Bourdieu might assert, it remains with consumption.

Durkheim's analysis of different types of suicide can, ironically, be redeployed to describe putative trends in consumption. He distinguished four kinds of suicide: egoistic, anomic, altruistic and fatalistic. According to Lukes (1975: 286), 'Egoism and its opposite altruism pick out that which ties an individual to socially given ideals and purposes; anomie (and its curiously shadowy opposite, fatalism) pick out that which holds an individual's desires in check, regulating and moderating them.' These constitute two dimensions, of embeddedness in group life and of regulation. Egoistic suicide was characterized by excessive individualism, 'a lack of "object and meaning" in "genuinely collective activity"' (Lukes, 1975: 207), implying a decline in social attachments, especially to religious institutions or marriage. Its opposite, altruism, entailed a lack of a sense of an autonomous self because of the extent to which the sense of self was invested in the group. Anomic suicide was precipitated by the condition of lack of regulation, the absence of 'a spirit of discipline', something that was overdeveloped in the fatalistic form. It is possible to analyse consumption decisions in a similar manner. If we reformulate Durkheim's account of the social pathology of suicide in terms of a set of social forces that affect the nature of social relations in western societies, we will see that similar forces still pertain.

The play of social forces

Proponents of the thesis of the declining importance of social class, though not agreed on the consequences of its dissolution for consumption, often isolate as vital two trends – individualization and informalization – which tend to reduce the social embeddedness and normative regulation that characterized class cultures.

Many authors would maintain that pressures towards uniformity of consumption within large groups of the population, and especially classes, have reduced recently, as part of the process of individualization (e.g. Beck, 1992; Giddens, 1991; Bauman, 1988). It is agreed that in the 1990s individuals integrate themselves into society by their own efforts at self-construction, creating a self-identity, a process wherein consumption is of great importance because appearance becomes the measure of a person's worth. Hence anxiety about the effectiveness of the exercise of the freedom to choose a self: 'the risk of the chosen and changed personal identity' (Beck, 1992: 136) cannot be avoided. In such an account, personal expression, whether in clothing, durable goods, leisure activities or aesthetic preference, becomes detached from affective communal norms and ideals, thus becoming socially disembedded.

Others authors suggest that there has also been a decline in 'the spirit of discipline' in the sphere of consumption (e.g. Bell, 1976; Martin, 1981; Lasch, 1978). This might be described as a process of informalization (see Wouters, 1986), wherein rigid, conformist, established and routinized patterns of consumption dissolve. Free rein is thus given to personal preference as moral, aesthetic and social standards are relaxed, so behaviour becomes irregular. Often attributed to the cultural revolution of the 1960s, informalization is discerned in dress, manners and social disciplines surrounding eating. Anomie, an absence of normative orientation, may result as strict rules governing appropriate consumer behaviour and ways of presenting self become less binding.

Though individualization and informalization are usually considered as dominant trends, there are, without doubt, counter-tendencies. Some authors claim that people bereft of social attachments create imagined communities, seeking to compensate for the lack of a sense of belonging associated with the excessive individualism of the modern condition. These imagined communities come in many guises. Sometimes the community is the nation or ethnic group whose integrity is proclaimed in nationalist ideologies (see Anderson, 1983). Sometimes belonging is sought through the nostalgic invention of traditions which give people a sense of their historical roots (e.g. Hobsbawm & Ranger, 1983). Regional and local identities have perhaps become more pronounced as part of the 'global–local dialectic' consequent upon the internationalization of production and communication (e.g. Savage, 1989). The search is for some natural rootedness or belonging, associated with the sense of sharing with people in similar circumstances a set of common standards and aspirations. This quest for social re-embedding might be called, for convenience of reference, 'communification'.

A fourth tendency, which might be called stylization, reintroduces a kind of discipline or regulation over self-presentation through consumer practice.

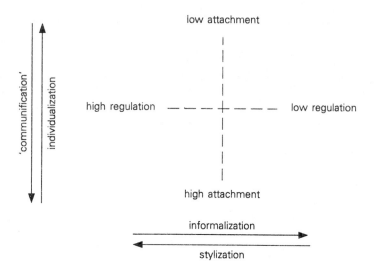

Figure 1.2 *Social forces*

Thus, for instance, some youth subcultures are highly conscious of style, and membership or sympathy is largely recognized through shared attire and aesthetic judgments (about music, etc.). Some, though not all, definitions of lifestyle identify precisely that – voluntary, aesthetically derived, style groups based on shared taste. New groups with disciplined purchasing habits are emerging, smaller than classes, generations or churches, but nevertheless observing highly regulated patterns of appropriate consumption.

Figure 1.2 expresses graphically the four trends: individualization, informalization, communification and stylization. All operate on consumption practices. The first two are inherently corrosive of group, or class, alignments; the others could in principle further deepen divisions between groups.

1.4 Explanations of changing consumption

One way of categorizing contemporary accounts of changing consumption patterns is to map, on the same axes, the trajectory proposed by different theories accounting for the transformation or dissolution of the class structuring of consumption. These are to some degree artificially constructed by me for the purposes of exposition. However, they roughly represent the competing theoretical positions of authors who have described significant changes in consumption patterns occurring since the 1960s. I assume that the point of intersection of the two axes represents a condition in which class was primarily responsible for most visible differences in patterns of consumption.

Individual diversity and personal identity

One view (trajectory A) would be that there is simply much greater diversity in consumer behaviour, that rules have been relaxed and individual preferences released from the constraints of social group approval. This is the position, almost unqualified, advanced by Beck in *Risk Society* (1992). For Beck, contemporary social change is characterized by individualization and deregulation. Part II of his book is mostly a statement about an outbreak of excessive individualism as attachments to class and status groups, and to marriage, atrophy. The cause of this is, almost entirely, the extension of market relations, which wrench social bonds asunder. There is a likeness to Durkheim's diagnosis of modern social bonds, though Beck assumes that it was class cultures, rather than attachments to society as a whole, that previously restricted excessive individualism. While Beck notes that risk provokes anxiety, his analysis and prognosis is largely optimistic. More pessimistic observers of the same processes might interpret them as pathological bases of anomie and egoism, of personal uncertainty and insecurity.

Identity has been a recent watchword of cultural analysis, and an individualist interpretation of postmodern culture might see recent historical change in the same way as Beck. The vision of the heroic consumer, as captured by Featherstone (1987), and pronounced the model of contemporary consumption, is also an instance of trajectory A. In the context of a calculating hedonism developing during the 20th century, Featherstone describes how individuals engage in a conscious project of autonomous, reflexive self-creation:

> Rather than unreflexively adopting a lifestyle, through tradition or habit, the new heroes of consumer culture make lifestyle a life project and display their individuality and sense of style in the particularity of the assemblage of goods, clothes, practices, experiences, appearance and bodily dispositions they design together into a lifestyle. The modern individual within consumer culture is made conscious that he speaks not only with his clothes, but with his home, furnishings, decoration, car and other activities which are to be read and classified in terms of the presence and absence of taste. The preoccupation with customising a lifestyle and a stylistic self-consciousness are not just to be found among the young and the affluent; consumer culture publicity suggests that we all have room for self-improvement and self-expression whatever our age or class origins. (Featherstone, 1987: 59)

The idea that consumer choice engenders uncertainty is easily derived from such a prognosis. Lacking social attachments that require shared appearance and accoutrements to demonstrate solidarity, and lacking any set of authoritative rules that might indicate appropriate ways of regulating wayward (that is, neither ethically nor aesthetically controlled) appetites, consumers are thrown back on their own, possibly idiosyncratic, judgment about what to buy.

Market segmentation and niche consumption

A second position (trajectory B), suggests that there is a growing differentiation of distinctive lifestyles as the era of mass consumption passes away. Disembedding from traditional social networks and groups (especially classes) occurs as individual choices become more effective and are deployed in search of new identifications. But the consequence is not patternless individuation, but rather new, more intricate and more specialized, small group formations.

One version of this is seen as leading to the proliferation of 'neo-tribes', elective groupings, exhibiting high levels of temporary commitment, whose boundaries are identifiable through the shared lifestyles of members (see Maffesoli, 1988; Bauman, 1990; Hetherington, 1992). Bauman (1983) proclaimed the demise of class culture somewhat earlier than Beck. His subsequent analyses of consumer competition and the postmodern condition (1988, 1991) accept from the start that there are no standards, no foundational bases for consensual, disciplined behaviour. There can be no universally binding moral code. The trend is one of sharply declining attachments, though without that necessarily entailing the total collapse of regulation. In various places he notes the emergence of elective attachments in the contemporary period: that is what the 'neo-tribe' represents, a small grouping to which people are intensely, if temporarily, attached by means of shared self-images (Bauman, 1990: 206–13, 1991: 248–50). In this way, Bauman recognizes the importance in social life of shared group identification, without which most people become distressed, because social approval is required to verify any given or assumed identity. The solution is the temporary attachment. Impermanence is symbiotic with its voluntariness: a preferred stylized group identity is chosen, but it can just as easily be discarded. So, lifestyle groups proliferate, visible through their differences, but not grounded in a social or material substratum.

A similar description of consumer behaviour is advanced on the basis of analysis of post-Fordist trends in economic production (see Aglietta, 1979; Harvey, 1989). The emergence of flexible production, which has ended the Fordist regime of accumulation, has been described and explained in a number of ways. In each account new patterns of consumption are represented as constituting new kinds of demand. The consumption patterns are sometimes described in the language of postmodern culture (e.g. Harvey, 1989), on other occasions in terms of market segmentation and niche consumption (e.g. Piore & Sabel, 1984). It is implied that tastes are becoming more determinate, more specialized and more discriminating. Unfortunately, most post-Fordism theses tend simply to deduce consumer behaviour from evidence about the greater variety of products that firms are capable of producing (see further Warde, 1994a). The possible logical error involved is obvious: consumers' behaviour should not be construed as simply a response to the needs of new production techniques, without recourse to evidence about what consumers do. Nevertheless, there is here a prediction about the proliferation of tasteful, symbolically recognizable, subcultural, consumption-based styles of life.

Massification

Much current speculation about consumption has been inspired by the attempt of cultural studies to rescue 'popular' culture from the condescension of those who described it as 'mass' culture, thereby denoting it a debased alternative to what was truly valuable, 'high' culture. There is, of course, longstanding debate about the existence and nature of mass culture and for writers like Adorno it was precisely mass consumption, of objects and of media messages, that eroded good taste and the capacity for critical judgment.[2] The mass culture thesis suggests that the culture industries increasingly feed anodyne cultural products to consumers who, receiving them in private, passively accept them. Mass media, because seeking to appeal to the largest possible audiences, tend to offer unadventurous and unimaginative entertainment. A dominant, mass culture, is generated, reflecting and refuelling the instrumental rationality of capitalist production and accumulation. Aesthetic values and discriminating taste atrophy. Uniformity and apathy characterize the sphere of consumption. Hence a third trajectory (C) is proposed: that the passing of class differentiation leads to much greater uniformity of consumption behaviour.

It is not difficult to find evidence consistent with Adorno's diagnosis of cultural trends. Differences of class, gender and nationality fade before the ubiquitous presence of McDonald's burgers and Coca-Cola, symbols of the extension of common taste across continental boundaries. Multinational corporations exist to produce often identical items, in the largest possible volume: food, cars, clothes and many other items are mass produced for sale in many different countries. Mass consumption, on a national or even international scale, has a uniformity resulting from economic rationalization and the globalization of media messages and corporate advertising. Ritzer (1993) nominates 'the McDonaldization of society' as the master process of the current epoch, countering illusions that the aspiration to individualized expression has finally triumphed in the world of commodities. In this view, class, lifestyle and personal variations are merely minor themes in a mass culture where established common popular cultural tastes predominate.

The retrenchment of social division

A final scenario, trajectory D, is that class, or some other structural social differentiating principle like ethnicity or nation, is becoming more intense. Earlier periods in history witnessed exclusive consumption practices, where privileged classes or estates marked their status very visibly. Few contest the persistence of vestiges of such stratification. In contemporary Britain, a widening of income differentials and a shift away from state services to marketed substitutes provides material circumstances for greater class

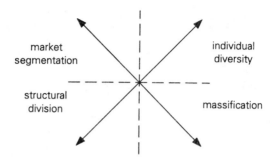

Figure 1.3   *Explanations of changing consumption*

inequality. Arguably, there was comparatively limited cultural expression of class differences in post-war Britain, and perhaps less than in the France of the 1970s as described by Bourdieu (1984). Yet it requires little imagination to envisage a system of distinction in the UK just as rigid and exclusive as the French.

Although intensification of class differences is a logical possibility, scarcely anyone has claimed it as a significant trend in the last fifty years. However, there are solid grounds for maintaining that class divisions are no less severe now than earlier in the 20th century. Goldthorpe and Marshall (1992) have provided a persuasive statement of the view that in key areas like social mobility, educational opportunity and voting behaviour the influence of class remains basically constant. The same may be true of consumption, for while the items consumed may change following product innovation, the basic processes of establishing class distinctions and maintaining class distances might remain the same.

It may also be that differences between other types of social groups have increased. The re-creation of national, regional, ethnic and local identities may have some impact if consumption is used to mark distinctive group belonging. Changes in gender relations, to the extent that they give women greater economic and social independence, could increase sex differences in consumption. Also, and perhaps most likely, generations, or categories of people at different stages of the life course, may develop distinguishing collective practices. More likely than any of these is the null hypothesis, that the cultural differentiation of social groups remains basically unchanged. Such a conclusion would, of course, pose a serious objection to theories of change.

1.5   The complexity of consumption

Assessing the adequacy and accuracy of these theoretical positions and their accounts of recent trends is very difficult. Although a considerable amount of casual empirical evidence has been marshalled in support of each, no systematic empirical evaluation has been attempted as yet. Before this is possible some conceptual and methodological issues require attention.

The concept of consumption

Problems arise initially with the definition of consumption. Consumption is a complex field, covering a multitude of activities and a range of goods and services, many of which are provided in non-commodified forms. Neo-classical economics, and many analyses concerned with the symbolic aspects of consumption, focus on personal, private purchases in the market-place. However, under any generic definition of the purposes or functions of consumption there are several other sources of products that might be consumed. The role of the state in providing so-called 'collective consumption' services has been examined by urban sociologists (e.g. Pinch, 1986). Equally, much domestic work is directed to providing consumption services, as too are neighbourhood and kinship networks. Identifying different modes of provision of services contributing to consumption raises the question of how these articulate and how they develop over time. The analysis of the history of consumption can no longer be encapsulated in the question 'who buys what?', but must become one of 'who obtains what services (or goods), under what conditions are those services delivered and to what use are they put?' The rhythms of provision are complex, varying, for example, by country, region, class, gender and generation. Looked at in this way the history of consumption is a complicated one, influenced not just by what goods are retailed and at what price, but also by household arrangements, government policy, community organization and industrial conflict.

It might be argued that consumption is not a coherent conceptual field because the activities and items involved are heterogeneous. What can be said about fashion clothing may not apply to food; an enthusiasm for popular music may not have the same social logic or meaning as pigeon-fancying; state-provided services have a distinctive ethos and rules of access. It is possible that class differences in one field of consumption are declining while in another they are increasing. Equally possibly, there may be some highly visible examples of emergent neo-tribalism while the behaviour of the majority of the population tends towards greater uniformity. To decide between general theories applying to all spheres of consumption is, if not impossible, practically unachievable at present. Hence, an approach through case studies of different fields recommends itself, though even this is difficult since areas of study like food are themselves enormously complex and heterogeneous.

Trends and lifestyles

A further conceptual issue concerns the adequacy of the concept of lifestyle. Bourdieu defined taste by identifying unitary lifestyles grounded in

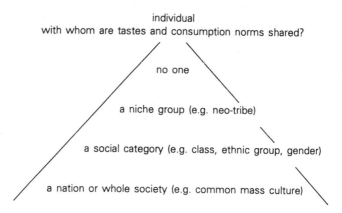

Figure 1.4   *Shared tastes*

competition between social classes. Two questions arise: are tastes still shared by socio-demographically distinguishable groups and are patterns of consumption as coherent as he presumes?

There are many competing ideas about the extent of shared taste. These can be represented by Figure 1.4. Possibilities range from there being no common taste whatever, each individual exhibiting unique behaviour, to there being a global uniformity of taste. At one end consumption is conceived as socially unconstrained, as people choose a lifestyle regardless of biography or social position. At the other extreme the flood of global culture incorporates all those it washes over. Determining the answer depends importantly on how the criteria of similarity and difference are applied; how homogeneous must a group be to justify being described as sharing consumption norms and what degree of internal differences between members of such a group will be accepted.

The second question is whether even individuals exhibit behaviour sufficiently coherent to permit the identification of style. One account suggests that nowadays it is not incumbent on people to adopt a coherent style of life. Styles, indeed, are often very fluid, people changing from one situation to the next. Featherstone points out that postmodernist culture to an important degree is *dis*orderly:

> The tendency within consumer culture is to present lifestyles as no longer requiring inner coherence. The new cultural intermediaries, an expanding faction of the new middle class, therefore, while well disposed to the lifestyle of artistic and cultural specialists, do not seek to promote a single lifestyle, but rather to cater for and expand the range of styles and lifestyles available to audiences and consumers. (1990: 18)

Indeed, Featherstone suggests, people are even encouraged to have more than one style persona.

Both questions raise formidable problems of measurement. Most obviously, if the patterning of consumption on the basis of class diminishes and no alternative socio-demographic indicators replace it, should the resulting patternlessness be interpreted as individualization or as uniformity? If the former, will lifestyle enclaves be sufficiently large to permit their detection as statistical regularities, which might indicate niche consumption rather than personal, idiosyncratic and arbitrary behaviour? Moreover, and germane to evaluation of most postmodernist arguments, can one distinguish between lifestyles whose organizing principle is incoherence, where meaninglessness is itself meaningful, and the absence of anything worth calling lifestyle? Thus, methodologically, it is difficult to establish which, if any, of the theoretically anticipated trends are occurring because the same evidence can be cited in support of more than one position.[3]

1.6 Conclusion

Theories of consumption vary in their explanations of the basic mechanisms involved in decision-making and in their historical projections. While many maintain that there has been a radical transformation in the nature of consumption, and that this occurred some time between 1970 and 1990, they are not agreed on the direction of the changes or the most likely outcome. Some of the most influential accounts emphasize the erosion of group constraints, of social embeddedness or normative regulation, and pronounce the effect individualization. Yet even they do not exhibit consensus. For some, like Giddens, individualization manifests itself as calculating, instrumental self-direction. For others, like Featherstone, it is a more expressive process, as people develop greater aesthetic sensibilities which they exercise through their consumption behaviour. For yet others, like Beck, the process is more one of progressive personal uncertainty, as the relaxation of norms and rules casts people into a sphere of anomic indifference.

Yet it is far from certain that counter-trends and counter-tendencies, ones which reproduce group commitments, and perhaps establish new forms of collective judgment, have been vanquished. One purpose of the case study of food is precisely to estimate the comparative strength of processes that lead to stylization and the demarcation and maintenance of social group boundaries through consumption. I will return to this in Chapter 9 where I argue that the role of commodity consumption in the formation of self-identity has been exaggerated, that such misinterpretation obscures the significance of further commodification, and that normative regulation and social embeddedness retain a tenacious grip on consumption behaviour. Meanwhile, in the next chapter I demonstrate that the trends and projections advanced by general social theories of consumption have parallels in accounts of the field of food and eating.

2
The New Manners of Food: Trends and their Sociological Interpretation

2.1 The sociology of food

For a sociology of consumption, food is a most instructive critical case study. Food, its preparation and consumption, is intricately connected to many other central processes of social life. The food system comprises an enormous industry: Goodman and Redclift (1991: 27) estimated that about 2.8 million people were employed in food production and distribution and catering industries in the UK in 1987. Food preparation also absorbs huge amounts of time: shopping, planning, storing, cooking, serving and clearing up are the regular activities necessary to sustain the habit of almost everyone eating several times a day. Much of that household labour is performed by women, at shops and in kitchens, though men fill some of the most prestigious roles in the formal economy. Food is also a significant means of cultural expression and is often used as a general means of commentary on contemporary culture. Though partly an aspect of bodily reproduction, culinary practice is also associated with lifestyles and, one supposes, is the ultimate metaphorical source of the concept of taste. In addition, food is a matter of considerable psychological and emotional significance – as a whole range of phenomena, from the meaning of Mother's cooking to illnesses like anorexia nervosa, indicate.

Because of this polyvalent significance, food practices can easily be used as a laboratory for the understanding of social relations. For instance, in one short essay, Furst (1988) describes ways in which food generates and reinforces gender divisions in the household, how food preferences are generation related, the symbolic and ritual significance to the preparation of 'traditional' meals at the weekend if quickly prepared supermarket food is used during the week, how different cultures preserve a sense of identity through their food practices (like eating rotting trout in Norway, for instance), how meals structure daily time, and also how they express emotion and caring. Yet the sociological literature on the production and consumption of food in the UK is minimal. Most of the work reported in a recent literature review, *The Sociology of Food* (Mennell et al., 1992), derives from anthropological and historical inquiries. This neglect of a vital set of social practices is surprising since, as the authors show, a satisfactory explanation of food preferences entails addressing issues of taste, status, class, gender identities, domestic power relations, tradition, migration, the civilizing process, new technologies, and commercial exploitation. These are areas of distinctive sociological insight which might usefully be applied in order to further illuminate food behaviour.

My principal concern is with recent change, especially as illustrated in the UK experience. Because of the many functions and aspects of food practices, analysing change is a complex matter. Both persistence and alteration in food behaviour can easily be exaggerated, so there is considerable controversy over the direction of change in the present period.

At the outset, consider some of the trends that readily come to mind when reflecting on present day experiences of shopping and eating. Enormous numbers of new products are constantly made available by food manufacturers, some of which fail, but others sell. Fresh produce from around the world is routinely available, the seasons and geographical distance apparently overcome by an increasingly concentrated retail sector. The proportion of income spent on food and on different kinds of foodstuffs continues to fall, as predicted by Engel's Law, from 33 per cent in 1958 to 18 per cent in 1992 (Family Expenditure Survey). The component parts of the average diet are changing, driven partly by more prominent concern with health and nutrition, a process promoted by government and documented in attitude surveys, but resisted in part by manufacturers and consumers. Domestic routines are altering: cooked breakfasts and midday meals at home are in decline, and domestic kitchens display a greater variety of equipment. The market has expanded for the commercial delivery of meals and snacks, at fast-food restaurants, in public houses, through home deliveries of take-away food, as indeed it has for complete, pre-prepared, chilled or frozen packages purchased from the supermarket and reheated at home. There is burgeoning publicity for food and cooking, with new magazine titles, television programmes, sales of recipe books, eating-out columns in local and national newspapers. The character of food production and delivery is changing, subject to similar pressures for industrial restructuring that affect other major industrial sectors. Competition generates more advertising and promotion. Meanwhile signs of popular resistance are apparent as movements for protection of the environment, animal rights and vegetarianism become prominent. Food scares, eating disorders and obsession with body shape equally suggest enhanced concern, and often anxiety, about food. All these processes are widely acknowledged, recognized and discussed. Together they constitute *prima facie* evidence of rapid and fundamental change.

However, sociological analysis needs to be sceptical of common sense. Some of these shifts may not be as extensive as they at first appear. Also, there are counter-trends. More importantly, though, we might distinguish another level of analysis. The question arises of whether these are better considered surface phenomena: it is certainly possible that the items people include in their diets alter completely, while social differences, the meaning of eating and the role of food in everyday life remain constant. An analogy with fashion might be pertinent: styles alter, but neither the logic of the fashion industry nor the rationales of the consumers change. For example, and more concretely, the widespread availability of many exotic or convenience foods in the 1990s does not entail that social class differences in their consumption have declined: neither need reduction in time devoted to meal preparation signify a lesser demonstration of care; nor need eating events, even if less regular and predictable, cease to structure daily time paths. Sociology is at least as interested in this second level of analysis which questions the social significance of changes at the surface and tries to infer whether less directly observable persistences continue to be structurally important.

Much of this book attempts to evaluate interpretations of change in practices relating to the consumption of food and a summary of my views is presented in Chapter 8. However, evaluation is almost impossible in such a complex field without some synthetic framework or overarching characterization of trends. So, against the backcloth of claim and counter-claim, I outline some competing interpretations of the developments in food behaviour over the last three decades. In the next section I examine Mennell's influential schematic notion of 'diminishing contrasts and increasing variety'. Finding it indeterminate, I then survey four, more precise but mutually incompatible, accounts of current trends. Their central theses parallel the four general explanations of changes in consumption that were isolated in Chapter 1. Each contributes something to an explanation of food choice, the endless series of micro-decisions about ingestion which are not compulsory, but are evidence of tastes formed in socially structured contexts and expressed through consumption.

2.2 Diminishing contrasts and increasing variation: Mennell's projection

All Manners of Food

Mennell's magnificent study, *All Manners of Food* (1985), explores changing habits and cuisine over several centuries in France and Britain. An examination of cookery books, diet, menus, accounts of banquets and assorted literary sources, it is the starting point for a historical and institutional approach to British food consumption patterns. Mennell is influenced by Norbert Elias and much of the book might be seen as demonstrating the applicability of his thesis about 'civilizing processes' to eating (Elias, 1978; 1982). From the Middle Ages to the present, Mennell discerns many changes including the emergence of bodily discipline, the rise and fall of class differentiation in diet, and the commercialization and internationalization of food production and distribution.

Since his is a study of long-term shifts it is a little unfair to challenge in detail Mennell's explanation of contemporary trends. However, I will argue that the bold and influential thesis about change in the 20th century, developed in the concluding chapter, is intriguing but indeterminate.

Mennell begins by critically evaluating versions of mass society theory in order to advance an alternative pluralist thesis. He endorses the Frankfurt School's rejection of a liberal notion, held by some American sociologists, of mass society, 'that contemporary mass culture is a response through the market to what people want' (1985: 320). Mennell accepts, after Adorno, that the possibility now exists for standardization of diet, for people can now eat perpetually the few items that they have come to like, because these are readily available all the year round. Indeed, this is a feature of what is described as unadventurous or 'fussy' eating among children. Moreover, mass production did eliminate many products: Mennell notes that in the mid-1950s there were only about six types of English cheese available because the mass manufacturers eliminated farmhouse cheeses. That trend has, however, since reversed. He also acknowledges the unplanned vicious spiral resulting from corporate competition, which leads to the use of, for instance, dubious chemicals in agriculture and manufactured foods. But he denies that this amounts to the manipulation of consumers and rejects the idea that the concentrated power of food industries has any monolithic effects. So while acknowledging the relevance of the Frankfurt School to understanding recent change, he maintains that we should eschew mass society accounts. Overall the industries have led to 'the opportunity for more *varied* experience in eating and to develop *more* varied tastes' (1985: 321). In western countries

> more varied cookery as well as more plentiful food is more widely available than ever before. If commercial interests make people's tastes more standardised than they conceivably could be in the past, they impose far less strict limits than did the physical constraints to which most people's diet was subject for most of the period. (1985: 321–2)

Thus he concludes that

> 'underneath the many swirling cross-currents, the main trend has been towards *diminishing contrasts* and *increasing varieties* in food habits and culinary taste. One trend, not two: in spite of the apparent contradiction between diminishing contrasts and increasing varieties, these are both facets of the same processes. (1985: 322)

Mennell identifies many ways in which contrasts have diminished. Social inequalities in the quantities of food consumed have declined, as a greater sensitivity towards inequality in nourishment developed during the 20th century. Appetite has been civilized: more secure food supplies and a concern with self-control over the body, for example weight-watching, have produced more regular habits for all. Differences between the seasons and between festive and everyday eating have diminished. So too have those between town and country. Importantly, manufactured foods have become part of the diet of every social class. Also, whereas the emergence of *haute cuisine* increased differences when compared to the common culture of early modern Europe, its recent decline, which is also associated with 'the common participation of all social ranks in modern mass catering, convenience and fast foods, can be seen as restoring only in the very recent past some semblance of the medieval culinary unity' (1985: 324). Mennell further sees a decline in ostentation and superfluity in cooking and eating, part of the 'democratization' and simplification of eating. An example is the disappearance of regular ten-course dinners for the middle classes at the end of the 19th century. Distance between professional and domestic cookery has also reduced, a function of cookery books and guides as well as improved domestic technologies. Mennell adduces a growth and successive transformation of the hotel and restaurant trade, chain caterers like Lyons Corner Houses, steak bars, and so forth, providing for those who never had access previously. While popularization may be rued by some, international hotel cuisine is an improvement for many. Finally, he notes a change in the hierarchical connotations of individual foods, the association between prestige and expense being eroded.

Mennell attributes increasing variety to a different set of processes. No longer is there the dominant, rigid, stylistic hierarchy in food which used to characterize an older Europe. In its place, pluralism and contest emerge, celebrating a diversity of coexisting tastes, encouraged partly by fashion, but also by the spread of international restaurants. Mennell claims that magazines and cookbooks have diversified so that, for example, there is no longer a single leading cookbook. The food discussed in magazines is 'more diverse and cosmopolitan' (1985: 330). Furthermore, the growing inter-dependence of professional and domestic cookery is said to be central. This occurs first through more eating out and, second because food technology and marketing bring to ordinary tables a variety of food unimaginable in light of the monotonous diets in the past. Finally he detects a growing diversity of motivations of those involved in the field of food, which results in a wider social distribution of relevant experiences.

The enlightenment of the domestic cook

The detailed evidence for Mennell's projection is distributed throughout the second half of the book, but most appears in two chapters, on the influence of professional chefs and, especially, on change in domestic cookery. His chapter, 'The enlightenment of the domestic cook?' considers the food-related contents of a few women's magazines in France and England between the late 19th century and the end of the 1970s. He considers them a valuable source of information for a number of reasons, including the fact that they seem to reflect normal practice, there being a strong correla-tion between published recipes and what is reported about food in contemporary memoirs, journalism and fiction.

Mennell argues that there has been more change in the 20th than in previous centuries, and lists as key factors the development of new food-stuffs, the importation of foods of other countries and more copious and accessible writing about cookery. Nevertheless, he sees little change in the way French magazines treat food during the 20th century, though he detects rather more in the English ones. Prior to the First World War, French recipes are lighter and more varied; 'there is not the obsessive concern with economy found in England, nor is cookery assumed to be a burden' (1985: 240). In the inter-war period in England, he sees a 'hesitant progress of the trend towards relatively greater social uniformity in eating' (p. 243). The Second World War itself had little lasting effect, though for the duration it entailed more tinned and processed food, considerable ingenuity, equalization through rationing, and a reinforcement of the Englishness of cooking – cakes, bread, oatmeal, dumplings and leftovers were prominent foodstuffs.

After the end of rationing in 1954, England experienced 'fairly rapid changes' (p. 255). By comparison France changed less: 'by the late 1970s it was surprising how little had changed in the French magazines. There is still no preoccupation with short cuts, no obsession with economy, no assumption that cooking is a time-consuming burden, and little implication that cookery is particularly difficult' (p. 255). Among the shifts in England were more reference to new foodstuffs (especially frozen, tinned, 'instant' and pre-cooked) and some reference to cookery as both as an enjoyable hobby and an element of competitive social display, dubbed 'hostess cookery'. Mennell sees a new preoccupation with style emerging in the UK in the late 1950s and 1960s. By the late 1960s, he claims, 'the sensitivity to nuances of social gradation was being applied with renewed vigour to the culinary domain' (p. 257). However, he maintains:

> The nearer we come to the present day, the more difficult does it become to discern any clear trends in the cookery columns. Since the 1960s there appear to have been fluctuations and even contradictory developments. Overall, the emerging pattern could be described as 'diminishing contrasts, increasing varieties'. (1985: 259)

Mennell illustrates this for France by noting the increasing prevalence of 'the contrasting influences of the nouvelle cuisine and of convenience foods'. This was less apparent in England, though he lists several tendencies, including more specialization between magazines and the emergence of gastronomic legislation for good taste in the early 1960s. But although 'posher nosh with less effort' was one value promoted, gourmandizing was overshadowed by the concern for convenience. By the 1970s he notices a 'more cosmopolitan air' (p. 261): photographs include wine and glasses; recipes by famous male chefs appear, as do articles on French cookery techniques; and readers' recipes become more varied. However, this amounts to 'no clear trend or policy in the cookery columns . . . . Start-from-scratch, back-to-the-farmhouse recipes alternate with others representing the most ruthless short cuts with convenience foods' (ibid.).

When summing up, Mennell emphasizes three recent developments: a sense of excitement about food emerged; more cosmopolitan sentiment became apparent, even when associated with greatly increased stress on convenience; and columnists seemed to be less consciously 'addressing

housewives of a particular social class', as the distinction between women
with paid and unpaid work became the main observed difference among
readers.

Mennell's indeterminacy

A thorough critique of Mennell's general thesis of 'diminishing contrasts,
increasing varieties' must await the empirical evidence about detailed
changes in domestic cookery since the 1960s. However, it is probably
helpful to briefly preview the themes to be challenged.

There are three potential avenues of empirical criticism. First, if looked
at closely, Mennell seems to be suggesting trendless fluctuation in the
representations of food in the magazines after the 1960s: no trends or
systematic shifts are apparent; patterns are simply dissolving. This is much
less precise a notion than the phrase 'increased variety, diminishing
contrasts' suggests. Second, the diminishing contrasts claim has limited
justification. Mennell's account, though heavily nuanced, is primarily a
'decline of class' thesis, which I will challenge on the basis of systematic
quantitative evidence. Third, his evidence of increased variation is largely a
function of changes in production, of changes in commercially available
products, rather than of consumers increasing the range of items they
ingest. The empirical adequacy of the trends identified by Mennell is a
matter returned to in Chapter 8.

I am sceptical of the claim that diminishing contrasts and increased
variations are part of a *single* social process. Mennell never explicitly states
what distinguishes those phenomena exhibiting diminishing difference from
those undergoing diversification. Without some clear distinction between
the two categories of process, between contrasts and variations, the neat
phrase merely says that some phenomena become less diverse, others more
diverse. The strong implication, however, is that the diminishing contrasts
are *social*, almost all being concerned with the erosion of differences
between social classes in particular.[1] Access to foods of all kinds becomes
more equitable, a result of changing material circumstances, innovations in
the food manufacturing and catering industries and shifts in ideology.
Increased variety is premised on the belief that people do actually take
advantage of greater opportunities to diversify their consumption, but the
clearly identified causes mostly have their origins in changed commercial
practices.[2] Generally, Mennell understates the importance of commercial
interventions which make consumption patterns more uniform.

Mennell's causal reasoning is obscure. In effect, he does little more than
describe two concurrent trends: reduced inequalities of class and income,
and growth in variety of products available. Initially, the most plausible
interpretation of their relationship is that greater variety is a consequence
of the decline of social class. In the long run, since the 18th century, that
thesis is hard to resist (see also Burnett, 1989), but whether it accounts for
change during the 20th century is contestable, for it is neither clearly

demonstrated nor explained. Greater affluence means that people are able to afford a wider range of products, providing that is what they desire. Mennell emphasizes the democratization of judgment as a cause of greater pluralism, presumably envisaging the emergence of a plurality of smaller groups each with its own distinctive pattern of food consumption. But not only is no clear evidence of an emergent pluralism advanced, he also fails to specify satisfactorily what form that pluralism takes. Moreover, the larger part of his evidence relates to diminishing contrasts and he never eliminates the possibility that such a trend towards social uniformity will not continue to the point of forming the mass culture that he earlier dismissed.

Mennell's account of 20th-century trends is consistent with several different projections which largely parallel the consumption trends illustrated in Figure 1.3 (p. 18). *If* diminishing contrasts *entail* increased variety, it is unclear which of three quite different outcomes would transpire. It might lead to much greater individualization of diet, to a situation where there are no social patterns or regularities in diet. Second, class differences could give way to other dimensions of social-structural variation, leading to new social contrasts that reflect new types of social division. Or, third, it could lead to a more uniform national diet. Of course, the third is not consistent with 'increasing variation', if that term is genuinely describing *consumer* behaviour. By suggesting in various places all three outcomes, his formulation is rendered indeterminate. Other accounts of changing food habits, examined in the next section, give support to each of four possible outcomes.

In sum, Mennell underestimates the link between commercial innovation and emergent variety and overestimates the extent of class decline and the erosion of social differentiation. In his account increased variety is primarily a function of commercial production rather than consumer preference.[3] His principal theme, the shift from class determination to plural tastes, results more from intuition than from the evidence cited. He says little about how social and commercial processes form such plural taste, nor does he consider how such tastes might subsequently redivide the population.

2.3 Four sociological theses on changing food habits

There are four alternative ways to clarify the developments that Mennell's account leaves suspended. Though I construct them somewhat artificially, each corresponds to one of the more general theoretical accounts of consumption outlined in Chapter 1. The first revolves around the proposition that the decline of constraints associated with social differentiation leads to a pathological situation of individual uncertainty about what to eat. A second alternative, suggested in many accounts of contemporary cultural trends, is that there will be *increased* rather than diminished contrasts. As constraints diminish, people might become more consciously aware of alternative styles, as pluralist niche consumption spreads through the British population. I shall refer to this, more precisely, as the post-Fordist interpretation. A third thesis, probably orthodoxy among nutritionists and redolent of a mass society thesis applied to national cuisine, anticipates, and indeed would probably encourage, uniform, disciplined, national norms of consumption. A final view is that differentiation based on longstanding, major social-structural divisions persists or even augments. Some theorists anticipate the continuing provenance of subtle but highly significant class differences, although the displacement of class by powerful gender, generational or regional divisions might equally be envisaged.

Thesis one: towards arbitrary individual diversity

The eminent French sociologist of food, Claude Fischler, has diagnosed a contemporary crisis in modern western societies over food choice which has become, for the individual, a source of anguish and obsession, anxiety and suspicion (1993: 394). He identifies many tensions that arise from the collapse of traditional and authoritative external rules about what should be eaten. While eating is acknowledged to be a human pleasure, everywhere people seek to exercise restraint because of the desirability of having a lean body. Moreover, the commercial system supplies a multitude of foods, some fresh, most manufactured, but people lack confidence in its wholesomeness. In historical perspective there is an abundance of food widely available, but for the individual there is no reliable guide as to what to choose. Fischler's basic explanation of the crisis is that 'Now the modern situation is characterized more and more by manifestations of individualism, more and more by autonomy and anomie, and less and less by heteronomie (the imposition on the subject of external rules)' (1993: 390)[4]

Fischler shares many ideas with Mennell but is convinced that the current trend is towards a splintered, uncertain and confused situation, where, in the midst of conflicting advice, the individual is left alone, ill-prepared, to make decisions about food consumption. '"What to choose?" becomes a tormenting, invasive and occasionally insurmountable question' (1993: 391).[5]

His brilliant and much quoted article (1980) identifies the source of the problem as 'the omnivore's paradox': omnivores need variety, but unknown foodstuffs may be poisonous. Food is thus always a source of some anxiety, but is heightened in the modern period: 'The hypothesis I suggest is that modern society develops in such a way that it tends to *increase the anxiety of the paradox instead of regulating it*' (1980: 945). Fischler sees currently a 'crisis of cultural patterns', a *weakening* of cultural constraints in urban modern society which causes the crisis. In preindustrial societies, there were enormous economic, social and ecological constraints – few things to buy, seasonality, dearth, monotony except for feasts: 'In such a situation the social and cultural framework of eating habits is remarkably stable, rigid, almost coercive. There are religious prohibitions and prescriptions, all sorts of ritualized occasions. There is a fixed number of meals, each with a precise "grammar" or "syntax" to it. There are particular foods for particular people' (1980: 944). Today, with a continent-wide division of labour, with regions concentrating on particular products, there is an abundance of food.

> This determines two different paradoxical effects on individual consumers: (a) a wider range of possible foods, including exotic ones, and far fewer constraints, seasonal or other; but at the same time, (b) a process of homogenization of foods consumed throughout the industrial world, and a loss of specificity (if not identity). Food items tend to become largely identical from one country to the other, from one supermarket shelf to another. (1980: 945)

In this respect Fischler points to some counter-trends to increasing variation that are minimized by Mennell.

The central element of Fischler's argument has a Durkheimian theme, the collapse of normative regulation. He uses the example of snacks replacing meals. He is averse to 'grazing', because eating thereby is 'becoming less of a social, and more of a strictly individual, practice' (1980: 947). This causes yet more anxiety:

> Food selection and intake are increasingly a matter of individual, not social, decisions, and they are no longer under ecological or seasonal constraints. But individuals lack reliable criteria to make these decisions and therefore they experience a growing sense of anxiety. (1980: 948)

He sees this change in food habits as a corollary of the disintegration of rules and norms more generally in other spheres of social life. Ultimately Fischler relies on an orthodox diagnosis of anomie, that in the absence of consistent and authoritative rules people behave in unpredictable, unregulated, and idiosyncratic ways. Hence his delightful pun: the contemporary transformation of diet represents a shift from gastronomy, knowledge of the rules of food, to gastroanomy, a condition bereft of rules.

In his assertion that deregulation is a course of anxiety and uncertainty, Fischler exhibits strong parallels with Bauman's (1988) more general analysis of the contemporary consumer. He observes that organizations and occupations like nutrition, official medicine, alternative medicine, food manufacture and their advertising agencies proffer advice. These increasingly commercially marketed advice services seek to persuade and thereby to allay anxiety. Increasingly too, industry and the market offer the solution to self-regulation and restraint through the selling of 'diet' and 'light' products. Yet these are part of the origin of the problem. Fischler observes that a 'dietetic cacophony reigns', a view endorsed by Levenstein (1993). Where personal and collective resistance does occur, it is the behaviour of a minority reactive to the pervasive anomic condition. The search for a distinct dietary regime is an understandable response to social detachment and deregulation. Hence,

Other substitutes for traditional gastronomies arise from individuals particularly anxious to find and cling to valid criteria for food selection. Food fads, fad diets, food sectarianisms, even new trends in culinary aesthetics and the generally growing interest in cooking, may be better understood in the light of the aspiration for new individual dietary goals and norms. (Fischler, 1980: 949–50)

For Fischler, the behaviour of individuals grows more diverse but without any secure foundation. As a consequence of individualization and deregulation, people are deprived of confidence in foodstuffs, in expert advice and in their own abilities to select what to eat. In this view the current period is not one of flourishing styles, plural market niches, or the aestheticization of everyday life, but a mire of personal uncertainty and discomfort.

Thesis two: post-Fordist food

Claude Fischler interprets food fads, fashions and sects as evidence of atomization and the disintegration of social regulation. However, what Fischler disparages as cultish may be seen by someone else as commitment to a set of values or mode of life, not pathological but admirable practice. These phenomena might instead be evidence of stylization, niche consumption and neo-tribalism. Such might be the condition of post-Fordist consumption, a growing differentiation of distinctive lifestyles as the era of mass consumption passes away. This situation might be described, apropos of Mennell's thesis, as increasing variety *and* increasing contrasts. Consumption in such a scenario is subject to a process of greater stylization whereby people become more capable of appreciating perceptible differentiation on the basis of observing the behaviour of others. Despite some work on food fashions (Simmonds, 1990) and restaurants (Finkelstein, 1989), there are no good examples of this thesis being examined specifically in the context of food habits.

Casual observation suggests the existence of fashions and styles: some groups of people appear to eat in distinctive and different ways. In the UK, as elsewhere, fashions exist for foreign cuisines and restaurants, new food items, manners of presentation of food, and so forth. A very large proportion of the population at any point in time claim to be on a diet of some sort, and even simple weight loss diets have brand labels to differentiate them. There are groups of food enthusiasts: not only does the traditional, exclusive gourmet survive, but there are also the so-called 'foodies', an object of British humour in the 1980s because of their excessive dedication to stylish and pernickety eating. But perhaps the most significant example of all is vegetarianism. Vegetarianism has become a social movement of considerable significance in the UK, where around 6 per cent of the population claim to be vegetarians, a much higher proportion than in other European countries. Although studies of contemporary vegetarianism are few, there is evidence that vegetarianism coincides with other lifestyle attributes and often with political, ethical or religious commitments (Hamilton, 1993; Beardsworth & Keil, 1992; Fiddes, 1991). This might be exactly the sort of development that a theory of post-Fordist or neo-tribal consumption would anticipate.

Post-Fordist and neo-tribal trajectories are rarely specified precisely, but by implication they exhibit certain general and common features. Both imply a growing cultural pluralism. Both should expect an increasing number of distinguishable groups, each with distinctively different rules, norms or standards about food, which constitutes a stylistic unity, and whose consequent behaviour is perceptibly different, both to those within and those outside each group. However, they offer competing explanations of the nature and origins of this group differentiation. In the neo-tribal version, differences between groups would not be explicable at all by socio-economic or socio-demographic characteristics, since membership is voluntary, temporary and a matter of personal choice. In this it bears some similarities to market research techniques for identifying lifestyles on the basis of shared attitudes and values.[6] The post-Fordist account is more agnostic about the basis of group formation and would probably expect some socio-demographic differentiation in behaviour.

John Urry (1990: 13–14) offers arguably the only developed definition of post-Fordist consumption, which he contrasts with Fordist, or mass, consumption. In analysing 'the tourist gaze', he sets out:

two ideal types of Fordist mass consumption and post-Fordist differentiated consumption.

Mass consumption: purchase of commodities produced under conditions of mass production; a high and growing rate of expenditure on consumer products; individual producers tending to dominate particular industrial markets; producer rather than consumer as dominant; commodities little differentiated from each other by fashion, season, and specific market segments; relatively limited choice – what there is tends to reflect producer interests, either privately or publicly owned.

Post-Fordist consumption: consumption rather than production dominant as consumer expenditure further increases as a proportion of national income; new forms of credit permitting consumer expenditure to rise, so producing high levels of indebtedness; almost all aspects of social life become commodified, even charity; much greater differentiation of purchasing patterns by different market segments; greater volatility of consumer preferences; the growth of a consumers movement and the 'politicizing' of consumption; reaction of consumers against being a part of a 'mass' and the need for producers to be much more consumer-driven, especially in the case of service industries and those publicly owned; the development of many more products each of which has a shorter life; the emergence of new kinds of commodity which are more specialized and based on raw materials that imply non-mass forms of production ('natural' products for example).

Though something of a *mélange*, with no very obvious central generating principle, Urry's is one of the few summaries of the positive characteristics of a system of post-Fordist consumption. As with other accounts there is a tendency to pay rather more attention to what the producers are doing than to consumer behaviour. The consequent danger is that the undoubted existence of many more specialized products (exotic fruits, speciality cheeses, pre-prepared meals, etc.) will be interpreted as implying that consumers select as connoisseurs, in accordance with scripts of differentiated unitary lifestyles. But this does not necessarily follow. Urry's definition suggests five distinctive attributes of consumption behaviour in a post-Fordist world: (1) consumers will make more use of commodified provision; (2) there will be 'much greater differentiation of purchasing patterns by different market segments'; (3) there will be 'greater volatility of consumer preference' (hence products have a shorter life); (4) consumer movements will proliferate; and (5) there will be a, presumably conscious and active, 'reaction of consumers against being part of a "mass"' – which will involve seeking out specialized, and perhaps 'natural', raw materials. There is some evidence for each of these.

The further extension of commodification might be seen in higher absolute spending on bought meals, take-away foods, cook-chill products from the supermarkets and so forth. Yet this was equally a tendency of the era of mass production, there having been a perpetual decline of domestic provisioning, petty agricultural production, gardening and jam making since the onset of urbanization and industrialization (see Cowan, 1983 for an account of American households; for the UK, Burnett, 1989).

Many people in market research and the advertising industry are heavily committed to the truth of the second proposition; indeed many commercial strategies, and hence reputations and jobs, depend upon it (see Lury & Warde, 1997). Advertisers, sellers of media space and market research organizations operate by giving advice to producers about the probabilities that different sorts of people will want particular products. Their business is matching products to segments of the consumer market and there is much dispute about the optimal diagnostic methods for divining consumer preferences. The degree to which they are successful is contestable, but there is no doubt that the culture industries operate to encourage people to behave as if they did belong to discerning and distinct segments. When sociologists redeploy market research data they certainly do discover some patterns. For example, Savage et al. (1992) indicate differentiated patterns of consumption within the middle class, finding a 'health and champagne' lifestyle segment as well as an ascetic grouping, each of which mapped roughly on to a specific socio-economic stratum within the class.

The degree to which people have become more volatile in their consumption is an empirical question. It probably characterizes some people and some products more than others. For instance, preferences for different leisure pursuits and for the paraphernalia associated with sports seem more ephemeral than food tastes. In the sphere of food, volatility perhaps characterizes adolescents and children, but there is good reason to think that food tastes are generally fairly conservative. The same staple foodstuffs, which in some instances have characterized regional and national cuisines for centuries, continue to be central. Many of the bestselling manufactured food products have survived a long time: Smith et al. (1989)

note that chocolate is among the comestibles with durable sales: the oldest chocolate bar still in production in the UK was first sold in 1876. The same impression, that it is difficult to alter people's food habits, arises from the high rate of failure of new food products despite the extent of producer and media encouragement of innovation. To be sure individuals and household members probably do 'go off' certain foods, and they may change brands of cereal or yoghurt, but it would be surprising if food preferences altered sufficiently rapidly to justify describing individuals as 'volatile'.

The fourth condition, that there should be consumer movements, is also partly met because there are consumer organizations and pressure groups politicizing food production and consumption. Thus in the UK, there are specialized food movements like the Vegetarian Society, the London Food Commission and an associated organization 'Parents for Safe Food' (see Parents for Safe Food, 1990), the Consumers' Association who test products and publish the *Good Food Guide*, and some quasi-governmental bodies. These are supplemented and complemented by movements for animal rights, mystical eastern religions and sportsmen's diets (which have fashions too). There have also been some extremely successful pressure group activities to preserve traditional varieties of products, the earliest and most outstandingly successful one being the Campaign for Real Ale (CAMRA) which reversed a very powerful trend towards industrial concentration and the rationalization of beer production through pasteurization. The empirical question is whether these movements are fuelled by enhanced concern with consumption and lifestyle, or by anxiety and perceptions of risk, as suggested in Fischler's explanation for instance.

There are many possible examples of the fifth condition being met, both in general and with respect to the promotion of natural products. Not only has the variety of commercial British beers regularly available sharply increased in the last twenty years, the same is true of bread, farmhouse cheeses, apples and so forth. That they are produced is, however, no guarantee that they are bought by consumers who are resisting becoming part of a mass and it is quite possible that it is a fairly small proportion of shoppers who have, even unconsciously, such a general motive. This may be true of gourmets and of people with cultural capital tied up in public eating as a form of entertainment. However, it is probably less important in explaining the very specialized demand exerted by purchasers of organic and whole foods who exhibit a concern with 'natural', health-giving and uncontaminated produce.

So there is some supporting evidence for all the shifts towards post-Fordism listed by Urry. There is some evidence of pluralism, of voluntaristic practices, of fashions and of stylization, although it is not yet proven that these are independent of the socio-demographic characteristics of the people involved. Nor is the evidence sufficient to demonstrate this to be the overarching tendency. Other forces could be more powerful and some of the features may not clearly separate post-Fordist from mass consumption.

Interestingly, all but the first of these five conditions apparently require that consumers have a great deal of knowledge and are highly skilled in their aesthetic appreciation. Undoubtedly there is an expanding cadre of experts or pundits employed to inform people about the options available to them. Unfamiliar and specialized products have to be identified both for their uses and their symbolic significance, in order that people can make technical and socially relevant distinctions. There is need for interpretation of the food industry, for giving meaning to products, for the composition of diets that combine different foods, and so forth. British supermarkets provide free recipe cards for unfamiliar meals and leaflets on what to do with a mango or a guava. There are, obviously, many people so involved, journalists and marketeers, as well as nutritionists and political campaigners. The extent to which they deliver information that will encourage or allow people to construct a coherent food style is, however, debatable. It is not clear that these features affect a significant proportion of the current western, or British, populations. Nor, despite the fact that contemporary consumers are skilled and sophisticated readers of signs and styles, is it certain that they are *sufficiently* active, discriminating, knowledgeable and self-reflexive. The case for neo-tribalism and niche consumption is not yet secured. Indeed, the material discussed in the next section makes it seem unlikely that it is the dominant trend.

Theses three: mass consumption in a mass society

One of the great fears of the bourgeois mentality since the 17th century has been of uniformity: the idea that all people might share similarity of condition, experience or taste offends against the dominant favourable image of individuality. In cultural matters, this fear has most often been expressed from an apparently elitist position of regret about the erosion of the values and achievement of 'high' culture; mass culture promoted by mass media has been vilified for its poor taste. Mass consumption was one primary source and indication of cultural deterioration. It has been one of the great achievements of cultural studies to rescue popular culture from the condescension of such judgments about its inferior qualities. Moreover, as did Mennell, sociologists have challenged empirically the notion that such a mass culture exists. As Bell said back in 1962, 'What strikes one first about varied uses of the concept of mass society is how little they reflect or relate to the complex, richly striated social relations of the real world' (1988: 25).[7] Nevertheless there remain many forces encouraging uniformity rather than diversity.

One possible consequence of a collapse of class cultures is precisely the emergence of very widespread shared tastes and preferences. Ray Pahl, for example, proclaimed the irrelevance of class to sociological analysis in the late 20th century, and saw the successor social regime as characterized by an increasingly large 'middle mass' (1989). By definition this does not include all groups, for it would be implausible to proclaim equality of condition, opportunity and aspiration for everyone. Obvious exceptions are ethnic minorities, the very rich, some groups of cultural intermediaries, and the very poor, none of whom could be considered part of a middle mass consensus. But, it could be argued, these exceptional groups comprise a relatively small proportion of a population which is otherwise basically homogeneous.

The manufacturers of goods and commercial providers of services retain an interest in selling their products to as many people as possible and, providing there is demand, the more uniform the product the more competitive the price at which it can be offered. It is not coincidence that the food industry provides some of the most striking instances of mass consumption. The plausibility of a mass society thesis is suggested by the title of a popular overview of social trends – in *The McDonaldization of Society* (Ritzer, 1993). Primarily an account of the continuing process in the western world of rationalization (with its characteristic concerns with efficiency, calculation, predictability and control), the operating principles of the global chain of fast-food producers are taken as metaphor for social trends more generally. Certainly, the spread of a chain of very popular fast-food restaurants, across the globe, which prides itself on the delivery of identical products, of uniform quality, appears to be an instance of mass food culture. The number of outlets and extent of the markets for McDonald's meals, the ubiquity of Kelloggs cereals, Coca-Cola and Pepsi-Cola, are legendary examples of massification which other manufacturers surely try to emulate. Much of contemporary, very extensive advertising for foodstuffs is for mass-manufactured products and targeted at a mass, not a segmented, audience (see Warde, 1993). Of course, the aspirations of the producers, as Mennell notes, are not easily achieved, and indeed in Britain, the increasing, and internationally exceptional, concentration of firms in the retail sector results in it being profitable to provide a huge variety of items. The four largest chains of supermarkets were reported to sell two-thirds of all packaged groceries (*Guardian*, 20 September 1995).

Some of the tendencies towards massification within food manufacture and distribution occur today on a global scale. As yet, governments and state agencies are probably more important in that they provide a mixture of constraints and incentives towards certain dietary choices. In the UK there is regular controversy about government health and safety in the light of food scares, restraints on international trade, and national guidelines for a healthy diet. The latter are interesting for many reasons: they make visible the sectional interests involved in the politics of food provision and they induce indignant debate about the adequacy of scientific statements and the fallibility of experts. But nutritional information and instruction too will always appear to be directive, in some measure, and thus potentially in default of the image of the sovereign individuality of the western shopper. The nutritionists' mission is to persuade everyone to consume a similar set of nutrients in order to maintain a healthy body. That this standard appears to change is a source of public disquiet and much advice is ridiculed because it is not the same as that of twenty years ago, even though the circumstances may have changed and diets are a package of items.

Besides health promotion campaigns, there is also a certain homogenizing effect associated with the idea of the national community. To have a distinctive national cuisine has become an important stratagem for the tourist industry and, often with the support of governments, traditional national dishes and even cuisines are either exhumed or invented for the purpose. A campaign like 'A Taste of Scotland', run in 1992, appeals to, and perhaps enhances, a sense of national identity for native and visitor alike. Similarly Appadurai (1988) shows how cookbooks serve to foster an impression of national unification in India.

There are in addition some parts of routine food practice that are widely shared within national cultures. Mary Douglas's (1975) often-quoted account of the structure of the British meal is a case in point. There is a basic, language-like code to eating events which is shared and uniform in the UK, even though the actual food items might vary. Similarly, and another reason for postulating the existence of mass food habits, there is empirical evidence for the universality of the notion of 'the proper meal'. It bears the unmistakable imprint of what might be considered orthodox British dietary practices and is held by most women, irrespective of age, class or region. Described first by Anne Murcott (1982) on the basis of in-depth household interviews in South Wales, a larger survey in the north of England by Charles and Kerr in 1982–3 suggested its widespread diffusion in the UK. One of the most striking aspects of the work of Charles and Kerr (1988) in their study of food in 200 households in the early 1980s is the uniformity of behaviour in their sample around the continued central importance to the British family of 'the proper meal': hot meat (or sometimes fish) and two vegetables. Moreover,

> a proper meal is defined not only by its contents but by the way it is eaten and what happens during the meal in terms of behaviour. It is also defined by who is present. It is ideally a meal which is a 'family' meal and this, by definition, requires all members of the family to be present. It is also a meal cooked by the woman in the household for herself, her partner and her children. (Charles & Kerr, 1988: 21)

Around this family meal, children were socialized into appropriate gendered behaviour as well as learning table manners and food tastes. Main meals in the 1980s did not always consist of meat and two veg, but that was the ideal, and alternative food ideologies, like vegetarianism, were restricted to a minority of middle-class households. Similarly a shared sense of propriety is apparent from the foods that accompany ritual celebrations: the Christmas dinner and the wedding cake (see Charsley, 1992) bear traditional and uniform meanings.

Thus, some powerful homogenizing forces do exist. Charles and Kerr's evidence does not suggest an enormous amount of variation or differentiation in actual household practices in the 1980s. There could be a convergence of the vast majority, whose uniform pattern of behaviour may prove to be a feature which overpowers stylization or individualization. So while one can agree with Mennell that there is no simple, automatically successful manipulation by industrial producers, and that there is an enormous variety of items available, it remains plausible to argue that the principal characteristic of recent times is mass conformity in dietary matters.

Thesis four: the persistence of social differentiation

Empirical and theoretical sociologists have typically operated on the presumption that social differences in behaviour are structured along some fundamental dimensions – described by concepts like nation, class (measured as occupation, income and education), gender, ethnicity, generation and life-course stage. These are treated as key dimensions underlying variation in social experience, affecting resources, respect, interests and legitimate capacities for personal and collective action. The three theses examined so far in this section have all asserted that there has been some reduction in degrees of regulation and the level of social embeddedness governing food practices, such that the power of these structural features of social differentiation have become less salient. All would be sympathetic to some version of Mennell's claim about 'diminishing contrasts'. All would agree that the diminution with respect to the dimension of social class has been most marked and the most sociologically significant. No one, however, claims that class has become totally irrelevant. Mennell admitted that social differentiation, and specifically class differences, had not disappeared; it had merely declined. Charles and Kerr detected still significant class differences among the households that they interviewed, though the evidence was not enormously strong.

Though Mennell was concerned with other sources of 'contrast' besides class, as between urban and rural areas and between professional and domestic provision, the other three theses pay little attention to other structural lines of differentiation. One possibility is that if class differences diminish, then other structural divisions will become more significant. On the face of it, on the basis of our knowledge of household decision-making and the changing composition of households, we might expect growing differentiation between men and women. Increasing income inequalities, often identified in terms of social polarization, might have an impact. Certain aspects of generational change, which are partly implicit in the post-Fordist thesis, might also be important. The fourth thesis suggests that structural differentiation in general, class differentiation in particular, is likely to persist in the field of food.

The most thoroughly developed position anticipating continued differentiation in the realm of food practices is Bourdieu's (1984) application of his general approach to French eating habits. *Distinction* recognizes the symbolic significance of class practices and relates these cultural or symbolic aspects of taste to class reproduction. Food consumption is less about eating enough to survive, more about social meanings. Bourdieu considers food as one means of expressing 'distinction': different social classes, and different groups within the middle class (owner-managers, established professionals and intellectuals, and 'the new *petite bourgeoisie*' – e.g. professionals in popular culture industries) eat different food items.[8] He singles out levels in a hierarchy of practices where those which are rare are designated 'distinguished', those 'both easy and common' are termed 'vulgar' and those with an intermediate position deemed 'pretentious' (1984: 176). He suggests that peasants and the industrial working class exhibit 'an ethic of convivial indulgence' and thereby resist 'the new ethic of sobriety for the sake of slimness, which is more recognised at the highest levels of the social hierarchy' (1984: 179). Clerical and commercial employees behave quite differently: Bourdieu sees the main boundary in food practices as lying between manual workers and clerical staff, for while they earn about the same, they spend on different categories of commodities (white-collar workers spend less on food and more on body maintenance) and also on different items of food. Meanwhile, fractions of the French middle class in the 1970s displayed immensely significant symbolic aspects of difference in their diets, as well as in other areas of cultural capital. Interpretations are offered in terms of symbolic attributes of different social positions, for instance:

> the taste of the professionals or senior executives defines the popular taste, by negation, as the taste for the heavy, the fat and the coarse, by tending towards the light, the refined and the delicate. The disappearance of economic constraints is accompanied by a strengthening of the social censorships which forbid coarseness and fatness, in favour of slimness and distinction. The taste for rare, aristocratic foods points to a traditional cuisine, rich in expensive and rare products (fresh vegetables, meat). . . . [By contrast] the teachers, richer in cultural capital than in economic capital, and therefore inclined to ascetic consumption in all areas, pursue originality at the lowest economic cost and go in for exoticism (Italian, Chinese cooking, etc.) and culinary populism (peasant dishes). They are almost consciously opposed to the (new) rich with their rich food. (Bourdieu, 1984: 185)

Bourdieu demonstrates that eating habits express class differences. The account is of the situation in the 1970s and the data was not collected with a view to exploring change. Though he would probably accept that the items consumed might change over time, he implies that the social class structuring of the field and the ends to which it operates will persist over time. Bourdieu's critics suggest that his theoretical approach is oriented to social reproduction and hence privileges continuity over change: for Bourdieu, one suspects, any deregulation of behaviour in a particular field would, of necessity, simultaneously involve re-regulation (Calhoun et al., 1993; Jenkins, 1992). Furthermore in the absence of systematic international comparison it is quite possible that Bourdieu's analysis, despite his claims to the contrary, applies most effectively to France. In Britain food probably has lower cultural significance than in France. Class distinction has been expressed more obviously by accent, residence, education and leisure pursuits than through eating. However, it has been suggested that food is becoming a more significant cultural marker, an effect of greater media attention, more eating out and wider exposure to foreign cuisines. In this way Britain might be becoming more like France, and class distinctions may even have grown in the field of food, as Levenstein (1993) claims has been the case in the USA since 1960.

The fourth thesis, then, maintains that there remains very significant structural differentiation in eating behaviour, indicating its social embeddedness and its social regulation, and which is primarily manifest as hierarchical class difference.

2.4 Conclusion

Each of the four theses examined in the previous section anticipates the dominance of different trends in the current period. The general pressures identified as lying behind dispositions in food choice are illustrated in Figure 2.1. The tendencies envisaged as dominant are, respectively, individual diversity, niche specialization, standardization and collective distinction. Each thesis is stated at a general level and most acknowledge some of the evidence cited by the others. Thus for instance, Fischler accepts the growth in the attraction of specialized group diets, among them the vegetarian option, but he deems this a minor rather than a dominant theme of the present period and consequently he offers a different interpretation of its significance. Undeniably, evidence for all four projections can be found; complexity and the contingency of food selection prevents any trend from becoming all-encompassing. But all cannot be simultaneously equally powerful. It is on the matter of the relative strength of the competing forces that I seek to adjudicate between these accounts.

Since the field of food is enormous and sociological analysis of it is in its infancy, the capacity to discriminate between these theories on an empirical basis is necessarily restricted. Not only is Wood (1995: 45) sensible to advise modesty in theoretical claims about food practices, but the same applies also to our expectations that empirical investigations will prove decisive between competing positions. Nevertheless, it is essential to begin such inquiry and Part II is concerned with the description and analysis of a specially selected body of material about food in Britain that bears on the processes isolated by the four theses.

The diverse evidence about changing food behaviour was primarily collected with a view to examining whether there was a fundamental shift in consumption behaviour during the 1970s and 1980s, as anticipated by general theories of post-Fordism and postmodernism. In fact, the findings show many key continuities through the relevant periods, as well as developments that cannot be attributed to, nor considered consistent with,

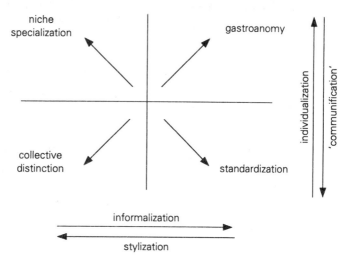

Figure 2.1   *Forces influencing dispositions in food selection*

such theories of transformation. I found no major turning point and no radical transformation consistent with their projections.

Mennell correctly emphasizes the increased variety of foodstuffs available. Variety provides the key to understanding contemporary consumption, since it is central to the legitimation of the dominance of the supermarket in food distribution and because it poses a perpetual practical problem for consumers, of what and how to select. Examination of advice given by experts in the mass media suggests that some basic principles are used to recommend foods, dishes and cuisine and that the importance of each, while never disappearing, fluctuates over time. The discourses of judgment have an enduring structure. So too does practice, in so far as it can be measured by food-purchasing patterns and domestic arrangements for the preparation of meals. Contrasts in behaviour between socio-demographic groups, or the social distance between them, altered little over the relevant twenty-year period and the distribution of domestic tasks at the beginning of the 1990s appeared much as before. While many specific and detailed changes occurred, continuities are very pronounced. In Part III that evidence is reapplied to Mennell's prognosis of 'diminished contrasts and increased variety' in an attempt to identify the most important changes in the last quarter of a century and how these reflect developments in consumption more generally.

3
Measuring Change in Taste

3.1 Introduction

Sociology, when commenting on the nature of contemporary societies, probably tends to overestimate secular change (Abercrombie & Warde, 1992: 7). Claims about radical transformation are often not subjected to the test of systematic comparison. In a new field like that of consumption, where there is relatively little relevant systematic knowledge about past practice, there is even greater temptation to invent, whether from theoretical deduction or by pure speculation, a picture of a past against which to contrast a sketch of the current situation. Some of the results of such temptation have already been reviewed. Those aspects which are empirical can only be sensibly adjudicated on the basis of: (1) precise specification of the hypotheses in question – what length of time should be considered, how fast is the change supposed to be occurring? etc.; and (2) the preparation of adequate and relevant time-series data, which is rarely simply available and often very hard to construct. Because the major theses about changing consumption patterns have been inadequately specified, their rigorous testing is by no means easy.

This chapter describes briefly the variety of different methods used and data sources compiled to begin the process. My sources, while internally systematic, are not entirely comparable; for example the years to which the data refers are not identical. Nor is it easy to combine the interpretations of expenditure figures, recipe columns and household interviews. Nonetheless, they derive from systematic empirical investigation specifically designed to address issues of change relevant to the assessment of the various competing theoretical accounts.

The rest of this chapter describes briefly the three main sources of data deployed to explore changing food habits. The first was women's magazines, whose recipe columns were systematically sampled and compared for two twelve-month periods in 1967–8 and 1991–2. I discuss the character of the magazines, the structure of the sample and the outline of the framework for the analysis of the recipes, which was the basis of coding for content analysis. The second source, the *Family Expenditure Survey*, was reanalysed for the years 1968 and 1988 (the latest annual data set available at the time of conducting the research) primarily using the statistical technique of discriminant analysis. The third principal original data source was a household survey conducted in the north of England in 1990 which asked some questions about food preparation. The difficulties associated with each source are also briefly discussed as the problems of obtaining and interpreting systematic data must be borne in mind when considering my account.

3.2   Representations of food: the contents of women's magazines

Messengers of taste: of recipes and magazines

Women's magazines are influential vehicles of popular culture. Almost all contain a standard set of features (beauty, health, food, fashion, problem pages, etc.) but in different proportions. The magazines themselves are probably becoming rather more differentiated in their content, with popular ones dividing between those with an emphasis on families and those for working women. The magazines generally purvey 'visual fictions around consumption' (Winship, 1987: 64) and appeal to 'feminine pleasures'. Their description as being based upon 'survival strategies and day dreams' (ibid.) holds good, though perhaps the battery of strategies and the contents of dreams may have diversified somewhat. Winship notes that image and image projection became rather more important in the 1980s: improvements in photography and page-making certainly enhanced their presentation. Nevertheless, some of the most successful new magazines of the 1980s were primarily practical guides.

My study is unusual in examining a comparatively unglamorous and practical aspect of the contents of the magazines. The terseness of recipe columns, whose understanding requires considerable tacit knowledge (Tomlinson, 1986), suggests that they exist primarily to convey helpful and useful information. However, high-quality photography, and the impracticability of some of the recipes for domestic purposes, suggests that they also have a role in expanding readers' general knowledge about and reflection on cuisine and, through visual imagery, in fuelling the imagination about food, style and pleasure. McKie and Wood (1992) suggest that in addition recipes in popular journals have a moral role, setting standards, often unattainable, for the preparation and presentation of food. Within their particular literary and commercial context, the food columns in the magazines offer an implicit set of answers to the questions 'what and how shall we eat?'

To explore the contents of the food columns I selected a sample of UK magazines. My primary sources were the five most widely read women's weekly magazines and the five most widely read monthly magazines in each of two twelve-month periods in 1967–8 and 1991–2. The magazines are sampled at the mid-point of the months of November, February, May and August in each year, in order to control for seasonal variation in the contents of food columns.

The magazines together have an enormous readership; though the figure has fallen substantially since 1967, each tranche of ten magazines in 1991 would have been seen by around 29 million people (see Appendix Table A.1, p. 211). The weeklies have the largest circulation and their potential capacity to influence people is augmented by their more frequent appearance. Each of these magazines devotes a significant proportion of its space to food articles and advertisements: means were 8 per cent to articles and 9 per cent to ads in 1967; the figures for 1991 were 12 per cent and 13 per cent, respectively (see Appendix calculated from Table A.3, p. 213). It can be assumed that these food columns would come to the attention of a large proportion of British women and thus have some influence on the determination of food taste and knowledge.

Given the enormous circulation it is not surprising that the readership is not highly differentiated. There is a class difference between readers of the weekly and the monthly magazines: the latter are more glossy and more expensive to purchase. Within both weeklies and monthlies, audiences exhibit age differences (see Appendix Table A.2, p. 212). The degree of differentiation between magazines has not changed a great deal since 1967, class differences have remained constant, while age differentiation has increased a little.

From the selected magazines I drew a systematic sample of recipes. This produced 114 recipes in the earlier year, 124 in the later period which, given their random selection, should be sufficient to make some provisional generalizations about recipes and any changes over time. A larger sample would be preferred. However, as the sample was subjected to content analysis, involving 55 coding categories, significant extra resources would have been necessary to increase its size.

Content analysis uses some quantitative techniques to make inferences from text and can be used for many different purposes. In this instance it was designed to estimate the extent of change in the types of food recommended in magazines published twenty-five years apart. The procedure involved classifying items of text – adjectives, verbs and phrases used to commend dishes – into many fewer content categories and then counting how often each was referred to. The choice of content categories was determined after extensive examination of the magazines and reading of the secondary literature on food consumption which identified themes likely to be important in understanding continuity and change in British food habits. The themes considered worthy of investigation were many and included: the persistence of tradition; the spread of ethnic cuisines; the attraction of novel foods; the preservation of health; the spread of vegetarianism; the origins of pleasure derived from food; the constraints of time on food preparation; the symbolic significance of home cookery; the reproduction of domestic cooking skills; the significance of cost; the sensual and utilitarian values of foods; the structure of meals; the impact of household composition on food behaviour; the presentation and style of dishes; and the impact of the seasons.

The themes thus targeted by the coding scheme resulted in two sorts of information being recorded. The first was primarily factual, like how many people a dish was expected to serve, or from which ethnic cuisine it was said to derive. The second was evidence of the vocabulary used to recommend a dish: whether it was fashionable, healthy or tasty, for instance. Changes in the frequency of occurrence of particular types of dish or reasons for their recommendation is some indication of the changing standards by which food is judged desirable or useful. The basic content categories are listed in the Appendix, Table A.4, p. 214.

Content analysis has limitations, but for my comparatively simple purposes the method was sufficiently robust. Seeking only general confirmation of the impressions of change acquired by my detailed reading of the recipe columns, estimates of the frequency of appearance of items was adequate.

Principles of recommendation

Foods, dishes and menus are recommended to readers of magazines, sometimes in a preamble to a set of recipes, sometimes recipe by recipe, sometimes both. In some instances, recommendation involves extensive discussion, in others merely a few adjectives that introduce the recipes in the article. These introductions I will call, adapting the terminology of Tomlinson (1986), *recipe promotion devices*. Many different words are used to recommend foods, but they do seem to be reducible to a fairly small number of regularly employed classificatory concepts.

Some general functional criteria probably have always been used to encourage people to eat. *Utilitarian* invitations claim that people will accept, and thereby gain sustenance from, a particular dish, e.g. good, nutritious, satisfying, perfect, adaptable, useful, glorious, filling. There are also some functional criteria that trade on a *sensual* appeal, e.g. that food is tasty, delicious, delicate, fragrant, hot, fiery, mouthwatering, flavoursome, spicy, red hot, tangy, juicy, subtle, etc. However, the appeal is vague and imprecise, tantamount to saying 'pleasing to the senses', but without any guarantee that, or any information as to how, this might transpire. These recommendations go no further than promising physical satisfaction.

Other lines of recommendation are more substantive, containing some information about the raw produce, the end product, the history of the product, its belonging to a tradition, or its being positively beneficial for one. The promise is that the dish will be desirable for some additional reason besides merely being palatable and capable of quelling the feeling of hunger. Informative proposals, which tend to vary historically, go beyond abstract properties specific to foods and their sensual (visual, olfactory, tactile or tasting) attributes. They are concerned instead with social or socially relevant benefits that arise from their consumption; they are associated with, and symbolic of, social relationships.

This distinction between physical satisfaction and social significance is hard to draw at the margins, but there is a set of social recommendations, ones which have a bearing on social relationships or on the social standing of the provider or the consumer. Specific and substantive information and judgments about the interpersonal affects or meanings of the food are encoded into these kinds of recommendations. Such foods may perhaps alter emotional states ('comfort foods'), enhance social status (through display of wealth or power), exhibit personal identity (as style and connoisseurship), or confirm family relationships (as in a mother's cooking).

In general, it is useful to think in terms of eight social appeals, imperatives or *principles of recommendation* that give meaning to food items. These categories have been derived from inspection of recipe promotion devices and seem to make sense of magazine contents at the separate dates. They were constructed in an iterative process of looking at magazines, exploring their meanings, making inferences from language used, and subsuming specific messages under more abstract concepts. The eight categories should not be unfamiliar and are readily applicable to popular representations of food practices. The categories that people customarily use change over time and there is no way in which the social analyst can escape from reflecting the common usage of such categories.

Novelty One feature of contemporary social life is the positive value attached to new experience. This appears prominently throughout the magazines, including in the food columns, in many nuanced ways. Among the terms that intimated novelty in the content analysis were: experiment, exciting, 'interesting and a little unusual', exotic, 'bewitching ideas', foreign, less orthodox, creative, different, alternative, fresh ideas, 'for a change', 'for variety'.

Tradition Analysts of policies directed towards altering people's diets have usually been impressed by the durability of food preferences. One adjective widely used to sell foods is 'traditional', appealing to the certainties, and perhaps the social belonging, associated with well-tried practices. A recipe was coded in terms of the appeal to tradition if it included words or phrases like authentic, classic, like Granny used to make it, old-fashioned, 'ancient recipe, perhaps a family secret' and sometimes – depending on the context – national, regional speciality, popular, or famous.

Health Experts increasingly pronounce what is good for us to eat. Gronow (1991) has convincingly interpreted the advice of the nutritionists as a *disciplinary* discourse, in Foucault's sense, transmitted by state and experts, and concerned with disciplining the body more generally (see also Turner, 1982). The kinds of elements in a recipe indicating a concern with health are partly explicit recommendations that dishes are healthy, but are also indicated by the recording of calories, fat and fibre contents, and by terms like light and non-fattening. Discussions of slimming, of which there are many, are taken as an indication of concern with bodily discipline.

Indulgence   It has become state policy that we should look after our bodies properly and protect them against over-indulgence. Nevertheless food columns make just such indulgence a point of recommendation in some instances. The phrase from the advertisement for cream cakes, 'naughty but nice' recurs, and foods are described as wicked, tempting, rich, enticing, treats, feasts and the like. Incitements to 'spoil the family' or enjoy 'a touch of luxury' may, depending on context, also imply indulgence.

Economy   The cost of food is also relevant. Recipes are recommended because they 'go further', are cheap, budget, low-cost, inexpensive, not extravagant, economical, contain reasonably priced ingredients, and use foods that are in season.

Extravagance   By the same token, it is sometimes appealing to think that food is luxurious, extravagant, elaborate, expensive. Such food may be appropriate when in need of personal comfort or in order to give the family a 'treat'. More often, special occasions, festivals and entertaining create a desire for explicit or ostentatious use of expensive, rare, out-of-season produce – an extravagance because of the cost in monetary terms. Recipes were coded as extravagant without reference to the time expended in their preparation.

Convenience   Time, however, is precious and often recipes are recommended because they are quick, easy, clean, fast, requiring limited preparation of ingredients, minutes-only, manageable, for the busy housewife, take seconds or moments, etc. Convenience is a value. This virtue is announced routinely in recipe instructions that give preparation as well as cooking times, as well as in instructions about freezing or microwaving as means of saving time and energy.

Care   People learn tastes and tend to like what they are used to, often expressing strong preferences for their own mothers' cooking, for instance. One popular adjective depicting wholesome food is 'home-made'. The connections, however, are also with the personal, emotional and domestic significance of food. Columnists routinely assume the familial context of food provision and, within it, that women are carers, providers and producers. That home-made food symbolizes such concern is recognized by phrases like home cooking, cooking for the family, family meal. Foods may be comforting, remind one of Mother or Grandmother's cooking, or display care for one's children, and so forth. It is implicitly assumed that quality, freshness, taste and goodness will be enhanced by the addition of domestic labour.

These categories embrace general, substantive and socially relevant themes. They subsume a variety of words, phrases and more elaborate justifications of why a person might cook and eat a particular dish or dishes. They are primarily inductively derived from the explicit propositions, and sometimes implicit presuppositions, in the passages, often sketchy and rudimentary, that constitute recipe promotion devices. These eight principles constitute four pairs of antinomies which structure contemporary food choice. They present real, contradictory appeals, representing social pressures that operate on food choice. Conceivably, they make selection a difficult, anxiety-provoking and under-regulated, activity. They are the context of cultural deliberation about what it is proper to eat.

The evidence arising from the study of magazines is used to illustrate the ways in which foods recommended to people have changed since the late 1960s and to substantiate the claim that four central antinomies underpin contemporary taste. It should be stressed that this evidence is about the way in which food is represented and not about what people actually eat or cook. If, as Hermes (1995: 14) argues, women's magazines are 'low-involvement media', where the readership is not highly attentive to the content, then their direct capacity to alter practice is likely to be limited. Nevertheless, the magazines may both reflect current practice, as Mennell believes, and, even more likely, reflect and reproduce contemporary categories of judgment.

3.3 Household food expenditure

Governments have collected data on people's eating habits by means of household surveys since 1940 when, for purposes of wartime regulation, the National Food Survey (NFS) was instituted. Run under the auspices of the department of state responsible for agriculture (now Ministry of Agriculture, Fisheries and Food), it has been principally concerned with collecting commercial intelligence for food producers and estimating achieved nutritional standards for the population in general. The Family Expenditure Survey (FES), first conducted in 1953–4, and primarily an instrument for fiscal policy, also obtains information on food. It inquires about household spending on many items and was preferable because it contains more comprehensive and sociologically relevant socio-demographic information than the NFS. In this section the FES is described and the statistical techniques deployed for its analysis are briefly noted, as are some of the difficulties of interpretation over time.

Family Expenditure Survey and discriminant analysis

Patterns of social differentiation in food habits in the UK were explored by applying discriminant analysis to data from the Family Expenditure Surveys of 1968 and 1988.[1] This source has the advantage of a large sample size, over 7,000 households in each year. It also contains a substantial amount of information of a socio-economic nature: income, demographic characteristics, socio-economic group, etc., are all available. The data on food expenditure is broken down into food categories, for example different types of meat, milk products, take-aways, etc. Unfortunately, however, the expenditure categories for 1968 are not the same as 1988 and so to make a precise comparison some categories have to be merged, with the inevitable loss of some detail.

Discriminant analysis is a multivariate technique which generates a system of equations (similar in some respects to regression equations) that can discriminate between different groups of cases within a sample, the groups usually already having been ascertained. The method can also be used to see which variables serve to discriminate most efficiently between groups. The best summary expression of the results of a discriminant analysis is to show how effectively the classifying model predicted the group to which an individual household belonged on the basis of its food-purchasing patterns. The summary statistic shows the level to which the variables (in this case food items) allocate households correctly to the classifying groups to which they belong. If patterns exist then we should expect the number of correctly classified cases to be greater than would be expected by chance. So, for a four-class system, we would expect significantly more than 25 per cent of cases to be correctly classified by the discriminant functions if the analysis is working. It is possible to make inferences from the patterns revealed by the misallocation of households to class groupings. It is also possible to identify key food items that distinguish one grouping from another. However, the statistical data generated in these last two exercises is copious and there is insufficient space ever to report it in full detail.

Change, measurement and categories

The question was explored whether patterns of differentiation in food habits in the UK, primarily with respect to social class, had altered by applying discriminant analysis to data from the Family Expenditure Surveys of 1968 and 1988. This research design seemed initially to have a range of desirable characteristics: precise comparison, large samples, very detailed food expenditure, and acceptable socio-demographic data on households. It did throw up a number of interesting and important methodological considerations that bear on the measurement of social change generally and on the interpretation of changing taste in particular.

Strenuous efforts were made to estimate precisely the extent of change. Exact and systematic historical comparison is, however, fraught with difficulty. Few sets of data are strictly comparable at different dates and even studies explicitly designed as replications find it hard to ensure similarity in all respects. For example, using food items as an indication of lifestyle presented difficulties because different spending heads were used by the FES in 1988. Therefore categories of food items were reduced to the most discriminating set of categories that were consistent at the two time points. This, however, eliminated a good deal of information pertinent to depicting lifestyles. Some of the items which were most discriminating in

1968 were not available by 1988 (for example a differentiation between luxury and ordinary vegetables), while some of the most discriminating items in 1988 (for instance spending in different kinds of public eating establishment) were not distinguished in 1968. A 'collapsed' set of spending categories thus lost some of its most relevant discriminating elements as a result of trying to achieve precise comparability over time, though it remained possible to make some additional inferences on the basis of the more detailed spending figures. The same problem arose with some of the independent socio-demographic variables, especially occupation.

Expenditure patterns give an indication of differences of behaviour between social groups, but often without the detail that would allow interpretation of the cultural significance of purchases. Nor does fact of purchase provide information about subsequent use, a matter of particular importance in households containing several people since it cannot be assumed that all consume the same items. Hence it was sometimes found most useful to examine single person households.

The results discussed in the text below, mostly in Chapters 5 and 6, make use of this data in its different forms as appropriate. Despite the problems, it was informative simply to compare the percentage of cases correctly classified at two dates as an estimation of whether the influence of specific social determinants had increased or decreased.

3.4 Household arrangements and eating: a survey in Greater Manchester

Though often described simply as consumption, eating at home involves large quantities of labour time as well as responsibilities for decision-making. The uneven division of these and other domestic obligations has been a source of political interest to feminists since the 19th century, and a topic of sociological investigation for the last fifty years. Recognition that alternatives to the conventional arrangement which allocates most such tasks to adult women has been one reason for empirical research: many tasks might be automated, industrialized, commercialized; or they could be undertaken by paid servants; or they could be distributed equally among all household members; or other friends and relatives could be called upon. The most recent phase of research on domestic divisions of labour was inspired by a desire to understand how the very many discrete work tasks – whether as paid employment, by informal agreement or through domestic allocation – are now distributed between individuals and households. One landmark study in the UK was Ray Pahl's (1984) investigation of the Isle of Sheppey. Sceptical of some of its findings, and of its applicability to other places, a team at Lancaster University replicated parts of the study in the north of England in both 1988 and 1990 (see Warde et al., 1989, 1991). On the second occasion, reported here, part of the survey devoted extra questions to the provision of food.

The research into household divisions of labour was done in association with schools and colleges in the Greater Manchester area. In the autumn of 1990 fieldwork was undertaken to repeat part of Pahl's (1984) study of divisions of labour and to extend it in certain respects. Using similar survey methods, we asked about sources of labour for particular household tasks, responsibilities, attitudes to domestic tasks and wider elements of lifestyles.

Questionnaires returned by 323 households were analysed. The sample is skewed towards a particular population as a consequence of instructing students following A-level courses in sociology to administer the schedule to one of their parents. Sixty-two per cent of respondents were female and 86 per cent of households contained a couple living as married; 90 per cent of the respondents, because they were almost all parents of an A-level student, were between the ages of 36 and 55. Consistent with their stage in the life course, households were larger and more affluent than average. About half the sample of households contained four people, counting children. Considerably greater proportions of household members were in managerial and professional occupations than is typical of the British workforce as a whole: 40 per cent of our households contained a male member of the salariat (i.e. engaged in professional and managerial occu-pations). Correspondingly, there were relatively few manual workers or unemployed persons in the households. Of the principal adult women in the sample, 43 per cent were in full-time paid employment, 38 per cent in part-time paid work and a mere 14 per cent were engaged full time in domestic work in the home. (For more details of the sample see Appendix, Tables A.6–A.9, pp. 218–19).

The results of the survey bear most closely on the issue of the work involved in the domestic provisioning of food. Respondents were asked which of a long list of tasks were done for the household and who had done each on the last occasion. The answer could include commercial firms or domestic servants as well as specific household members. Thus evidence about the quantity and source of services was obtained. This included information about cooking, shopping and so forth. It allowed estimation of the division of labour within the household, analysis focusing particularly on those households containing a couple living as married. Questions were also asked about frequency of eating out and use of take-away foods. Also included were some questions about tastes which were adapted from those asked by Bourdieu (1984) of his French respondents. Respondents were asked to pick from a list adjectives that identified their tastes with respect to some social and cultural activities. For example, they were asked, 'When you have guests for a meal, what kind of meals do you prefer to serve?: (choose no more than three).' Although the answers to these questions proved hard to interpret, they do give some direct information about people's expressed tastes.

Analysis involved estimating and explaining variations in the volume and nature of the tasks undertaken, their distribution between household members and respondents' tastes. To this end several scales were computed, including ones to measure the domestic division of labour between men and women in couple households. The simple statistical technique of cross-tabulation was used to explore the relationship between tasks and the social characteristics of households and their members. Household size and composition, its income and ownership of property and goods, the occupations, educational qualifications and class positions of its adult members were among the social characteristics associated with variations in domestic organization.

The survey provided useful information about detailed elements of food provisioning in households. It says nothing definitive about change, for it was conducted at a single point in time and there is no earlier study with which it can directly and systematically be compared. However, some inference is possible when the results are viewed in the light of the many sociological investigations of the organization of British households that have appeared since the 1960s.

PART II

Indicators of Taste: Changing Food Habits

Part II reports the findings of the different empirical research exercises designed to estimate the degree and direction of change in British food habits since the 1960s. It describes change in the nature of media recommendations about taste and in the domestic practices of food purchase and preparation.

The evidence is presented in terms of the more general issue about how and why consumers select what to eat. It presupposes that the unprecedented range of products that are made available for sale, increasingly in the UK by a small number of supermarket chains, poses a perpetual problem of selection for customers. There are many reasons why this problem is not disabling, one of which is the widespread currency of the principles of recommendation outlined in the previous chapter. These can be flexibly applied as a means of discriminating among a multitude of products. Hence I have analysed the data in terms of four antinomies of taste.

With respect to the guidance offered to people about what to eat, advice comes from many sources: from government, mass media and social contacts. On the surface, the advice is incoherent and inconsistent. Nevertheless, four 'antinomies of taste' provide a systematic basis for these contradictory messages. These oppositions – novelty and tradition, health and indulgence, economy and extravagance, care and convenience – are values which can legitimize choice between foodstuffs. They were derived inductively, by inspection of the food and recipe columns in women's magazines in 1968 and 1992, and refined in terms of the analytic categories of social and cultural theory. I examine systematically the changes and continuities apparent in these popular media representations and recommendations about taste.

The four antinomies are longstanding structural oppositions, claims and counter-claims about cultural values which can be mobilized to express appreciation of food and to make dietary decisions. These are very deep-rooted contradictions, probably irresolvable, and applicable not only to food, but to other spheres of consumption too. I maintain that these antinomies comprise the structural anxieties of our epoch: they are parameters of uncertainty, apt to induce feelings of guilt and unease. Marginal adjustments to their content, and to their relative force, may give the impression of major changes in standards of social action, but they are permanent features of the modern predicament. They can be seen as the sedimentation in common consciousness of the most central dilemmas for individuals' actions in the current stage of the development of modernity. They apply to many situations of uncertainty where it is necessary to decide between alternative courses of action in the sphere of consumption. Thus the very mundane activity of feeding households indicates sharply some of the most trying contradictions or problems involved in regulating personal conduct and negotiating a decent life in contemporary Britain. Behind the uncertainty betrayed by antinomies in food recommendation lie the structural contradictions that render problematic security, identity and belonging in late 20th-century Britain.

These antinomies are widely applicable. They correspond to, and contingently reflect, principal institutional forms – the ambivalence of modern experience, a fetishism with body maintenance, the distribution of material resources, and gendered household relations. These are, in turn, derivative of abstract and predominant categories of modern culture, individuality, corporeality, money and time. The antinomial principles derive from fundamental cultural classificatory categories. They are irreducible and irreconcilable oppositions which frame the central dilemmas of contemporary consciousness and experience.

People regularly make use of each of the eight categories of judgment as guides to practical conduct and aesthetic appreciation. Vernacular phrases and homilies invoke the principles: 'it's time for a change', 'I deserve a treat', 'that is much too expensive', 'buying cheaply is false economy', 'life is too short to stuff a mushroom', and so forth. Because most are familiar, people can appreciate the attractions of both poles of each antinomy. But these are not always helpful in the process of decision-making. Often the opposite, as they become a source of anxiety about the best course of action. Food has probably always been a source of physiological concern, with respect to its chemical properties, the sufficiency of its provision and its capacity to sustain the body. But also, and arguably increasingly in late modernity, it is a source of cultural anxiety. The structural anxieties of our age are made manifest in discourses about food.

Each of these antinomies is explored in turn, in Chapters 4 to 7. The analysis is based on a combination of detailed commentary on texts, content analysis of magazines and advertisements, and survey data. These are deployed, as and when appropriate, to illuminate the nature of the antinomies and their tendencies to change since the 1960s. The analysis of change is completed in Part III, Chapter 8, where trends in food behaviours are summarized as a means of clarifying the ambiguities of Mennell's thesis of 'diminished contrasts and increased variety'.

4

Novelty and Tradition

4.1 Change and continuity in the British diet

Baudrillard (1988: 48) posited that to experience pleasure by consuming new items has become an obligation; a citizen's *duty* is constantly to try new pleasures. 'A *universal curiosity* . . . has as a consequence been reawakened in the areas of cuisine, culture, science, religion, sexuality, etc. "Try Jesus!", says an American slogan. *Everything* must be tried.' This spirit of restlessness, the cultivation of novelty, and the associated pursuit of fashion, pervades contemporary society. The constant development of new products and the endless creation of new desires on the part of consumers are the essential mechanisms for the reproduction of modern capitalism and its consumer culture. The requirement for ever renewed innovation among producers is well recognized. The process whereby consumers can be persuaded that they want more, and new, items is rather less well understood.

Many accounts of consumer culture point to the capacity for people sincerely to desire something that they don't have, or have never experienced, only to feel disappointment when they actually consummate that desire. This notion lies behind Campbell's (1987) portrait of the modern consumer who daydreams about self-improvement through acquisition and, one of my favourite expressions of the condition, that of Hirschman:

> The world I am trying to understand . . . is one in which men [*sic*] think they want one thing and then upon getting it, find out to their dismay that they don't want it nearly as much as they thought or don't want it at all and that something else, of which they were hardly aware, is what they really want. (1982: 21)

If an item or an activity can be represented as 'new' its appeal probably increases. Thus, in the magazines, novelty constitutes a basis of appeal for foods, as well as for clothes, body images, tourist destinations and so forth. Newness is a property which promises excitement and adventure for individuals and progress at the institutional level.

But constant innovation has its disadvantages. Perpetual change causes social and personal disruption. People come to feel insecure and anxious. New practices or products might prove unsatisfactory, might give fewer rewards than those being discarded. Worse, the new might prove positively dangerous, but once introduced it might be impossible to restore prior conditions. This has been described by Berman as the paradoxical 'experience of modernity': 'To be modern is to find ourselves in an environment that promises us adventure, power, joy, growth, transformation of ourselves and the world – and, at the same time, that threatens to destroy everything we have, everything we know, everything we are' (Berman, 1983: 1). This is much the same dilemma that is recognized by Fischler's more deep-seated omnivore's paradox: new foods often induce anxiety because they are seen as risky, so there are always also grounds for continuing to consume those foods which one knows can be trusted.

The paradox of modern experience is reflected in the food columns of the magazines. For many people probably the most immediately impressive feature of contemporary British foodways is the extent to which they have changed as new items, products and practical options have become available. The vast number of items on sale in large supermarkets – items which have been imported from all corners of the globe, thus making easily accessible tropical fruits and continental delicacies – is spectacular. The same supermarket will stock products, manufactured by the food industries, that our grandparents would have marvelled at: packages for the microwave oven, frozen foods, and pre-prepared, complete chilled dishes which permit meals representing most of the cuisines of the world to be eaten at home. And should one choose not to eat at home, then there is a huge range of restaurants, at varying prices, with different degrees of formality, exhibiting the cooking styles of many countries. The use of such commercial outlets is one source of changing routines of eating which have seen reduced numbers of meals taken by whole families in their homes. To a population inured to observing change, the field of food provides an abundant stock of examples.

However, there is a danger of exaggerating the extent of change. An alternative principle of recommendation can also be found in the magazines, when the food columns appeal to the familiar, the well tried and the traditional. Most sociologists of food suggest that it is extremely difficult to change eating habits fundamentally or rapidly. Despite cultural 'modernization' in Scandinavia, Ilmonen (1991) claimed that the ten most popular main dishes in Finland in the late 1980s were all traditional ones, popular for many years and not representing a powerful trend towards the modernization of food behaviour. Similarly, there are many stable elements to British eating habits. Not all pressures are for change. Many people are resistant to suggestions that they should alter their diets, whether for health or other reasons. It is not hard to find evidence of nostalgia and attachment to foods that remind people of their childhood experiences. Nutritionists despair because the tastes learned in childhood are difficult to alter: fixed dispositions to which people become accustomed are relinquished slowly, if at all. In addition, the large food manufacturers try hard to maintain mass markets for their more successful products which have a very long life. Smith et al. (1989: 37), in a study of confectionery, observe that 'product maintenance, brand loyalty and product stability are the watch-words of management, rather than innovation, crisis and change'. (They record the survival of Fry's Chocolate Cream bar since 1876!) They go on to say that

'The same story of brand stability can be repeated for alcoholic drinks – one only has to think of the durability of Guinness – biscuits, cakes, cereals, tinned vegetables, fruits and meats, jams and numerous other processed foods.' Given these considerations, tension might be expected between competing principles of recommendation of the novel and the familiar.

4.2 Novelty

Just as Eskimos have many words for snow, a culture like ours has an enormous number of subtly different ways of expressing novelty. We can distinguish between completely (or brand) new; unusual and exotic; out-of-the-ordinary, as measured against some ideal or the routine of mundane daily life; unfamiliar to a particular person, though familiar to other cultural groups; adventurous, experimental and innovative. These several meanings of the word 'new', often hard to differentiate in their abbreviated representations in recipe promotion devices, appear regularly in the magazines.

Recipes draw upon and discuss diverse and unfamiliar cuisines – national, ethnic and regional. The appeal to 'foreign' cuisines has been a key element of the magazines, which have introduced more diverse food styles to British readers since the 1960s. Unfamiliar products are examined and the ways of preparing them discussed. In 1968 such articles typically identified the available varieties of a general product category: pasta, species of fish, wines and European liqueurs were included. There were rather fewer examples in 1992, and these targeted more specific items: the avocado, the globe artichoke and the kiwi fruit. The magazines also intermittently offer advice about the basic cooking techniques required by alien cuisines. Occasionally a celebrity chef provides a recipe for an exotic and currently fashionable dish. In addition, and very importantly, new is used to indicate a break with routine, having things for a change, including alternative ingredients in popular dishes, and so forth.

If, as Baudrillard suggested, curiosity is mandatory, one might expect extensive and growing appeal to novelty by food columnists and advertisers. The content analysis of recipes uncovered more frequent appeals to novelty than to familiarity. However, the evidence from the recipe promotion devices suggests that in the last quarter of a century the appeal to novelty has *declined*. In 1968, 43 per cent of recipes sampled made some positive reference, explicit or implicit, to novel aspects of the dish, compared with only 22 per cent in 1992. In 1968, some 13 per cent of recipes (fifteen of them) assumed that the reader would be unfamiliar with either the ingredients or the techniques required; another 11 per cent claimed to be being adventurous or experimental with more conventional ingredients; and a further 13 per cent were recommended primarily on the basis that they were exotic or stylish. By 1991–2, experimentation with new ingredients accounted for a mere 2 per cent of recipes; simply being different, that is to say offering fresh ideas, occurred in 5 per cent; and 6 per cent were promoted as unusual, exotic or stylish.

This shift is not compensated, as it might well have been, by greater attention being paid to foreign cuisines. The proportion of recipes where the ethnic origin of a dish is an explicit or implicit part of its appeal did not change significantly: it was 28 per cent in 1968 and 27 per cent in 1992. This degree of continuity obscures some real differences. Ethnic attribution was more likely to be explicit and precise by the 1990s. The proportion of recipes originating in the British Isles (Irish, Scottish, West of England, etc.) declined, from 9 per cent to 5 per cent. More significantly, there was a sharp increase in the number of recipes explicitly originating from non-European cuisines. In 1968, 86 per cent of recipes mentioning geographical origin were either British, French or Italian, and only 10 per cent were non-European. By 1992 Italian cuisine was still the most widely represented type, but there was a wider coverage of European cuisines and 39 per cent of ethnically identified recipes originated from outside Europe, from places like China, the Caribbean, Africa and Mexico.

In 1968 there was an assumption that readers would not have experimented with different cooking techniques, nor with a range of unfamiliar ingredients, and that they would have a limited, conventional set of techniques, recipes and tastes. They were considered in need of introduction to a wider range of culinary possibilities, despite any reluctance on their part to try. Readers were encouraged to experiment, to be audacious, which usually meant to be open to foreign influences.

Articles in this vein were almost entirely published in the monthlies. They were about the creation of desire and aspiration, thus to escape the presumed limitations of conventional and orthodox cookery. It was a matter of *arousing curiosity about the unfamiliar*. *Family Circle* ran an International Cookery Course, which included recipes for scampi *alla livornese*, moussaka and *tarte aux pommes*. The use of foreign-language names for dishes was typical. Advice, often proffered in a very straightforward and didactic manner, covered the basic knowledge necessary for the preparation of foods like pasta and pizza, implying that they were unfamiliar. Pull-out supplements with a wide range of foreign dishes also featured. Several magazines applied the adjective 'gourmet' to recipes, columns or supplements in which foreign dishes were predominant. The overall impression was of a partly coherent project, advanced by the columnists, to extend knowledge, improve quality and increase variety among British domestic cooks. One effect was to bestow style on food by association of innovation and internationalism with sophistication. This process of cultivating culinary sophistication was, nevertheless, uneven: the monthlies still remained fond of recipes for sausages, gave advice on the use of Angel Delight and suggested trips to the moors to pick your own bilberries. Moreover, the much more widely circulated weekly magazines had hardly embarked on the project.

Overall, in 1968, while there was a strong ethos of innovation, experimentation and the cultivation of taste in the monthly magazines, the weeklies exhibited less coherence and were more matter-of-fact. They appeared to be rerunning routine instructions for family food preparation, with a significant proportion of their food-related material appearing in letters pages, which itself presumes shared and common knowledge relating to food.

The spirit of adventure in the 1960s monthlies was much less evident in 1992. In particular, there had developed a routine acceptance of ethnic variety, so that truly exotic and strange recipes could be introduced without much comment or reflection. Perhaps a certain ennui, or disenchantment, had accompanied the global spread of information and access to different cuisines. Alternatively, the presence of the totally unfamiliar had become so great that it had to be subjected to a more routine and matter-of-fact approach. By 1992, relatively little attention was being paid to new ingredients; few exhortations were made to experimentation and adventurousness; and less explicit reference was made to the exotic and stylish, though that certainly remained important.

The process might be described as the *routinization of the exotic*. By the 1990s it came to be assumed that people would accept other cuisines as appropriate; the gleaning of recipes from overseas did not have to be defended, or even much discussed. This may be the result of globalization more generally, both of messages and raw materials. In some respects, the appeal of Baudrillard's homily that 'everything should be tried' is a mode of experience redolent of the rather less confident, but more open, experimental and expansive 1960s. It is now routine that we should partake of foreign and international cuisines; and also perhaps that we need not necessarily or explicitly Anglicize them. Readers were having to be cajoled and encouraged in the 1960s, whereas in the 1990s they might know about the ingredients, or be able to make their own improvisations, or be prepared to try anyway because they have learned more varied tastes. That the weeklies had become as familiar with foreign foods and international variety as were the monthlies twenty-five years earlier is evidence of this routinization. They also adopted some of the same sense of style in food, so that the differences between weeklies and monthlies in these respects was less than before.

4.3 Tradition

Another reaction to rapid cultural change is to reaffirm the value of tradition. Established conventions, proven procedures and well-tried practices carry appeal for many people. In the face of the cult of the new, some people seek out authentic or shared sets of customs that can be protected, defended or reproduced. Much popular discussion of change in all areas, and perhaps more in the area of food than some others, assumes that there once was a set of shared and common practices that have recently passed into desuetude.

Tradition as legitimation

Beardsworth and Keil (1990) suggest we might understand recent changes in terms of the declining hegemony of a 'traditional menu' now challenged by competing alternatives. Certainly at any period some behaviour might appropriately be deemed customary, being repeated regularly without reflection, but it is debatable whether it ever made sense to talk of a traditional British diet, if by that is meant the long-established behaviour of the vast majority of the population. The term 'tradition' often conveys spurious notions of longevity and uniformity. Historical accounts (e.g. Burnett, 1989), suggest both that the content of the British diet evolved rapidly throughout the last 200 years and that food habits were neither stable nor widely generalized across the population. It is important at least to appreciate that the term 'tradition' may serve as a rhetorical device for the legitimation of a particular set of preferences.

On 26 November 1991, an issue of the weekly *Woman's Realm* ran a four-page cookery special under the title 'A Taste of Scotland'. Readers were invited, in their imaginations, to sample the fare of two exceptional 'cooks' who provide dinner, bed and breakfast in central Scotland. The article included information about the women in charge, about the kind of establishment they ran and a few recipes from each, which were endorsed as 'tried and tested'. Much is made of the regional suppliers of their raw materials, as well as about home-produced vegetables, herbs and eggs. The recipes printed are specialities of the respective houses. From the first come traditional roast gigot of Scottish lamb, wild Tay salmon, tomato stuffed with haggis, cloutie dumpling, bramble fool and Drambuie chocolate pots with shortbread. The second establishment offers cullen skink, saddle of roast venison or Scottish beef, clapshot and whisky & coffee *parfait* with white chocolate sauce. This is described as the effect of 'liking to experiment with traditional Scottish dishes, using top quality produce served in new and imaginative ways'. Clearly the dishes involved are being strongly associated with Scotland, some being 'rediscoveries' which have become fashionable lately.

Most significant were the pictures. Each woman was photographed twice, itself very unusual in food journalism. Elma Barrie poses behind her dining tables, with dishes upon them, in surroundings of old wood, silver, glassware and china. Traditional luxury ingredients abound, with plenty of cream, a whole salmon and a large joint. She is also photographed 'picking brambles' on a clifftop. There is a shot of the house, apparently isolated and fronting on to a shingle beach. Anita Steffen is photographed in a similar setting, but with large open fire and fireplace, copper ornaments, and prettily presented dishes. She also appears 'collecting the newly laid eggs' in the garden. A third picture shows the approach to the house, with geese on the grass.

Pictures of grass, cottages, a shoreline and the open spaces present a highly romantic image of rural Scotland: part tame, part wild nature contrasts with the achievements of culinary culture. Tradition is directly associated pictorially with nature, a comparatively rare phenomenon in food journalism or advertisements (see Warde, 1993). The artefacts represented give the impression of solid values, longevity, history and the survival of tradition. The narrative introductions glorify the small business of the self-employed craft worker producing high-quality, small-quantity personal services; Anita Steffen's 'cosy dining room can only accommodate six people at one table', Elma Barrie's 'cosy dining room can accommodate up to three tables'. While epitomizing the celebration of tradition, the extent to which any of this constituted a typical form of life or common food culture in Scotland is highly debatable.

The invention of traditions

Hobsbawm and Ranger (1983) coined the term 'the invention of tradition' to describe a common social process whereby comparatively, or entirely, new activities are given legitimacy by the pretence that they are timeless. Such inventions are as old as modernity and have fulfilled a great variety of political and social purposes, but the world tourist trade during the last thirty years has been uncommonly active in creating impressions of regional and local customs to attract visitors. The tourist industry is pre-eminent in its responsibility for the re-creation or invention of spectacular events, rituals or practices. Local food habits or specialities have played a role. The Automobile Association's guide *Food Routes* is one example of the association between food provision and leisure travel in the UK: the places listed to visit on a journey are the purveyors of high-quality, and usually locally sourced, comestibles like cheeses, beers and cakes. Similarly, the determined tourist might find newly invented culinary traditions in local and regional recipe books, in *Recipes from Wales* or *The Geordie Cookbook*.

Probably the tourist industry is more advanced at inventing traditions than is the food industry. Food columnists sometimes make connections with travel, and in 1968 as well as in 1992 there are articles that deal with an unfamiliar cuisine in the context of a visit to its geographical home. 'A Taste of Scotland' was one striking example of the way in which tourism, food and invented tradition are brought together. Incongruously, the achievements of Elma Barrie and Anita Steffen are made possible by regional suppliers of foods from far afield, by car hire firms and the aviation industry. The article was accompanied by a pre-publication reference to the Scottish Tourist Board's *The Taste of Scotland Guide*, implying co-promotion; and gratitude is expressed for the courtesy flight provided by an airline company. The article thus operates partly as a tourism column promoting Scotland as a destination and partly as a celebration of the potential virtues of discovering a 'traditional' cuisine.

One suspects that tradition is being invented anew, begging the question not only of why this should happen but also what the term 'tradition' might mean. The appeal to tradition, pursuit of the objective of returning to traditional behaviour, indeed the search for traditions to which one might return, is a perpetual feature of modern thought. One reason is that there are commercial gains to be derived from enacting or displaying tradition. Another is the widespread feeling of insecurity or uncertainty induced by declining normative regulation or social belonging. To claim that a practice is traditional is to deem it continuous over time and to accord it some legitimacy because of its moral or aesthetic value. Adherence to a tradition can provide grounds for a conscious justification of conduct. Customs may be distinguished from traditions by virtue of their being unreflective, habitual practices which are intrinsically neither good nor bad. The recommendations in the magazines draw on, without distinguishing very clearly, appeal to both tradition and custom.

The meanings of tradition

Four distinct senses of the term 'tradition' are apparent in the food columns of the magazines. The first suggests that an item is a well-established customary item belonging to the national cuisine which will therefore be *familiar* to all readers. A second sense, of *longevity*, is obtained by describing a dish as old-fashioned but still valuable, a stratagem that sometimes conjures up nostalgia and on other occasions demands action to rescue it from obscurity or extinction. Third, sustaining the continuous development of a practice sometimes necessitates embellishment or adaptation, and creativity in this regard may be praised as valid *improvisation* on tradition. A fourth sense is that of a dish being *authentic* within a particular culinary tradition, not necessarily the British tradition. In this sense we may talk of classic Italian or traditional Indian recipes.

In 1968 recipe promotion devices primarily invoked the first two senses. The accolade of tradition was almost entirely restricted to the weekly magazines; ten of the 44 recipes in the sample from the weeklies appealed to tradition. *Woman's Realm* (Aug. 1968) contained the most overt example, an article entitled 'Susan King backs British cookery'. She says:

> At its very best British cooking is second to none in the world. And most of us have nostalgia for those plain but perfectly cooked dishes granny served. This week we present traditional recipes from England and Scotland.

The symbols of English tradition that she chose included 'junket for breakfast instead of yoghourt', saffron cake from Cornwall, apple dumplings, and steak and kidney pie. Significantly the English savoury dish featured was a pie. Another featured recipe was for bread pudding, a dish that appeared elsewhere in the sample too. It was introduced with a rhetorical question, 'How many young housewives know how to make bread pudding?', to be followed by a reassuring promise 'We have given a really authentic recipe.' Baking is the most praised aspect of Scottish cuisine: 'when it comes to tea-table fare, the Scottish housewife can outbake anyone. There are baps, the traditional shortbread and Dundee cake, of course, plus dozens of different kinds of scones, oatcakes and so on.' This patriotic rendering of tradition looks backwards along with other nostalgic references, as when it was suggested we remember 'all the delicious trappings of tea-time of the when-we-were-very-young days', which preceded recipes for sticky Swiss buns and scones for tea (*WW*, Feb. 1968). The only recipe in the monthly magazines appealing to British traditions was one for lemon pancakes for Shrove Tuesday.

Explicit use of terms like 'nostalgia' and 'old-fashioned' in the magazines of 1968 was especially likely to be reserved for reference to cakes, puddings or biscuits. Of the ten recipes in the sample invoking tradition, only one was a savoury snack, though even it involved the use of crumpets; another was for oatcakes, four were for puddings and four for cakes or scones. Clearly the magazines in the 1960s regarded the baking of sweet items as the most distinctive element of the British tradition. By contrast, endorsement of novelty and a diversifying cuisine was concentrated on main courses.

The number of appeals to tradition as a credential of recipes increased quite significantly, from 14 per cent of recipes in 1968 to 25 per cent in 1992. This was, however, largely because the character of the references to tradition altered. In fact, the proportion appealing to familiarity and longevity of British traditions remained more or less constant, at about 10 per cent of all recipes, which comprised slightly more than one-third of references to tradition in 1992. However, the thematic components were less coherent than in 1968. Some of the suggestions were still for cakes and puddings: bread and butter puddings appeared yet again, alongside Christmas cakes, but strawberry cheesecake also featured. In 1992, most traditional dishes were savoury, including both recognizable ones like creamy haddock fishcakes and farmhouse vegetable soup, but also including smoked haddock and watercress soufflé and lamb escalopes with oatmeal. There were few continuities as regards the types of dish deemed traditional and those so designated had become very heterogeneous. The only recipe in the sample repeated at both dates was bread and butter pudding. The bread and butter puddings of the 1960s (*WW*, Nov. 1967; *WR*, Aug. 1968) were made from stale white bread, shredded suet, mixed fruit, mixed spice, Demerara sugar and golden syrup. *Good Housekeeping* in 1992 (March) described an 'alternative' version – brioche and butter puddings – where mixed fruit and brown sugar were the only ingredients in common, brioche, Amaretto, almonds, skimmed milk and eggs being the components of the concoction. Thus, custom remained an important consideration, but without an appreciable explosion of nostalgia for British cooking.

It is peculiar that appeal comes to be made to alien traditions, to the traditions of someone else, of some other society. A further third of the references in 1992 concerned foreign dishes, when instruction was given in the art of cooking a dish in accordance with its own tradition: for example an 'authentic' Chinese braised chicken or Thai steamed prawns with golden egg nests. In 1968, only three recipes in the sample referred to non-UK traditions, offering *fritto misto* as classic Italian, and *dinde aux truffes* and quiche lorraine from France. There was, thus, increased concern with the authenticity of foreign recipes: 7 per cent of the sample insisted on the accuracy of a non-British recipe in 1992 (the comparable figure was 3 per cent in 1968). In 1968 it was not untypical that one magazine suggested leaving out the mussels and squid from paella because they might not be to British taste.

The final third of the references to tradition in 1992 involved the suggestion of improvisation on orthodox British recipes. Brioche and butter pudding was a notable example! Others included proposals like 'New ways with old favourites' (*WW*, Aug.), an article partly alluding to the use of microwave technology, which contributed recipes for roast chicken, bread and butter pudding and creamy haddock fishcakes.

The appeal of tradition

Overall, the 1992 magazine laid more emphasis on improvisation and authenticity, the more cerebral and reflective sense of tradition, compared to 1968. Also by 1992, reference to tradition was more likely in the monthly than in the weekly magazines. The monthlies made more frequent mention not only of authentic foreign cuisine but also of old-fashioned and familiar aspects of British cooking. Tradition became a little more fashionable.

The dual sense of the attractions of tradition can also be inferred from the data from our survey in Greater Manchester. When respondents were asked 'When you have guests for a meal, what kind of meals do you prefer to serve?' more than a third of respondents replied 'traditional', a response more frequent than any except 'well presented' and 'plentiful'. Traditional meals were most likely to be preferred by older respondents, of lower social class, where the principal woman household member was not in full-time employment and where there were no children under 15 in the household. But interestingly, not only respondents with no qualifications, but also those holding degrees, were likely to like traditional food. This probably reflects the two different senses of the word in contemporary discourse on food, as the customary or as the authentic.

Behind invented traditions lurks the imagined community, a site of social group membership that promises collective security and group identity. Acceptance of the authority of comparatively fixed and shared dispositions or customs of a social group is a comforting antidote to the uncertainties of personal adventure and innovation. Such customs may be founded upon, or defined in terms of, nation, region, class, cult, ethnic group, generation, and so forth. Food columns call up local, regional and British traditional recipes. Ironically, the prominence of localized identifications with food coincides with the general decline of spatial differences in consumption patterns. In the UK, regional differences have subsided since the 1960s, as documented in official statistics. This was also one of the few social variables examined in the statistical analysis of household expenditure that showed an unequivocal trend towards greater uniformity. Comparing the four countries of the UK, we could identify correctly the location of 58 per cent of households in 1968 on the basis of their expenditure on food, but only 47 per cent in 1988. Northern Ireland was the most distinctive in both years, and Scotland retained some characteristic patterns while those of Wales and England reduced. Probably the internationalization of food supply is the primary cause, reducing regional differences that were based on local availability and price differentiation of ingredients between parts of the UK. There remain geographical variations in popular taste, but they are subsiding.

The paradox of the contemporary situation is that despite powerful globalizing tendencies local differences continue to matter. Despite international communications, trade and a worldwide popular culture, people arguably show a greater awareness of cultural diversity and perhaps attachment to their own locality. Savage makes the point that people's possessions and their daily routines may actually be very similar from place to place while affections for their own locality may be very strong. He speculates that while people's lives may well be becoming more uniform across Britain, 'their *imagined* community identification may have increased' (1989: 267). The greater prominence of 'invented' traditions in 1992 also perhaps indicated more difficulties in legitimizing taste.

4.4 The antinomy dissected: the ambivalence of modernity

Novelty and custom are contradictory sources of appeal in popular representations of foodways. Curiosity about unfamiliar food panders to the desire for new experience, new styles and new tastes. However, this is less common in recipe promotion devices than it was twenty-five years ago. Appeal on the basis of national custom, to familiar and established foods, remained more or less constant during the period, though strengthening concerns with innovation around British standard fare and with authentic foreign cuisine have meant that the notion of tradition appears more frequently overall. The implication is that the strange and the familiar are equally valuable objects of desire. These contradictory imperatives replay, within popular discourses about food, the ambivalence of modernity, the tension between the excitement associated with new experience and the familiarity of that to which one is accustomed. So, new dishes are exciting, interesting, perhaps fashionable, stylish, and so forth; but they may be awkward to resource, difficult to cook, hard to appreciate, perhaps even distasteful. Customary dishes are a source of security, certainty and are often represented as emotionally gratifying. However, they do not necessarily carry social kudos, and may at worst be perceived as boring and out of date.

An advertising tactic, occasionally deployed, epitomizes the antinomy of ambivalent modernity. In 1992 an advert was run in several of the magazines for Bisto beef granules, which were presented as an essential ingredient of *boeuf bourguignon*. In 1967 the same ploy was used to advertise HP brown sauce, recommended by a named French chef as his special ingredient for *coq au vin*. Both appeal simultaneously to two contrary principles, of what you know and what you don't know, the familiar and the foreign, the customary and the exotic; and they suggest an imaginary reconciliation. While it is not entirely clear whether these were meant, or would always be read, as a joke, they can probably be reconciled only through humour.

The predicament of persons confronting the ambivalence of modernity in other situations may be more serious and troublesome. Pathological diagnoses of the ambivalence of modernity abound. Social theorists express concern that it leads variously to personal insecurity, anxiety in situations of choice, narcissistic individualism and social disorganization (Bauman, 1988, 1991; Beck, 1992; Giddens, 1991). One very prominent and important thesis maintains that, today, people define themselves through the messages they transmit to others via the goods and practices that they possess and display. They manipulate or manage appearances, thereby creating and sustaining a 'self-identity'. In a world where there is an increasing number of commodities available to act as props in this process, identity becomes more than ever a matter of the personal selection of self-image. Individuals are obliged to choose their identities.

Anthony Giddens (1991) analyses the emergent difficulties of sustaining self-identities in late modernity. For Giddens, self-identity is 'the self as reflexively understood by the individual in terms of his or her biography' (1991: 244). A principal organizing feature of the modern experience is the maintenance of self-identity through the construction of a coherent narrative about self, which is reflexively monitored over time and tested out in different circumstances. The handling of choice is critical. One of the great challenges to the self is the fact that 'Modernity confronts the individual with a complex diversity of choices and, because it is non-foundational, at the same time offers little help as to which options should be selected' (1991: 80). A major consequence is the primacy of lifestyle, which 'can be defined as a more or less integrated set of practices which an individual embraces, not only because such practices fulfil utilitarian needs, but because they give material form to a particular narrative of self-identity' (1991: 81). In modernity, lifestyles are open to change in the light of reflexivity:

> Each of the small decisions a person makes every day – what to wear, what to eat, how to conduct himself at work, whom to meet with later in the evening – contributes to such routines. All such choices (as well as larger and more

consequential ones) are decisions not only about how to act but who to be. The more post-traditional the settings in which an individual moves, the more lifestyle concerns the very core of self-identity, its making and remaking. (ibid.)

If actors are deemed to have chosen their self-images they can be held to account for the end result. Zygmunt Bauman emphasizes this in his account of *Freedom* (1988), where he maintains that choice entails being *responsible* for one's decisions and that one can make the wrong decision, thereby potentially provoking anxiety. While for Giddens individualization is unproblematic and providential, for Bauman it is hazardous.

The problem of choice appears greater in 1992 precisely because of the importation of examples from many new cuisines. Choice has become enormous, yet little guidance is offered by the magazines as to which principles might guarantee appropriate selection. This supports at least a mild version of Fischler's gastroanomy thesis. No means is offered to decide whether the Caribbean chicken is better than the Thai or the Moroccan. There is a huge range of options, but collectively the experts fail to guide. There is no authoritative canon, no foundational wisdom to provide a basic initial orientation among cuisines. There are no criteria or guidelines for making the first, and more general, choice. The routinization of the exotic has not only sabotaged the magical elements of foreign cuisines but may also have created a vacuum of judgment. However, once the choice has been made, much of the uncertainty is removed, as the recipes themselves are so precise in their details that one might feel confident in accomplishing successfully the final dish.

The problem may be conceived as a loss of social embeddedness. Bernice Martin proposed that the stage of development of advanced societies in the period after the Second World War was characterized by a key contradiction: 'What it gives is affluence and a new possibility of freedom and individuality; what it takes away is a natural rootedness and automatic structures of belonging' (1981: 16). In terms of food we might interpret this as a tension between increasingly personal choice between foods and the unavailability of recourse to fixed, group-sanctioned dispositions. This is expressed by the contradictory imperatives of novelty and custom. The anxiety associated with personal choice might be one reason for the invention of traditions and the attempt to imagine community where none exists. However, the problem of choice is not solved by reinvented traditions because many participants are usually at least half aware that these traditions are recent artefacts. It is doubtful whether invented traditions and imagined communities successfully offer sufficient comfort. On the other hand, declining access to collective judgments in accordance with well-tested group dispositions may not be of great concern. Some scenarios of postmodernism would suggest that people are increasingly at home with, and capable of negotiating, the dilemmas of choice, the rewriting of biographies and the opportunities for less unitary identities. Whether people become anxious in the face of uncertainty is arguable.

4.5   Novelty, custom and generation

The concept of generation

The sociological concept of generation might help to explain the vacillating importance of notions of novelty and custom. Some scholars suggest that generation is becoming an ever more important social division affecting consumption (e.g. Schulze, 1992; and with respect to food, Riley, 1994). When attention is directed towards generation it is usually young adults who come under the microscope, their innovative behaviour being perpetually capable of surprising, not to say shocking, their elders. Such concentration of attention is not always appropriate, as the evidence concerning the food preferences of different age groups suggests.

Age differences in consumption patterns are unsurprising since people at different stages of the life course will differ in their wants and needs. A recurrent problem in interpreting age-related data is deciding whether observed differences in behaviour arise from the practical obligations and constraints that occur at a specific stage in the life course, or whether people born in a particular period experienced distinctively different socialization processes. For instance, single and childless young people behave in ways different from parents in their thirties and forties who have co-resident children. If this were an effect of stage of the *life course*, then it would be anticipated that as these young people age they will adopt the responsibilities, and therefore many of the practices, of the older age group. More regular domestic meal times, less eating out, adaptation of diets to suit the nutritional needs and special preferences of children would be obvious examples. Alternatively, if preferences different from those of their elders were learned in early adulthood, then these might be maintained throughout a lifetime. This, a *generational* effect, would mean that with the passing of time the pattern of food preferences of the British population as a whole would shift. In the extreme case of generational taste formation, age groups might become homogeneous in their behaviour. For example, people growing up during the Second World War might exhibit a strong preference for the meat and chocolate that was denied them, while those brought up in the 1970s might have developed an enduring taste for carbonated soft drinks, TV dinners and pasta. This scenario suggests the existence of a shared collective basis for a food culture, of strongly shared tastes rather than highly individualized choice, with cohort membership overriding other social divisions. Incidentally, if this were the case, then variation in taste might be explained primarily in terms of food production: what was made available at a particular time, either as a result of shortages of products, or due to waves of innovation among food manufacturers and the hospitality industries, would be likely determining factors, supporting a production-led model of consumer behaviour.

There are several reasons why this scenario might be pertinent to recent British historical experience. First, young adults of the 1980s were perhaps the first cohort in the UK to have been exposed throughout their lives to an established mass consumer culture (see Warde, 1994a). Socialized at the hands of mass media, this group might be more effective in managing, exploiting and using the elements of such a consumer culture. Second, for those born in the 1960s, as the post-war boom began to increase disposable income for ordinary households, and simultaneously for young people, more resources were available to experiment with commercial food and drink products. Finally, there were simply many more, and therefore sometimes different, items which first became available for purchase during this period. For these reasons, recent cohorts of the British population might have distinctive consumption habits.

Patterns of consumption

The evidence of age-related food preferences is well established. Domestic struggles around food are frequent, with children and adolescents especially likely to register protest about the foodways imposed on them by their parents. The times of meals, their contents, table manners and behaviour expected on special occasions are all sources of domestic conflict. Particular disquiet has recently been expressed regarding the decline of the family meal, a worry based on the assumption that eating together regularly is a basis of stable family life. Mismatching time patterns are probably as important as youthful rebelliousness, but the habit of grazing may be more common among younger adults. Age-related behavioural differences are also prominent in eating out. People under 25, asked their favourite type of restaurant, choose Chinese and pizza houses more frequently than other age groups (Payne & Payne, 1993). Auty's (1992) local study showed that students, who eat out comparatively frequently, are more likely to visit pizza restaurants and burger bars than pubs or restaurants, which are favoured by older people. Similar patterns exist in other countries: Toivonen (1994) shows that it is younger people who eat out in fast-food places in Finland, and Fantasia (1995) makes the same point about the recent incursion of fast food into France. Finally, market research data on segmented markets for food purchased in shops also shows differentiation by age (e.g. Riley, 1994; Bartlam, 1993).

Households without dependent children drink significantly fewer litres per person per week of soft drinks (NFS, 1992). This is not a new phenomenon: prohibition of alcohol and frequent aversion in childhood to hot drinks containing caffeine is longstanding, so these individual habits might be expected to alter in later stages of the life course. The preferences of retired people for fish and lamb is much more likely to be a generational effect, there being no reason to think that their younger successors will discover a taste for such items simply as a function of getting older. In these two instances, interpretation is relatively unproblematic. Identifying causes and anticipating trends is more often difficult. The tendency of children to rebel against their parents through adopting a different diet is most probably an effect of their life-course stage, though if expressed as vegetarianism, currently especially popular among the young, it may persist to become a cohort effect. Without longitudinal data on individuals it is hard to determine whether statistical relationships with age are the effect of life-course stage or generational socialization. In addition, although age-based differences are undeniable, we do not as yet know, empirically, whether differences between age groups are changing. Some suggestive, though ultimately indeterminant, findings arose from reanalysis of the Family Expenditure Survey.

Generation and food expenditure 1968–88

The principal concern in the discriminant analysis exercise was to estimate the degree of change in the impact of social class on food purchasing behaviour. However, the analysis also threw up some preliminary and less systematic insight into the impact of other socio-demographic variables on food purchasing.

Some attempts were made to predict food purchase by age for the occupants of single person households. Considering all single person households, in four age bands (under 30, 30–44, 45–59 and 60+), and using the full set of purchasing items at each date, the models were very successful in their predictions (see Table 4.1).

The model for 1968 correctly predicted the age group of a person in almost 65 per cent of cases, that for 1988 in almost 64 per cent of instances. In other words, on the basis of a person's food bill, we can predict their age in about two cases out of three, confirming that age group is an important variable affecting food preference. The pattern of incorrect attributions was at each date very similar, it being easiest to predict those over 60 years of age, and hardest to identify those in the two central age groups.

The evidence about age groupings indicates that impact of age on food choice has become simpler, the model suggesting a more direct and linear association between age and food expenditure in 1988 than in 1968. This suggests some tendency during the last twenty years towards the establishment of tastes shared by cohorts which might be a consequence of the moulding of taste by producers, through their new products, their advertising, and so forth.

The most important items distinguishing between age groups were very similar at the two dates. In 1988, 87 per cent of the explained variance among all single person households loaded on to the first canonical function, which showed a simple and straightforward relationship between age and eating preference. The younger a person was, the more likely he or she was to buy food outside the home, especially at the cheaper end of the market, to purchase alcoholic drinks on licensed premises, and to buy soft drinks and potato products. Items avoided included tea, sugar, butter, bakery goods, milk, flour, jam, cooked ham, lamb and eggs.

Table 4.1 *Age differences in food expenditure among single person households, 1968 and 1988*

(a) Classification results: 1968

Actual group	No. of cases	Predicted group membership			
		1	2	3	4
Group 1	40	24	8	2	6
< 30		60.0%	20.0%	5.0%	15.0%
Group 2	82	13	33	17	19
30–44		15.9%	40.2%	20.7%	23.2%
Group 3	239	12	33	97	97
45–59		5.0%	13.8%	40.6%	40.6%
Group 4	800	18	58	126	598
> 60		2.3%	7.3%	15.8%	74.8%

Percentage of 'grouped' cases correctly classified: 64.77.

(b) Classification results: 1988

Actual group	No. of cases	Predicted group membership			
		1	2	3	4
Group 1	239	135	47	27	30
< 30		56.5%	19.7%	11.3%	12.6%
Group 2	220	58	78	56	28
30–44		26.4%	35.5%	25.5%	12.7%
Group 3	284	22	41	122	99
45–59		7.7%	14.4%	43.0%	34.9%
Group 4	1093	33	24	200	836
> 60		3.0%	2.2%	18.3%	76.5%

Percentage of 'grouped' cases correctly classified: 63.78.

In 1988, the effect of age was overwhelmingly linear, but the comparable data for 1968 was slightly more complicated. In 1988 the effect of being in mid or later stages of a career, and therefore somewhat richer if perhaps a little more home centred, was very small. In 1968 this was more pronounced.[1] Prediction of respondents' ages was based on rather similar items: younger people spent proportionately more on eating out, alcohol, potato products, soft drinks, canned fruit and vegetables, and proportionately less on tea, fresh milk, bread, flour, butter and jam. In addition, however, in 1968, people under 30 spent less than others still of working age, on bread, bacon, fish or tea.

The similarity of the items, and of the pattern of inaccurate attribution, suggest that generally it is the life cycle rather than the cohort effect which is strongest. In both years, about 80 per cent of persons aged 45–59 were allocated to one of the two groups aged over 45. This implies a point of maturation of dietary practice. In both years, the group 30–44 was the most difficult to predict, and it is probably significant that this was even more so in 1988, when only 36 per cent of cases were correctly identified.

There is, however, other evidence, especially clear when looking at women only, that there may be a generational effect in this particular instance, making it an exception to the rule that generally life-course stage is of primary importance. Women under 30 in 1968 were *very* distinctive in comparison with other women.[2] Their characteristic preferences were for meals out, sandwiches purchased away from home, 'luxury' vegetables (canned, fresh and frozen), 'luxury' fresh fruit, wine, soft drinks and milk products. (In 1968 the Family Expenditure Survey divided fruit and vegetables into two categories, ordinary, which were most commonly used, items like carrots, sprouts and apples, and superior, which included asparagus, endive, yams, guavas and pineapples.) So, in 1968, those women born since 1938 were adopting the most distinctive of diets *vis-à-vis* all older women.[3] This appears to isolate a cohort effect causing some significant alternation to patterns overall. A customary maturation of diet (the effect of life-cycle change, domestication, the use of fresh ingredients and more eating at home) was ruptured by one particular cohort which, though obviously in part subject to the constraints of domestication, has retained some of the characteristics learned as young adults in the late 1950s and 1960s and which have proved resistant to alteration. Hence, the same cohort, aged 30–44 in 1988, were a less homogeneous group, among which many individuals exhibited food consumption patterns typical of the cohort coming after them.

We might speculate that this particular cohort learned different food habits as young adults in the period after the end of rationing in the 1950s and in the early stages of a mass consumer culture in Britain. Women might have been influenced by 1960s changes in evaluations of good and stylish food reflected in the new tranche of recipe books.[4] This same cohort of women was also most powerfully subject to the quite dramatic increase in the proportion of women who, after marriage, were to continue in, or return quickly to, paid employment. The magazines in 1968 could, indeed, have been appealing to new developments in the behaviour of their younger readers. By 1992, the youngest group had become less distinctive. This suggests behaviour consistent with evidence from the magazines that curiosity was greater in the 1960s and that a routinization of the exotic occurred subsequently.

Age is a significant variable which is not declining in importance. Indeed, it is perhaps becoming more important, in that there is a very simple relationship between age and preferences, not much complicated by greater income or domesticity in the middle years. On the other hand we could say that there was, uniquely in 1968, a considerable difference between under-30s and the rest. That key, and sharp, difference has subsided, suggesting perhaps that the next, succeeding, cohort learned some of the post-war generation's ways.

The evidence adduced bears on speculation about increasing stylization of life. Great concern with novelty and fashion, and equally obeisance to tradition, might disclose aesthetic leanings that delimit particular styles of life. However, much of the variance between cohorts seems more effectively explained by the constraints of life-cycle stage than as style. For most of the century as cohorts aged, they tended to shift their behaviours towards some norm for mature family households. Young people have always purchased foods that require limited preparation time and skill. They have also always drunk away from home and eaten out more.[5] The tendency for young people currently to purchase much take-away food, to eat irregularly and to be absent from family meals is probably, firstly, a life-cycle effect. However, it seems likely that there was a specific generational effect, probably a process of stylization followed by more informalization. The increasing linearity of the statistical relationship between food purchase and age does not suggest the emergence of specialized, subcultural, niche differentiation.

4.6 Summary

Representation of food exhibits restlessness, novelty and fashion, even while there is reason to believe that food habits are more resistant to change than some other aspects of consumption. Both in the mind and in practice, innovation and custom coexist. In many respects, the appreciation of novelty requires one to postulate the existence of a traditional past imagined to exhibit permanency, even though no such fixed past may ever have existed. Conversely, people perceive perpetual flux while living and consuming in a profoundly routine manner. Custom and novelty are inextricably intertwined in the modern mind and in modern institutions. Ontological insecurity is the corollary of modernity, at the personal level there being an uncomfortable trade-off between autonomous self-expression and belonging (Martin, 1981). Self-expression may be achieved by enacting quasi-traditional behaviour, or by permanent experimentation with new experiences; a sense of belonging equally may be achieved by attaching oneself to an established and entrenched culture or to a new cult. These stratagems are, however, very much features of modernity, and do not of themselves herald postmodernity or post-Fordism.

Individualization is often glorified because it gives the personal freedom to pursue self-determination. But such freedom is paradoxical, modernity ambivalent. Curiosity may be unrewarding; adventure may be pointless, false or inauthentic; pursuing the novelties of fashion might even be a hindrance to innovation; diversity may confuse. Food columns in 1992 offered a haphazard bricolage of recipes. They positively encourage a promiscuous approach, in the sense that there is no overall direction or fundamental rationale for selecting one dish rather than another. Selecting with discrimination among a huge range of possibilities may easily remove any *meaning* from food choice. What is presented is an endless chain of items whose principal feature is their equivalence. By comparison, the columnists of the 1960s seemed to have had a project for the improvement of British taste and culinary practice which involved innovation and experimentation, rather than the simple display of diversity.

Nevertheless, there is a great deal of detailed regulatory information in the food columns. Even the foreign cuisine recipes are being described and transmitted in great detail to encourage reproduction of an accurate version of their authentic origin. There is evidence of concern for greater variety and greater precision in ethnic cuisine. The detail is in the form of regulations, but there is little guide or guarantee regarding the overall menu. What we see is rather less a confident plurality of styles, each with its own coherence and inner logic, rather more an anomic array of culinary options. The nature of uncertainty itself altered between the 1960s and the 1980s.

It is doubtful that there was much coherence to national food practices by 1968; there was not then a uniform and customary repertoire governed by national and regional standards. Nevertheless, in the 1960s the weekly magazines exhibit a degree of complacent boredom about food which was founded on some shared and common knowledge regarding appropriate ways to construct a domestic food regime. By contrast, the magazines of the 1990s presume few shared assumptions in culinary matters. They display a phenomenal range of options about which they are blasé. They celebrate choice, but refuse to rule on which are the best choices. The routinization of the exotic and rationalization at the level of detailed instructions on procedures might be seen as two concessions to consequent uncertainty.

Despite the uncertainty about what might conceivably constitute traditional British eating habits, the magazines made regular appeal to tradition. Much of the time this was a matter of inventing traditions anew; the change in the items considered 'traditional' between the 1960s and the 1990s is instructive. Nonetheless, there may have been some customary practices still in existence in the 1960s which are less secure now. That the 1960s magazines presumed a set of shared customs and practices might be inferred from the fact that the monthly magazines in particular were eager to encourage people to break out of their monotonous routines. Meanwhile, the weeklies were providing practical advice about how to sustain those routines and there was a certain humdrum normality about their food columns: readers reported their favourite recipes; the resident cookery writer answered readers' questions; recipes were provided without explicit rationale, as suggestions for things to eat that would be acceptable to most people. The manner of address anticipated much common ground between readers. Better though that this is not conceptualized as 'tradition' *per se*, but as custom, a sedimented and established way of doing things. By 1992, there seems to be less taken-for-granted common ground and greater need to invent tradition, as one ploy among many to help resolve the general problem of guidance. In the absence of overarching or foundational principles for food choice, tradition confers some legitimacy and is therefore a term attractive to beleaguered food writers and their audiences.

Mennell (1985) declined to consider the impact of generation on food habits. He may thereby have ignored one potential counter-trend to his thesis, that cohorts may have been becoming more rather than less differentiated. However, overall, the social distance between age groups remained constant. The statistical association between age and food preference, as measured in the discriminant analysis, was very similar in 1968 and 1988. This perhaps should give pause for thought to those who, particularly by concentrating their attention on the consumption behaviour of young people, interpret age-group differences as generational. For most of the 20th century it would seem that age differences in food preference were primarily an effect of the life course.

However, there were some signs that one particular generation, born in the 1940s, was responsible for a significant shift in food habits. This generation, while still under 30 years of age in 1968, was very distinctive in its food preferences, and was less likely than preceding cohorts sub-sequently to have developed practices common to mature households. It is not unreasonable to imagine that the women of this generation were the audience for the magazines that were encouraging culinary experimentation during the 1960s. The innovations of that period have subsequently become the norm, such that the cohort born after 1958 is not so sharply distin-guished from the previous one. If this is the case, then the major turning point in food tastes probably occurred earlier than a post-Fordist thesis would anticipate and for reasons that had little to do with a postmodern structure of feeling.

5

Health and Indulgence

5.1 Disciplining the body and pampering the soul

The November 1991 edition of *Cosmopolitan* ran an article entitled 'Comfort food'; 'say goodbye to the wintertime blues with shepherd's pie followed by a sinful pud'. Written by a columnist, Richard Ehrlich, it reported a conversation with a friend, Lucy, and her choice of food in a restaurant. It starts from the justifications for selecting something that is perhaps unhealthy, certainly fattening and bearing little established style value – bangers and mash (sausage and mashed potatoes). Explaining herself she says: '"Every so often, you have to break the rules. Sometimes salad just won't do it."' Lucy, it is explained, is 'very health conscious. Not a fanatic, but someone who looks after herself in every respect.' Indeed, as the author agrees, who would want to be a fanatic?:

> It's important to eat with an eye on your health, but a narrow view of what's 'healthy' doesn't always correspond with what your mind and body need to keep themselves happy. We are talking about the food you eat when your heart is broken, your boss is being impossible . . . in short, about comfort food.

Comfort food, our journalist says, 'is a term that has been much used lately, now that the fashion for dainty dishes served in gerbil-sized portions has passed'. This is clearly a style ploy: if the term is much used, it must be fashionable and that is a matter of importance for those who would like to be fashionable. 'The new trendy food is more like what Granny used to make', and we are subsequently assured that some really important chefs have been copying Granny in a respectably stylish manner! After proclaiming that 'High-quality comfort food has recently made some notable conquests', a few names are dropped. Gary Rhodes, a 'brilliant' chef, previously awarded a Michelin star for elaborate food, who as head chef at London Greenhouse Restaurant but is now doing something different, is taken as exemplary: 'There are nods in the direction of France and Italy, but mostly this is plain old British food cooked to an extraordinarily high standard.'

Ehrlich then offers an adaptation of Rhodes's recipe for onion gravy. Subsequently, to ally suspicion of his being parochial, he says 'Of course, comfort food doesn't have to be British', citing the virtues of 'a plateful of spaghetti carbonara or macaroni cheese' to comfort him if he's 'feeling down'. Nevertheless, the article is in large part nostalgia for Britishness and the sausage: 'British cuisine undeniably excels at simple dishes that raise the

spirits while filling the stomach. Bangers and mash is comfort food par
excellence and, when made with good sausages, it's one of the all-time top
10 treats.' Other such dishes include shepherd's pie, roast beef and
Yorkshire pudding.

What, then, has happened to health? Well, of course, Lucy would only
eat things like this sometimes and we have been told that she is in good
shape. Maybe if she took too much notice of the suggestions for dessert she
would not be so for long:

> To finish off what could be better than a steamed or baked pudding which
> Matthew Fort, Food and Drink Editor of the *Guardian* (and the 1990
> Glenfiddich Food Writer of the Year) calls 'England's greatest contribution to
> world cuisine'.

Once again the writer cites an authority, expert advice being a sort of
reassurance in a world of culinary confusion. The article concludes:

> Whatever you're feeling down about – and even if you are feeling terrific – these
> are dishes to warm the heart and cheer the spirit. Dig in and enjoy – you can
> always have a salad tomorrow.

Of course I'm probably being unfair in taking at his word a columnist
writing in a magazine that is being read primarily for fun. But the article
exemplifies one of the most important of mixed messages regarding
contemporary food. We should eat healthily; but not if it makes us sad.
Implicitly hedonistic consumption is justified in terms of what the mind and
body need: since the body doesn't need unhealthy food, it must be the mind
that is in need. This juxtaposition of indulgence and bodily self-discipline
identifies a profound contradiction. Its only resolution is by eating
something different tomorrow. Bangers and mash is for a special occasion,
when feeling blue; and that is a most important condition in the world of
self. You deserve to be happy, and to be comforted when not. Then
indulgence may be craved for a transgression of the rules. Ultimately, this
is a tale about good and evil, and what is being encouraged is evil. But you
can be forgiven because you feel miserable; if you aren't happy, try sin!

Many other key themes of contemporary culinary wisdom are present in
the article: health, indulgence, tradition, style, experts who are glamorous
and have an opinion worth more than yours, news about fashion, ideas
about the emotional self and its protection. The article as a whole comprises a ragout of some prominent elements of contemporary culture and
illustrates a very deep-rooted antinomy.

5.2   Health in the recipe columns

The assumption that Lucy would routinely eat healthily reflects one of the
most striking developments in recent representations of food. In 1968
health was rarely alluded to in cookery columns. In 1967–8 only 4 per cent
of recipes were coded as having recommended food explicitly because it

was healthy and none of these was in a monthly magazine. Even then, the references were scanty and tangential: honey was a healthy ingredient (*Woman*, May 1968), bacon 'a protein food' (*WR*, Feb. 1968). Healthiness was not an issue, even to the extent that there was little appeal to the functional aspect of nutrition. Except occasionally in relation to children, food intake was not associated with anxieties about risk to health.

Some time thereafter, concern for health escalated. The language of health came to permeate routine cookery articles and the recipe promotion devices. In the 1991–2 sample, 16 per cent of all recipes made explicit reference to health features in the food columns. The concern for health was partly instanced by the emergence of articles whose central identity was nutrition; *Cosmopolitan* ran a regular column 'Eating Light, Eating Right', for instance. Most commonly, especially in the monthly magazines, there was an assumption that healthy food would be light, and though rarely recommended specifically for its propensity to reduce calorific intake, there were overtones of concern with physical appearance, body shape, skin tone and the like. But food columns became likely to refer to the desirability of consuming five portions of fruit and vegetables per day, advice which emanated from government sources, or to the fact that stir-frying was a healthy form of cooking. The columnists also discussed the valuable nutrients obtainable variously from 'healthy, oily fish', watercress, potatoes and kiwi fruit, by way of enhancing the attractiveness of their featured recipes.

Another major change was the increased amount of factual information given about fat, fibres, calories, etc. In 1991–2, 15 per cent of recipes estimated fat or fibre content and 54 per cent gave calorie counts. Such facts were almost never recorded in the earlier year. Additional precise measurements are part of a more general and long-term tendency towards providing more exact instructions in cookery columns, a process best understood as the *rationalization* of domestic cookery. It is nonetheless significant that some extra information is provided about nutrition, implying increased concern with health. If it is accepted that the inclusion of specific nutritional information in recipes is a reference to health, then the percentage of recipes recognizing the principle of healthy eating increased from 9 per cent to 65 per cent between 1968 and 1992. Regardless of reservations about the ambiguities of coding procedures in content analysis, a major change occurred. The incorporation of health concerns into recipe columns, and the extensive coverage given to food in the health and beauty columns, implies that the scientific evidence about links between health and eating had been widely absorbed by 1992.

5.3 Policies for health

An emergent, socially pervasive, notion of 'healthy eating' appears in advertisements, in conversation, as apology when people excuse their choice of food (being caught eating cake usually requires the excuse that this is irregular behaviour), when poor mothers account for not giving their children an appropriately nutritious and healthy diet because they cannot afford good food, or as instruction on posters in doctors' waiting rooms. The change in part reflects the impact of government policy and propaganda regarding healthy eating, whose messages surely reached the food columnists. According to Murcott (1990), the British state began its first serious campaign to persuade people of the link between diet and health only in 1969. Since then there have been a number of documents and campaigns, though, according to Cannon (1993), the British government was both late and hesitant, in comparison with international counterparts, in introducing guidelines to counteract those 'diseases of affluence' related to diet, like heart disease and various cancers.[1] According to Cannon, the report of the Department of Health's Committee on the Medical Aspects of Food Policy, *Dietary Reference Values for Food Energy and Nutrients for the United Kingdom* (June 1991) was the first official document to recommend specific targets for reduction of intake of fats for the population as a whole, as opposed to specific vulnerable groups. Among the questions that arise are: who has absorbed the messages? who believes them? and who acts upon them?

Knowledge and practice

According to the *British Social Attitudes* survey of 1989, the population had become generally aware of the link between diet and health, though there was still some confusion about which foods were good for people and which not. Twenty-eight per cent of respondents said they were 'fairly' or 'very' worried about the sorts of food they eat (Sheihan et al., 1990: 147). This level of perception of risk is higher than in Sweden, but much lower than in the USA and Japan (Wandel, 1994). Despite their concern, few of the worried British respondents were planning to alter their diet. Nevertheless, most people described having made some moves in the previous three years towards eating more healthily: 88 per cent claimed to have implemented at least one of five changes, namely, grilling instead of frying, eating wholemeal brown bread, having fish instead of red meat, using skimmed rather than full-fat milk, boiling or baking potatoes instead of roasting or frying (Sheihan et al., 1990). However, people also report eating less confectionery while the total volume of the industry's sales has increased, casting doubt on the accuracy of their perceptions. The impression given about the prospects for more healthy eating by the survey was positive with respect to attitude, but reasons remained for doubting whether practice has yet altered decisively.

One effect of publicity has been an increase in the sales of some commercial products whose appeal is that they are light or that they contain low levels of fat or sugar. Skimmed milk, low-fat yoghurts and sugar-reduced variants of soft drinks have all increased sales quickly in the last few years. However, individual purchasers do not necessarily thereby eliminate from their diet the less healthy versions of the same items: people drink diet Coke *and* ordinary Coke (see Bartlam, 1993). That there are changes in the representation of foods in the magazines, and in attitudes reported in surveys, does not necessarily mean that behaviour is altering. As regards some of the more risky foods, there is some evidence that an increase in both consumption and expenditure, per head of the population, between the early 1950s and the late 1960s was subsequently reversed. Taking the national average for the nutritional value of household foods (NFS, 1991: 114, Appendix C, Table 8, p. 218), energy intake and carbohydrate intake peaked in the mid-1950s, fat and protein intake at the end of the 1960s, and both have continued to fall since. However, the *proportion* of energy derived from carbohydrate (an official sign of healthy eating) has fallen throughout the period since 1940. Thus, the trends for the individual components indicate healthier eating, but the overall pattern does not. Similarly ambiguous tendencies are apparent with regard to individual food items. More brown wholemeal bread is eaten, specifically denoted health foods have increased sales, while full-fat milk and sugar sales have declined. On the other hand, consumption of vegetables and fish has fallen, while that of cheese has greatly increased. The health message alone is insufficient to persuade people to purchase that which is good for them.

Moreover, healthy foods tend to be purchased by particular social groups; for example, young women drink diet Coke, the middle-aged and the middle class take low-fat dairy foods. There are class differences in the purchasing of healthy products. One of the ways to identify professional workers in the discriminant analysis was through their disproportionate spending on fresh fruit and vegetables, white meat, cereals and fruit juice. Routine white-collar workers shared their taste for cereals, poultry, fish, and fruit juice. It seems likely that these tastes reflect a greater preparedness of some sections of the middle class to adapt their diets to the rules of healthy eating. This is to some degree confirmed by the survey in Greater Manchester. Asked 'When you have guests for a meal, what kind of meals do you prefer to serve?', 84 out of 323 respondents selected 'healthy' from the list of options. Three social characteristics of a respondent significantly prompted the healthy choice: being a woman, living in a middle-class household, and being highly educated. The degree to which changes in practice significantly affect all the population is debatable.

Finally, one further possible counter-tendency to healthy eating is the decline of formal meals, which must make the recording and regulating of ingestion quite problematic. Although there is no inherent reason why snacks should be less nutritious than meals, some versions of fast food and of packaged products purchased off the shelf are notoriously unhealthy if consumed in large amounts. Moreover, when people eat out they often relax their concerns to monitor or restrict their appetites. Until 1994, estimates of the nutritional composition of the diet of the UK populace have ignored eating out: the National Food Survey for instance only collected detailed nutritional information on items purchased to be consumed in the home. Of course, it would be difficult for them, and equally for the average consumer, to obtain accurate information about the nutritional composition of dishes sold in pubs, cafés and restaurants. It is certainly possible, as the *Family Expenditure Survey* hints, that gains to health achieved by the professionals from eating light foods and fresh fruit and vegetables at home are counteracted by their habit of spending considerably more money eating out and drinking wine.

What is 'healthy'

One possible reason why diet has not changed more rapidly is that people are sceptical of the appropriateness of the advice offered by government and nutritional science. Nowadays, assessments of risk made by experts are frequently publicly challenged by other experts. Given the complexity of determining risk in many spheres, from the safety of nuclear installations to the effects of chemicals on foodstuffs, estimates can scarcely derive from other than expert sources (Beck, 1992). Yet their well-publicized disagreements, and apparent revisions to previously accepted beliefs, tend to undermine popular confidence in official recommendations. This scenario is perhaps most apparent in food scares in the last decade, for instance regarding salmonella in chicken and eggs or BSE in cattle. The handling of these, by government and the food industries, was lamentable in so far as their pronouncements simply gave the impression that they were intentionally covering up real problems in order to restrict loss of revenue for producers. The practical extent of the danger meanwhile remained obscure. By contrast, as Cannon demonstrates, there is expert consensus on more routine matters of diet. Reports from many countries and many sources over the last thirty years express consensus on the dangers to health of currently average levels of fat and sugar intake (Cannon, 1993: 9). Nonetheless, the concern with news values in mass media presentations does not always give that impression: the desire to offer an entertaining debate means that experts holding views shared by a tiny minority of scientists or practitioners are invited to participate in equal numbers. A misleading impression may then be given that each and every view is equally valid and that any advice is substantively groundless, a mere matter of opinion or faith. Additionally, the last decade has witnessed apparently growing scepticism of government, the state and its scientific advisers: whether justified or not, this may have inadvertently conferred greater credibility on other sources of information that are not necessarily any more trustworthy.

One among countless examples was the lead item on the BBC2 *Newsnight* programme (9 August 1994) which devoted many minutes to discussing a leaked document purporting to contain the Department of Health's new campaign to encourage more healthy eating and which was said to include targets for change such as that, on average, people should eat another slice and a half of bread per day, an additional 'egg-sized' potato daily, an extra half-portion of oily fish per week, and so forth.

Besides jokes about the size of eggs, the programme featured a clinical nutritionist who professed that we had no reliable knowledge about the effects of diet on health, a free-marketeer who maintained that governments should have no role whatever in health promotion and who warned of health fascism, a sociologist from a health care pressure group who approved the concreteness of the advice while expressing suspicion that it was self-interested food industries who were responsible for opposing the campaign, a spokeswoman for the Dairy Council proclaiming its products wholesome and a necessary source of calcium, a general practitioner from East London who said that the guidelines were totally inapplicable to ethnic minorities, and an interviewer who operated from the position that the sovereign consumer should not be instructed or encouraged in any way whatever on pain of infringing some right to spend one's own money in the way one personally sees fit. The cacophony arising from the combination of zealotry, promotion of sectional interest and editing for effect must have foiled any viewer seeking coherent conclusions and practical information.

The growing concern with healthy eating has generated new obsessions and new anxieties, as well as new commercial products which promise to alleviate such concern. Articles in the magazines, even entire books, are devoted to micro-properties of foods, to minerals and extra vitamins, usually considered good, and to additives, preservatives and chemicals, usually bad. The magazines carried articles concerned with food safety, specifically allergies, (*Prima*, Feb. 1992) and food poisoning (*WH*, May 1992). There were also articles on the micro-properties of foodstuffs and ways to ensure that sufficient proper nutrients were obtained, partly through appropriate cooking techniques, partly by surveying commercially available substitutes or supplements. Examples included 'Finding your way through the vitamin maze' (*Prima*, Nov. 1991), 'Minerals – a down-to-earth guide' (*Prima*, Aug. 1992), and 'Are you throwing vitamins down the drain?' (*Prima*, May 1992), an article which tellingly began with the phrase 'In the health conscious nineties'. Other articles lauded the value of a good diet for warding off medical complaints: examples included a feature about the role of special food regimens as a response to cancer (*WO*, Feb. 1992), a dietary solution to premenstrual tension (*WO*, May 1992), and instructions about weaning small children off junk food (*Best*, Feb. 1992). Some of these were in health columns, some in beauty columns and some were included in food columns, as has always been the case to some degree. Altogether, some fifteen articles were concerned with the health properties of food and how best to preserve health through diet. (A further eight articles were about slimming.)

Vegetables and vegetarians

Vegetarians often claim that their diets are more healthy than those of meat eaters, but the principal reasons given for conversion are ethical and

Table 5.1   *Types of dishes: recipes sample 1967–8 and 1991–2*

	1967–8	1991–2
Main dish[1]	59	61
containing meat	38	28
containing fish	15	13
containing only vegetables	2	12
other	4	8
Puddings	18	17
Starters (inc. soups)	7	12
Confectionery	27	27
Drinks	3	4
Other	2	3
N =	116	124

[1] Includes those specified as lunch and supper dishes.

political (Beardsworth & Keil, 1992). Health messages have, in general, sought to encourage people to eat more fresh fruit, vegetables, fish and fibre, at the expense of meat, sugar and fats. One indication of the impact of these messages is the content of the recipes themselves.[2] Table 5.1 shows the number of types of dish that were in the random sample of recipes at the two dates. If frequency of appearance in the food columns indicates changing practice, then the key shifts would be a decline in the prominence of meat in main meals, a corresponding growth of vegetarian main dishes, and some increase in starters and in other dishes associated with main meals (essentially accompaniments like sauces and side vegetables). That the proportion of main dishes remained constant, 50 per cent of all recipes in both years, arises partly from coding, a number of recipes (seven in all) in 1991–2 were described as lunch or supper dishes as main meals. While functional substitutes for main meal dishes, the implication might be that they were a little lighter in content and perhaps not intended for a family occasion.

By 1992 the magazines had come to give considerable prominence to vegetarianism. In British cuisine vegetables, especially green ones, symbolize personal virtue: they are good for you, you should have more even though you probably dislike them. This distaste and the general poor reputation of vegetables is partly the consequence of the appalling ways in which British cookery books and institutional food providers, like school canteens, have insisted upon murdering them. In the absence of a fine tradition of British vegetable cookery it is perhaps unsurprising that the vegetarian recipes themselves are often quite exotic, with a strongish Italian influence: of twelve examples in 1991–2, seven have foreign attributions, including *peperonata gougère, farfalle* with fresh tomatoes, *tarte provençale* and Mexican fondue. Their increasing prominence is, then, a feature of some importance.

It was not out of place for *Good Housekeeping* (Sept. 1992) to carry a 16-page pull-out booklet of vegetarian cookery. Two magazines contained directions for extensive vegetarian Christmas menus. *Family Circle* carried 'Look, no meat! Impress your vegetarian friends with these festive main courses' (Nov. 1991: 49). *Woman and Home* (Dec. 1991: 82–6) offered a complete vegetarian menu for Christmas dinner, 'Vegetarian grace. The alternative Christmas lunch menu', which included parsnip and almond parcels with curry sauce, pumpkin soup, cheese gougère with wild mushrooms and broccoli 'as a centrepiece for your Christmas meal', griddled vegetables, cloutie dumplings, and more. It was presumed routinely that readers might expect to prepare meals for vegetarians, so vegetarian recipes appeared without need for comment. Sometimes it was implied that vegetarian food was, *per se*, healthy (for example, *Prima* Feb. 1992 'Healthy cookery – vegetarian dishes') and sometimes it was associated with speed of preparation.

In addition, the magazines gave a clear impression that vegetable side dishes are becoming more important, attractive and varied. For example, as accompaniments to Christmas dinner in 1991, the magazines proposed an imaginative array including brussels sprouts with chestnuts, red cabbage with cranberries and port, roast hasselback potatoes and parsnips and carrots with lemon and garlic. In 1967, by contrast, little attention was paid to vegetable accompaniments, which were generally simple and plain. Roast and mashed potatoes and sprouts recurred repeatedly: the addition of chestnuts to the sprouts, stuffed tomatoes and cauliflower, each mentioned once, were the only other vegetables recommended in the ten magazines.

In this respect, the magazines are responding to the growth in the 1980s, and particularly perhaps to the publicity, given to alternative dietary regimens. Some diets are adopted as a consequence of physical ailments, like diabetes, some are a response to allergens. Other sections of the British population follow alternative, consciously self-imposed, dietary regimes directed towards maintaining personal appearance and body shape, towards fitness for sporting activities, and towards spiritual, moral or religious ends. Of the last types, vegetarianism is the most topical. Estimates of its extent vary. Beardsworth and Keil (1992: 255–6) quote Gallup surveys showing that 3.7 per cent of the British population were self-defined vegetarians in 1990, and that 10 per cent claimed to avoid red meat. Both figures were approximately twice as high as in 1984 when such questions were asked for the first time. There are many variants of vegetarian diets, so self-definition is preferred, even though this includes people who do sometimes eat meat or fish.

Of the four main motives for conversion, 'moral, health-related, gustatory and ecological' (Beardsworth & Keil, 1992: 269), the moral dimension, which includes both animal rights concerns and political concern about the effects on the food chain of the production of animal foodstuffs, was uppermost in the small snowball sample reported by

Beardsworth and Keil. Health concerns came next: although this is not primarily an issue of health, vegetarians exhibited considerable interest in, and knowledge about, food, its sources and its nutritional value, partly because it had until recently been maintained that avoidance of meat was unhealthy and that protein intake therefore needed to be monitored.

The centrality of the moral elements involved in the adoption of vegetarianism is important as an expression of alternative styles of life in the contemporary UK. It is possible to think of vegetarianism as a social movement, and in that sense to see it as part of stylization, as the emergence of a group of people, defined by their specialized consumption practices, in a manner consistent with notions of lifestyle politics. There is some evidence of an association between alternative diets, use of alternative therapies, health-consciousness and spiritual quests (Hamilton, 1993). As Atkinson (1983) notes more generally, the consumption of health foods is associated with holding alternative conceptions of medicine and science.

Beardsworth and Keil argue that food potentially gives rise to anxieties for everyone, and that adoption of vegetarianism is a response to three paradoxes of eating: 'it provides life, but at the expense of the death of other living organisms; it provides vigour, but may lead to disease; it provides pleasure, but may lead to disgust or nausea' (1992: 290). They interpret the specific resurgence of vegetarianism in the 1980s as following from the decline of a dominant, 'traditional menu'. They see the emergence of alternative menus, including 'moral menus', arising as ethical motivations in vegetarianism for instance, and 'rational menus', as in the propagation of food nutrition guidelines, as 'menu pluralism'. Options can now exist, due very importantly to major changes in the organization of the global food chain, which provide economic preconditions for vegetarianism to be viable on a mass basis. They suggest that an individual can now adopt an alternative menu, or indeed draw from more than one menu. The key lesson of the vegetarian phenomenon is:

> Given the fluidity inherent in menu pluralism, it is feasible for idiosyncratic combinations of menu principles to be assembled. In such circumstances, the resort to vegetarianism as a response to moral, health or gustatory concerns becomes an increasingly feasible option. Minority foodways are likely to proliferate and be received with steadily increasing tolerance (the great majority of the study's respondents reporting significant increases in the level of public acceptance of their dietary practices over the course of their adherence to vegetarianism). In this sense, the patterns of contemporary vegetarianism documented in this study can be seen as examples of shifts away from traditional menu principles towards menus in which moral or rational criteria play a much more explicit part. (Beardsworth & Keil, 1992: 289)

This argument suggests a pluralist, post-Fordist resolution of Mennell's indeterminacy problem. Vegetarianism is perhaps the best example of a stylized set of practices, in the sense that vegetarians constitute a minority group without any overwhelming socio-demographic cohesion (though vegetarians do tend to be younger women, and also to be highly educated, and in middle-class occupations). To the extent that this shared, minority form of consumption plays a key role in identity formation and social belonging, then it is one example consistent with the neo-tribalism thesis and offers a promise of greater tolerance of cultural minorities in the future.

5.4 Bodies and weight control: discipline and choice

Zygmunt Bauman (1990: 142) comments wryly that whereas one may be pitied for small stature, one's girth is a personal responsibility for which one can be held to account. Slimness, with its overtones of youthfulness and of proper self-discipline, is a much desired condition for many people. Pierre Bourdieu (1984) observes that slimness is associated with persons of higher social class and is itself a mark of distinction. Barbara Ehrenreich (1983), analysing the perversity of the pressures on women to remain thin, notes that while recent generations of American women have become larger than their predecessors, models in magazines have even smaller waists than in the 1950s. The ideal image gets further distant from average body size, which may be a contributory factor to current food disorders like anorexia and bulimia. Some authorities see obesity as the principal disease of affluence, while other writers disagree, pointing to the dangers and general ineffectiveness of intermittent dieting, and defending the right to be fat (see Shilling, 1993: 67). Others point to the absurdities and exploitative tendencies of the food industries which seek to persuade us both to eat and to diet, to slim and to consume heartily. The dieting industry itself is big business, manufacturing special foods, placing advertising copy, selling advice in magazines and books, and offering personal therapy. Articles and recipes in the magazines, while sometimes directly addressed to slimming, are more notable perhaps for the indirect means by which they stress the significance of body shape.

In 1992, one magazine in five contained an article explicitly about slimming. These articles demonstrate that slimming may be considered an issue of health, of fitness, of personal appearance, or any combination of these. By 1992, only 2 per cent of recipes were explicitly recommended because they aided slimming, compared with 5 per cent in 1968. In 1968 they included recipes for eggs which were 'non-fattening' (*WO*, May 1968), as was tuna (*FC*, May 1968). However, the additional nutritional information in the columns, especially about calories, is surely a substitute and indicates an even more routine concern with body weight than previously. The 1968 magazines rarely paid explicit attention to the link between food and health and were, comparatively, very relaxed, being forgiving and supportive about fat.

New formats for articles about slimming emerged in the 1990s and they differed in tone from the 1960s. One article, 'lose 5lbs in 10 days', in *Bella* (Aug. 1992), is typical in its partial deregulation of the weight-loss diet:

'Rather than a rigid, eat-only-this diet plan, both lunch and dinner are extremely flexible. *You* can choose what combination of foods to eat.' many offer a choice of items, rather than a directive regime. One paradox was the extent to which diets included 'treats'. *Best* (May 1992) for example encouraged its readers:

> Sin and slim. Enjoy a wicked treat each day and still shed those extra pounds on a diet that includes a naughty but nice factor. A little of what you fancy does you no harm so we've created the Sin-a-day diet that's low in fat and high in fibre. It lets you indulge in 250 calories' worth of daily treats such as ice cream, chocolate and crisps.

So, to the pasta, baked beans, chicken and many vegetables that constitute the three meals a day, can be added a slice of fruit cake, a chocolate bar or a glass of wine. A list of sixteen alternative treats was included, with a calorie count for each.

Another example was *Prima*'s (Feb. 1992) 'Chocolate lovers' diet' which said: 'If you want to lose weight, but can't face life without chocolate, try our diet that allows you to indulge every day!' The article noted that 'It is part of human nature to want those things which we are not supposed to have and chocolate is no exception.' It explained how the diet works:

> Each day you can choose five meals from each of three lists – each meal provides around 200 calories. It is up to you when you eat the meals – you can even combine two meals to make a more substantial main meal if you want . . . . On top of those five meals you can choose *one* item a day from the chocolate treats – it is best to keep this for your 'low point' of the day when the craving for chocolate is at its strongest.

Then followed lists of 'no-cook meals', 'hot meals', 'quick snacks' and 'chocolate treats'. So you might have in a day: one packet crisps with five dried apricots; a small can of spaghetti hoops on one slice toast; one carton of low-fat yoghurt with a banana and a kiwi fruit; three grilled low-fat chipolata sausages and two tablespoons of baked beans; a jacket potato with one tablespoon of cottage cheese and some chives; and one Creme Egg!

Besides echoing the counter-pressures of indulgence and discipline this article yet again reinforces the encouragement towards minimal food intake among women in the search for a slim body, but also indicates the emergent 'pick-and-mix' approach to diet more generally. Rather than suggest that a specific diet would be both appropriate and sufficiently attractive to everyone, which implicitly suggests mass norms for a mass audience, choice and tailoring to the individual are included. However, this is not true of all the diet columns on offer: offering general guidance rules is common, so specific foods are not always itemized; and invitations to choose between losing a lot of weight or a little (two campaigns that could be run one after the other, if desired) also appear.

All food columns in the magazines offer an implicit set of answers to the question of 'what shall we eat?' All such advice is precisely and importantly wrapped in the ideology and discourse of individual choice. There is no sense in which people will be commanded to do things; there is no ultimate prescription; no direct instruction will be given about the overall effect. Throughout the magazines, expert discourses of this sort currently offer a set of *restricted* choices, leaving it open for the reader to decide what is ultimately good or proper. This tendency is very apparent in the articles about slimming, as it becomes normal to offer people a list of equivalent foods to choose from, rather than prescribing a single week's eating.[3] This is an important aspect of the ideological force of the individualization process as it is presented to 'the consumer'.

5.5 Indulgence

Self-discipline is only required if people are inclined, encouraged, or tempted to break rules. As *Cosmopolitan*'s story about Lucy indicated, there are indeed some such temptations, or rather some occasions when it would be perverse not to be indulgent. For most people eating out is one such situation where rules about healthy eating are suspended (Martens & Warde, 1995). But advertisements also seek to encourage the subversion of the rules of healthy eating: one of the most prominent in the UK is perhaps the dairy industry's slogan for fresh cream cakes – 'naughty but nice'.

It might be anticipated that the growing concern with health would entail a decline in the recommendation of indulgent behaviour but, ironically, appeals to indulgence also grew sharply. Explicit recommendations to indulgence increased, from 2 per cent in 1967–8 to 7 per cent in 1991–2. In addition, recipes making implicit reference also became more frequent, from 6 per cent to 10 per cent. By the later year, incitement to indulgence appears mostly in the weekly magazines, the monthlies becoming more ascetic in respect of the body.

The recommendations to indulge operated with terms like irresistible and tempting. The recipe promotion device for Caribbean meringue and tropical fruit pie, 'Paradise Puds', exhorted the reader to 'go for a tropical taste with our refreshing and fruity desserts – they're too good to resist!' (*Bella*, Feb. 1992). 'Iced Delights: Indulge your family with one of these irresistible treats' (*Best*, Aug. 1992) heralded recipes for home-made ice creams and sorbets. *Woman & Home* (Mar. 1992) talked of 'wonderful wicked chocolate', and *Woman's Own* (Aug. 1992) incited people to a black forest gâteau described as 'Mouthwatering . . . subtly flavoured with kirsch . . . lashings of whipped cream . . . irresistible treat . . . perfect dessert'. And a version that is indirectly indulgent, the recommendation for savoury pie which ran 'Everybody loves a pie, so bake the family a delicious treat . . . tempting, tasty pastry dishes' (*WO*, May 1992). The dishes presented as indulgent are usually pies, cakes and puddings: other than these only marinated olives and watercress were described as tempting in 1992.

The motif of indulgence, while present, was less prominent in 1968. The caption to an illustration of 'Tea time bakes' ran, 'Fattening? Well who cares when the tea-table holds such irresistibly good things' (*WW*, Feb. 1968). Otherwise there were occasional references to 'tempting' or 'irresistible' biscuits, cakes or desserts. Presumably, in the absence of advice to take healthy options, the tendency to think of eating as wicked was less relevant.

It would also appear that readers, like Lucy, are considered more in need of comfort foods than before. This might be the result of the accumulating practical and emotional pressures that have impinged on women particularly in the last few decades, for they have been most exposed to the discourse of health and the glorification of the slim body. Alternatively, it may partly be psychological reaction to the impossibility for most people of achieving the idealized body forms. Or perhaps it merely indicates the enormous difficulty of exercising the degree of individual self-discipline required to resist the temptations of the pleasures of eating. As Fischler (1993) noted, it is only very recently that abundant food has been the normal condition for the majority of people in western societies and this is a condition that the evolution of the human body has not been well prepared for. The more normal problem has been shortage of food rather than an excess; and there is no obvious biological mechanism that restricts us from overeating. The rising proportions of obese people in the rich societies are surely evidence of this. An alternative explanation might be that the food industries are themselves responsible for subverting people's commitment to more healthy eating. Surplus agricultural produce is one of the principal political embarrassments of the European Union; farmers are over-producing. There is spare capacity for the manufacture of foods. There are many commercial incentives for encouraging people to eat more, especially of those products that industry is already set up to deliver.

The widespread appeal to indulgence also suggests that there is serious resistance to the notion of healthy eating. This comes in many forms. Feminist accounts have challenged the association between health and small body size. Objections to 'food fascism', expressed usually in new right circles, contests the legitimacy of the state instructing people about proper eating habits. Common sense, in the face of disagreements among experts and the discovery of toxic properties in many foods, often leads people to conclude that there is little good advice beyond that of having a varied diet. Others believe that good health is a matter of luck and beyond personal control: the *British Social Attitudes* survey of 1989 identified a small minority with such fatalistic attitudes. There is also, in Britain, a subculture that rejoices in the opportunity for indulgence, in the convivial behaviour described by Bourdieu as typical of the French working class. When respondents in Greater Manchester were asked 'When you have guests for a meal, what kind of meals do you prefer to serve?', only about a quarter of respondents (84 out of 323) used one of their three choices to opt for a healthy meal. Almost twice as many votes were cast for 'plentiful' meals. Being male or working class increased indifference to healthy eating.

5.6   The bodily condition

Thus, we might better understand Lucy and conclude that she is not alone facing her dilemma regarding the counter-attractions of self-control and emotional comfort. The counter-pressures of health and indulgence provide an instance of an antinomy that has expanded and intensified over the last twenty-five years. As you master the flesh you also need respite from the asceticism, just as the narcissistic *Cosmopolitan* article implied. A clear instance of change, it presumably has the effect of increasing guilt, concern, self-measurement, *calculation* and self-discipline, while at the same time responding to the desire to keep the self happy and satiated with pleasures. Rarely is it suggested that the care of the body might be a pleasure; rather it is an instrumental matter of efficiency and body maintenance.

This antinomy is widely diffused in everyday life throughout the British population, and concern with the body, its effective functioning and its appearance, is considerable. Savage et al. (1992), when examining the consumption behaviour of different sections of the British middle class, identified one substantial group whose style of life combined 'the new culture of health and body maintenance' with 'an older "culture of extravagance"' which was characterized by 'excess and indulgence largely based on a predilection for foreign eating styles and heavy drinking' (1992: 106). This new, apparently contradictory, lifestyle ('described – partly tongue in cheek – as "postmodern", where a binge in an expensive restaurant one night might be followed by a diet the next' (1992: 107)) was in the 1980s associated with predominantly high-income, southern, professional and managerial workers. If the 1980s postmodern 'yuppie' was the most extreme embodiment of the antinomy, there is evidence that the middle classes more generally share this somewhat inconsistent combination in their eating and drinking behaviours. The *Family Expenditure Survey* confirms that the professional middle class purchases more of the foods recommended as healthy. But the same class is also distinguishable by its high levels of expenditure on restaurant meals and on alcohol. It is, unfortunately, impossible to know whether this has changed much since 1968, but one suspects that in absolute terms, since eating out and alcohol consumption have increased, they are, in some senses, living through, in and amongst, this antinomy.

Lury (1996: 238, 242) argues that the type of behaviour described by Savage et al., of indulging one day and dieting the next, is a male prerogative. She refers to this, using Featherstone's (1991) term, as calculated de-control, an ability strategically to move in and out of the condition of self-control thereby to experience a wider range of sensations and emotions. Women, however, are denied the degree of self-possession that is a prerequisite for such behaviour. The instrumental and expressive modes of identity formation which provide the basis for the lifestyle of the new *petit bourgeois* may be applicable to men, but not to women. Indeed, the health and indulgence antinomy is one which is particularly marked by gender differences. Though most of the dilemmas apply to both men and women, their strength and nature vary. Women experience different forms of desire (Coward, 1984), tending to be more preoccupied with slender bodies and personal appearance, to be more subject to collective and personal policing of their sexual availability, to have restricted access to sport and recreation, and to have greater capacities for sacrifice (when in situations of scarcity they forgo food in favour of other family members). In response to restriction women may adopt other strategies for exercising control. Among them are the regimens constituting eating disorders like anorexia. As Bordo (1992) argues, the condition is as much about the conscious exercise of the will to control hunger and the body as it is about physical appearance. Being thin is an achievement resulting from having autonomously exerted personal control over one part of a life otherwise characterized by powerlessness.

While the recommendations to indulge might be seen as an endorsement of narcissism, the more prevalent discourse of discipline suggests that processes of re-regulation are also operative. Many Foucauldian scholars see not a collapse of discipline but a shift between modes of control in the contemporary era. Discipline becomes individualized and internalized, a matter of self-restraint. It is probably impossible to distinguish clearly in most instances in everyday life between those disciplined practices that are self-imposed and those that are externally imposed. Concerns with weight control and the manipulation of body shape are so pervasive in contemporary society that it would be difficult to deny the existence of some external social pressure to be slim, and surely the state in its health campaigns produces some propaganda to encourage such attitudes. But this remains more a matter of self-discipline than state intervention.

The imperative to achieve self-control is not just a matter of health, but pervades many fields of contemporary practice. Recent heightened appreciation of the reflexive component of subjectivity, implied when the self is conceptualized as a conscious 'project', has allowed some common practices to be read as regimes of self-monitoring or auto-surveillance (see Wernick, 1991). Through a variety of mundane devices, for example the curriculum vitae (Metcalfe, 1992), individuals in the act of constructing and reconstructing their own biographies monitor their own behaviour and thereby, at least half-consciously, discipline themselves with a view to self-improvement as defined through the lens of an employer's requirements. Ironically, some of the regimes for monitoring and disciplining the body today are just as severe as those once associated with ascetic religious observance, though now they are probably directed more towards personal appearance than moral rectitude.

Analogous processes operate to regulate food intake. People adopt dietary programmes from books and magazines. They count calories, sometimes in meticulous detail. They display charts that list the average calorific loss to the body of walking half a mile or spending twenty minutes jogging. They weigh themselves on bathroom scales regularly. They use tape measures, or the waistbands of clothes they have almost grown out of, to detect alterations in size. They enter upon crash diets, or longer-term campaigns – the vocabulary of war is never far distant. They join clubs and associations whose express purpose is to counteract the effects of having an appetite and whose efficacy derives from the collective and shared struggle against each individual's body. The collective aspect of personal self-discipline is interesting. It is apparently easier if you join a health club, an exercise club, Alcoholics Anonymous, a slimming competition, and so forth. Joining associations helps to maintain the fitness programme, to stimulate self-discipline. These are the elements of disciplinary regimes whose origins cannot be found in ethical or moral codes, such as Protestant asceticism, or in discourses insinuated by the state and policed by its agents. Rather this is a system of self-discipline of the body, of self-control, of self-monitoring, with a view to maintaining the appearance of good health. Probably sustaining such regimes has become even more difficult to the extent that eating events become more informal – though informality may make concealment, from self and others, easier. Keeping a count of quantity and balance of nutrients when eating a restaurant meal or snacks from a street vendor is well nigh impossible. Informalization compounds any personal anxiety that arises from food consumption.

The evidence perhaps implies a heightened or intensified degree of individualization. Probably the ultimate expression of individualism is an obsessive concern with the body as a vehicle of self-presentation. But the concerns with personal appearance are not ones that imply a decline of regulation. On the contrary, strict dietary and exercise regimens entail a severe mode of discipline associated with food consumption. The motivational complex that keeps this antinomy in existence is in some respects a vicious circle. Anxiety about bodily appearance requires regimes of severe self-discipline; self-restraint creates the sense of being unfree, but also of being 'displeased', being deprived of pleasures; hence the temptation to indulge, to transgress the rules of the dietary regime; and thus, again, a renewal of a sense of guilt and anxiety about bodily virtue. This is a potentially distressing antinomy, made worse because of the emotional significance of food, and one which affects educated middle-class women more than other sections of the population – partly explaining the uneven incidence of eating disorders.

5.7 Summary

Health is now a dominant value in discussions of food. There is some disagreement about what is a healthy diet, though most people know some version of official guidelines. However, they do not necessarily take a great deal of notice: the middle classes are more concerned and appear to be adapting their domestic food purchasing accordingly, though probably not their eating out or their alcohol consumption. Paradoxically, there is simultaneously a significant shift in the discourses towards indulgence. This arises partly because of the difficulty and unattractiveness of self-discipline and self-denial, partly because of the culture of hedonism that prevails in consumer societies. Especially interesting are the justifications for indulgence.

Particularly in the realm of consumption we are inclined to think that we have almost a right 'to please ourselves'. The hedonistic elements of consumer culture are much commented upon, and the appropriateness of considering first what might give one pleasure lies at the centre of the syndrome of narcissism in terms of which social theorists have often sought to characterize the current epoch. To please oneself implies being less prepared to follow established rules or conventions when they seem to run counter to personal gratification. Wouters (1986) identifies a prevalent process of informalization, particularly powerful in the 1960s and 1970s, which led to the deregulation of many social practices, including parents imposing less strict disciplinary rules on children and the acceptance of less formal ways of speaking. He maintains that informalization generally requires increasing *self*-restraint, for the less explicit are collective guidelines for conduct, the more the maintenance of social meaning and social cohesion depends upon individual judgment. The improvisations of the period underwent some retrenchment in the 1980s, for modern societies experience a perpetual oscillation between formalization and informalization, though in the 20th century the latter has tended to have greatest impact.

The field of food, especially those aspects of it that affect the body, conforms to this dialectic. Narcissistic tendencies, which thrive on the relaxation of rules governing food intake, are encouraged, as people seek pleasure in the choice to indulge their fancies. But, on the other hand, matters concerning the presentation of the body seem to require regimentation and self-discipline, which is the primary motif in programmes for a healthy diet. Indeed, in some cases the push for a healthy diet may include a degree of stylization, as with vegetarianism or perhaps even *nouvelle cuisine*. Re-regulation is involved, a re-regulation that is especially governed by the logic of calculation about nutrients: calorie, fat and fibre counts provide the numerical guidance making for self-imposed governance of the body that pervades contemporary food culture. The power of the tendency to formalization, through self-discipline and stylization, indicates a strong reaction to the informalization engendered by abandonment of any rules imposed by culinary tradition or scarcity. The striking aspect of this re-regulation is the extent to which it is presented as consistent with individualization; it is the message of self-restraint, of one's duty to control one's appetites without external surveillance. Yet, as the point about the need for associations to help achieve such control implies, this is almost a misperception of the possibility, or nature, of the contemporary self. Offering people choices with respect, for instance, to slimming diets, is to burden individuals with the project of living in practice the ideological programme of consumer choice and sovereignty. People are obliged to guide their actions in accordance with the dominant ideology of consumer society, as if following rules or guidelines suggested by others was a betrayal of the market.

The body is a particularly significant contemporary concern. The intense personal preoccupation of individuals with managing their bodies is reflected in sociological analyses of embodiment and bodily disciplines.[4] Much of this concern is expressed in terms of the importance of the body for conveying self-identity, for it is deeply implicated in the performative and cognitive aspects of gender, class and generation. Such concerns are becoming more prominent in contemporary discourses of food, with the women's magazines recommending dishes both because they promise good health and because they indulge physical and emotional cravings. The assumption of personal responsibility for the state of one's body is a central component of the trend towards individualization, but one capable of arousing serious personal distress and moral censure.

6

Economy and Extravagance

6.1 Material resources

One of the major contributions of the sociology of consumer culture has been to indicate the limits of approaches to consumption offered by neo-classical economics, which explains demand primarily as a simple relationship between the income of consumers, the price of goods and a universal desire to maximize utility. Consumption decisions are directed by concern with the symbolic meanings of goods, and indeed of different brands of goods performing identical practical functions, in addition to any consideration of cost. The sociological elaboration of this has, typically, been concerned with the processes of distinction, and thereby of exclusion, involved in the social interpretation of consumption. An impression of social superiority, as Veblen argued, can partly be achieved simply through the purchase and display of very expensive goods, but this will always remain a strategy open only to the rich. However, symbolic differentiation can also be achieved through the wielding and manipulating of symbols that are not deemed exclusive simply by their cost, but by their association with the good taste of knowledgeable or influential social groups. In the past, this typically meant association with higher social classes. It is this association that we might expect to be applicable to food since, as this chapter demonstrates, with some exceptions, it is generally not cost alone that makes for discriminating patterns in food purchase. However, influenced by some approaches in cultural studies, there has been a tendency for sociological accounts to go to the opposite extreme to that of neo-classical economics and to ignore almost entirely issues of prices and incomes. The strong materialist basis apparent in sociological accounts of the 1960s and 1970s has all but dissolved. This is unsatisfactory and is in danger of seriously misrepresenting food consumption.

Concern with cost is not much emphasized in the magazines. Concern with class is even less apparent. That the nature of economic relations between classes associated with food provision is obscured in popular media like women's magazines is predictable. They do not dwell on agricultural production, the wages of farm labourers, or the plight of the hungry or the starving, for these are not sources of the pleasures sought by readers. Where comment is made on the origins of ingredients in recipes, it is more by way of connoisseurship: discussion of the region of origin of the best Italian olive oil is more likely than a reference to the people who picked the olives in the first place. This is a process of legitimation, in so far as purchasers are helped to ignore the social effects of satisfying their preferences. It is precisely this that ethical vegetarians, animal rights campaigners and green activists seek to bring to the attention of a wider public. Similar lessons are taught by the specialist political economy literature which documents the processes of ownership, exchange and distribution that shift produce from field to table. It analyses the complexities, the exploitation and the inequalities of the global food chain. Vegetable protein is extracted from the Third World to feed western livestock. Agricultural workers are paid minimal wages to produce items for sale to multinational food manufacturing companies and supermarket chains. The food chain detrimentally affects standards of nutrition in exporter countries and has serious consequences in the form of malnutrition, hunger, migration and social upheaval in poorer countries. Such matters, though of the utmost importance, play little role in my account because they have low salience in routine food choice (but see, for example, Goodman & Redclift, 1991).

6.2 Income and food consumption

Less abstract aspects of the economics of food might be expected in the magazine recipe columns. Obvious issues include the price of food, the cost of nourishing a family, obtaining value for money, and difficulties in getting access to adequate amounts of decent-quality food. These topics do arise, but comparatively infrequently.

Thrift

Mennell commented on a dreary concern with economy in the British catering trade press, entirely absent in its French counterpart. The concern appeared in the earlier part of the 20th century as an obsession with the use of leftovers, and by the 1960s as 'avoiding the waste material arising in the first place' (1985: 193), to which end portion control, instant mixes, precooked catering packs and specially frozen foods became the solution. In line with his general view that professional practice has converged with domestic cookery in the 20th century, similar concerns with economy were detected in women's magazines, the period of the Second World War reinforcing and legitimizing this national tendency to be economical with food. That tendency certainly appears to have declined. Only one recipe sampled, from 1968, mentioned use of leftovers, when an article on cake-making noted 'There's a recipe that uses up those old yolks too'; (*WW*, Aug. 1968).

Nevertheless, there was little change in the extent of concern with economy. In 1968, 16 per cent of recipes were recommended as economical, as was a similar proportion in the 1991–2 sample (14 per cent). The typical terms remained the same, with 'inexpensive' more prevalent than 'cheap', and with reference to cooking on a 'budget' also prominent. In 1968 the weeklies made more direct reference to the virtues of inexpensive foods. When the monthlies expressed concern it was mostly to recommend the use of less expensive raw ingredients, which they did with slight apology but with encouragement to use methods of slow cooking or to add herbs and spices that will make for succulent dishes. Typically, an article entitled 'Cheaper fish with a taste of luxury' went on to assert that 'less expensive fish – with the addition of herbs and a special sauce or other harmonious flavours – can often rival their pricier cousins' (*GH*, Feb. 1968). Only one article in the sample of weeklies was concerned with entertaining economically; it advised collecting tins of fruit salad in the weeks before the buffet party, reminded readers that 'Good food need not be extravagant' and offered recipes 'with price in mind' (*WW*, May 1968).

By 1992, occasional columns appear with titles like 'Budget meals' or 'Budget cookery'. For example, *Best* (Feb. 1992) had a column 'Brilliant budget meals: feeding your family needn't cost a fortune. Follow our low-cost recipes'; and *Woman's Weekly* (Nov. 1991) recommended recipes for dishes made with mashed potatoes because 'Potatoes are really excellent value for money, and many of these dishes are really cheap – and also very tasty.' However, recommendations for economy now are as likely as not to be associated with entertaining comparatively cheaply as with simply preparing inexpensive family dishes. Thus, for instance, one article 'Budget meals; supper on a shoestring' (*FC*, Aug. 92), promised 'a gourmet dinner for six for under £15 including wine'; another (*Woman*, May 1992) suggested preparing meals for guests because 'few people can afford to eat out with friends these days'; and a third (*GH*, June 1992) inquired 'Why spend a fortune on entertaining?' and had experts each contribute an 'impressive, yet inexpensive dinner-party menu' (at £3 per head). Another column (*Best*, Nov. 1991), giving advice on economical Christmas presents, suggested 'luxury foods' because 'you can make them yourself at a fraction of shop prices'. In effect only half of the recipes in the sample were recommending cheap ingredients or dishes that might be appropriate for the hard-up family, compared with 85 per cent in 1968. The remainder in 1992 were oriented towards economizing on the costs of entertaining in one way or another rather than towards finding solutions to impoverishment.

Economy is a value, one that is appealed to in many contexts in modern market societies. Economists' accounts assume that economizing is the predominant consideration in exchange. Such an idea also used to be central to housekeeping manuals, and indeed was prominent in the magazines in the inter-war years. Good housewifery included paying careful attention to the cost of ingredients, adopting ways for ensuring that all nutritious foodstuffs were used up, and knowing how to make use of a glut of a particular food. Thus a recipe column might centre on how to make varied use of several pounds of apples in the autumn (e.g. *WW*, 23 Dec. 1922). Today we have what might be labelled designer seasons: a few recipes for plums appear in the October magazines, for instance, but the products are available all year round and are likely to have been grown somewhere other than the UK anyway. In other instances the 1930s magazines would suggest ways to cook very cheap ingredients, like herring or a sheep's heart (*WW*, 6 Nov. & 13 Nov. 1937). Such degrees of parsimony had disappeared by the end of the 1960s.

Between 1968 and 1992, however, the number of recipes giving the cost per portion of dishes rose, from 14 per cent in 1968 to 23 per cent by 1991–2. Again we see columnists becoming, above all else, more comprehensive and precise in the technical information they transmit; there is a strong sense of the rationalization of food preparation and, perhaps, more generally, of the art of living. Cost has become a technical specification rather than a household management problem.

In other contexts, the magazines primarily give the impression that the cost of food is negligible. Theoretically speaking, this might perhaps arise from a popular, if unconscious and exaggerated, appreciation of Engel's Law. This states that as household income rises, a smaller proportion of expenditure is devoted to food. This has occurred in the UK, as Figure 6.1 shows. However, while the proportion of mean household expenditure on food fell from 28 per cent in 1965 to 18 per cent in 1992, it remains substantial, still marginally larger than that for housing or transport, for instance.

The expenditure devoted to food varies between different household types, with larger and poorer families spending greater proportions of their budgets. In 1992 the poorest households', those among the lowest 20 per cent of incomes, mean food expenditure was £22.85 per week, or 24 per cent of total expenditure. Those in the highest income quintile spent £73.82, or 14 per cent of total outgoings (*FES*, 1993: 26, Table 8). The large absolute difference in amounts spent on food partly reflects variation in household size; households in the lowest decile contained on average 1.5 persons, while the highest decile contained 3.1. Calculating this expenditure another way, the lowest quintile spends just over £15 per head per week on food, while the highest spends just under £24 per head. Even in the UK in the 1990s, not everyone has access to abundant supplies of nutritious and socially acceptable food. It is no accident that recent poverty surveys have made what people eat one of the key indicators of poverty (Mack & Lansley, 1985; Townsend et al., 1988). For poorer households, the value of economy in food provisioning is of immense practical significance (Wilson, 1989; Graham, 1987).

Rich households spend significantly more per head on food than do poor ones. Unsurprisingly, income affects the quantity, and particularly the quality, of foodstuffs purchased. It might generally be expected that the relative differences between rich and poor in this, basic and contrasting, area of spending would have decreased since the 1960s. However, this is not the case. The *continued* prevalence of serious inequalities in food consumption on the basis of material resources can be derived from the discriminant analysis of the *Family Expenditure Survey*. A model identifying four groups by household income quartiles, standardized for household size, successfully

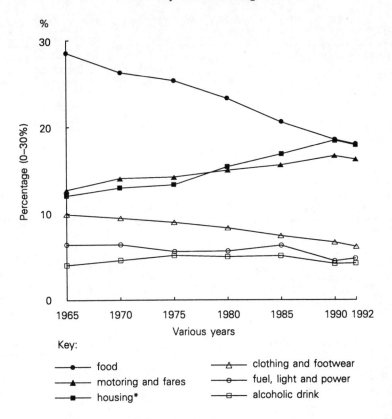

%

Figure 6.1 *Trends of expenditure for all households in the UK, 1965–92,
as percentage of total household expenditure.* Source: Family Expenditure
Surveys (various years)

Key:

——●—— food   ——△—— clothing and footwear
——▲—— motoring and fares   ——○—— fuel, light and power
——■—— housing*   ——□—— alcoholic drink

* There are discontinuities in housing expenditure series between 1982 and 1984 and
between 1991 and 1992

Note: Percentages are expenditure on commodity or service group as a percentage of total
household expenditure

allocated 46 per cent of households in both 1968 and 1988 (Tomlinson &
Warde, 1993: 7). There was, thus, no change in the effect of income on food
items. Significantly, per capita household income gave a less powerful
prediction than did models based on distinguishing between various
occupational classes. Using a model which grouped together employers and
managers, other white-collar workers, manual workers, and persons not
employed 52 per cent of households were correctly identified in 1968; in
1988 the same model was successful for 53 per cent of cases (see Table 6.1).
In both years the most distinctive groupings were the unoccupied and the
blue-collar workers. Moreover, close inspection indicates that these latter
groups became more distinctive over the period, giving some support to the
idea that there has been a polarization of those with and those without

Table 6.1 *Class differences in household food expenditure per capita, 1968 and 1988*

(a)Classification results: 1968

Actual group*	No. of cases	Predicted group membership			
		1	2	3	4
Group 1: employers & managers	643	258 40.1%	142 22.1%	116 18.0%	127 19.8%
Group 2: white collar	1207	235 19.2%	490 40.6%	252 20.9%	230 19.1%
Group 3: blue collar	3293	358 10.9%	519 15.7%	1675 50.8%	744 22.6%
Group 4: not employed	1770	161 9.1%	165 9.3%	277 15.6%	1167 65.9%

Percentage of 'grouped' cases correctly classified: 51.91.

* Classes: 1. Employers and managers; 2. Other white-collar workers; 3. Manual workers; 4. Retired and unoccupied.

(b) Classification results: 1988

Actual group*	No. of cases	Predicted group membership			
		1	2	3	4
Group 1: employers & managers	925	299 31.2%	258 27.9%	209 22.6%	169 18.3%
Group 2: white collar	1338	295 22.0%	509 38.0%	304 22.7%	230 17.2%
Group 3: blue collar	1623	147 9.1%	216 13.3%	871 53.7%	389 24.0%
Group 4: not employed	1770	161 5.0%	165 10.9%	277 16.4%	1167 67.7%

Percentage of 'grouped' cases correctly classified: 53.43.

* Classes: 1, Employers and managers (socio-economic groups, 1, 2, 3, 4); 2. Other white-collar workers (socio-economic groups 5, 6, 7, 8, 9); 3. Manual workers (socio-economic groups 11, 12, 13, 14, 18); 4. Retired and unoccupied (socio-economic groups 21, 22).

work. It also indicates the continued significance of the social boundary between the working and middle classes.

Luxury

In many societies, being able to eat copiously and well on a regular basis has been a sign of privilege. For most people throughout British history, feasts, celebrations and festivals were rare opportunities for pleasurable gastronomic indulgence. Equivalent culinary delights on a more regular basis would be considered extravagant, with money being wasted unnecessarily, a practice frowned upon in part because it was thought socially strategic, a way of displaying wealth that peers could not match. Social distinctions and divisions can be expressed through food.

Thorstein Veblen (1925) offered the classic sociological account of such behaviour in his analysis of the nature and role of 'conspicuous consumption'. The notion is a comparatively simple one, though his book is considerably more nuanced and insightful than the frequent summaries of its content might suggest. He observed the increasing importance of money as a means to rank people. In earlier societies the principal sign of being rich and powerful was the absence of having to work, thus his notion of the 'leisure class'. That mark of distinction had, by the late 19th century, given way to money as a measure of standing because free time is comparatively invisible in impersonal, urban societies. He maintained that in practice it becomes hard to estimate another person's wealth except in terms of the objects they display. Hence people use their possessions to demonstrate their pecuniary standing. The rich in late 19th-century America did not husband their resources, because it was more important to appear opulent than to save money. Thus reputation is associated with appearances; and people seek money as a means to achieve an outward display of the fruits of income through the possession of items that carry distinction simply because they are expensive. No longer is social standing a matter of being, for instance, ethical, comradely, trustworthy, honest, reliable or amusing.

One interesting aspect of this argument is that it implies that visibly to waste time or money may be an important strategic social objective. Another is that display can develop into a normative system, a set of practices and aesthetic judgments, which signifies status. According to Veblen, this encourages emulation among other social groups. Social groups lower down the hierarchy copy those higher up, such that there is what is often called a 'trickle-down' effect in cultural practices.

Veblen viewed social hierarchy as a continuum from rich to poor, where goods indicate a household's position on that continuum, and where the poor wish to possess the same symbols of status that the rich currently have. It thereby assumes a high level of agreement on which items are most prestigious and desirable, a shared structure of preferences throughout society. Veblen thus also offers an explanation of the perpetual demand for goods in consumer society and a counter-mechanism to the residues of Protestant asceticism in western societies. Expensive objects are coveted, luxuries sought, extravagance legitimized.

A contemporary application of Veblen's insight might be the fashion for *nouvelle cuisine*, with its emphasis on small portions of very fresh ingredients, with vegetables prominent, sauces light, and decorative presentation paramount. Meals constructed in this manner are not an instance of indulgence, for they neither represent comfort food nor contain rich victuals injurious to health or detrimental to body shape. They are, however, symbolically anti-utilitarian, designed to display exquisite taste, and more concerned with aesthetic effect than nutritional efficiency.

Moreover, such cuisine is exclusive, both because of its very high cost, its inaccessibility, its unfamiliarity, and its anti-popular ethos. The widespread popular reaction to *nouvelle cuisine*, puzzlement that anyone should pay so much money for so little food, is predictable. Nothing could be more extravagant. Nothing is further from the notion of value for money. Such behaviour is precisely conspicuous waste. *Nouvelle cuisine* is a vehicle for exhibiting status in the manner described by Veblen, moreover one that will principally be played out before an audience of peers, those other opulent people who can afford to visit the same restaurants.[1] Food, then, may exhibit extravagance.

Some foodstuffs are known primarily for being expensive – caviare, lobster and truffles, for instance. To serve these at home in the UK would be considered very special, and recipes using them are rare in the magazines. In 1968, 10 per cent of recipes were promoted in terms of their being extravagant. By contrast, only one recipe was so recorded in 1992, this because it included wild rice, described as an expensive ingredient. In 1968, one article noted that 'Truffles are costly but a speciality' (*IH*, Feb. 1968), and another picked an expensive joint as a special party dish (*WR*, Feb. 1968). However, much of the difference in frequency of reference arose primarily because the sampling frame resulted in the inclusion of an annual pull-out supplement in *She* (Nov. 1967) which bore the titles 'Cook Takes to Drink' and 'Food of Love'. All the recipes included some type of alcohol. The magazine observed, about Britons, that 'the addition of a glass of wine to a dish is looked upon as a wild extravagance' and, as if in mitigation, pointed out that this is not necessarily so if cheaper wines are used. It was the addition of wine that led dishes like chicken marengo, jugged hare and *ananas au kirsch* to be described as extravagant.

She was distinctive among the magazines sampled in 1968, partly because of its exaggerated consciousness of modern style, partly being very consciously aware of the practical problems facing younger working women, with or without parental obligations, who sought to combine career and social life. In addition, it contained a fair amount of copy devoted to the political issues affecting women and to current affairs more generally, as part of an appeal to educated, free-thinking, liberal or radical readers. *She* also represented most conscientiously new fashions in food and drink. It had a regular wine column, its food articles concentrated on either very quick or very elaborate dishes without concern for routine domestic provision for families, and it followed fashions in the restaurant trade, being unique in occasionally publishing reviews of restaurants. The recipes in its monthly column, 'Gourmet Nosh', explicitly addressed the would-be connoisseur. The dishes described during the year included several that were prominent on the menus of restaurants mentioned in the *Good Food Guide* for 1968: *blanquette de veau*, chicken in cream and port wine, quenelles of whiting in smoked salmon and chocolate chestnut cake. Other recipes featured included pizza, tournedos, lemon sorbet, mixed fruit meringue and pear and almond pie.

She's avant-garde role contrasted with rather more old-fashioned, established, middle-class pretensions of *Ideal Home* and *Woman and Home*, which were more likely to display food against backgrounds of oak-stained sideboards, formal dinner place settings, floral drapes and bowls of flowers. But they too promoted images of stylish and extravagant eating. *Woman and Home* ran a six page gourmet cookery pull-out (May 1968) which explained 'The word "gourmet" is inclined to conjure up thoughts of exotic dishes, of peacock and suckling pig, oriental spices and chefs in tall hats. But it means a connoisseur of good food, and Mary Meredith [its cookery editor] has produced for connoisseurs of home cookery this booklet of really luscious recipes for extra exciting dinner parties and other special occasions.' Recipes included baked gammon in madeira sauce, *coq au vin*, chicken *à la* kiev, guards of honour, soufflé Grand Marnier and blackcurrant lattice pie. The piece was run in association with a supplier of delicatessen-type products, which perhaps explains why 'fish salad platter' recommended use of tins of vegetable salad, potato salad, smoked oysters, sardines, shrimps, anchovy fillets and tuna, embellished with fresh cucumber and a few watercress leaves, and why game pie required a tin of whole roast grouse. Nonetheless, the acceptability of such convenience items was not atypical of the period.

These concerns with elaborate, usually rich, and decidedly special dishes coexisted alongside more prosaic columns in the weekly magazines. The latter, for instance, featured columns that published readers' own recipes, a format almost completely eliminated from the 1992 magazines. In 1968, *Woman's Own* still offered a prize weekly for a dish: 'We pay £2 2s for every recipe printed'. Popular were various sorts of meringues, biscuits, cakes and sausage dishes. Among them were: 'sausage special', a concoction of the contents of cans of beans, tomatoes, spaghetti and sausages; 'apple blobbies', 'an unusual and delicious pudding'; 'fried chicken with cheese sauce'; 'sherry cream', comprising custard powder and sherry; and 'spaghetti carbonara', the presence of which was explained by the fact of the contributor having an Italian husband. A number of important features are apparent. First this was just one of many outlets for exchange between readers and the editor. *Woman's Realm* had a 'Cooks' Club', *Woman* a 'Wooden Spoon Club postbag' for readers' queries and tips. As yet the expert professional adviser had not totally displaced the skilled domestic cook. Second, it was quite common and acceptable to make tinned and dried foods the central ingredients of a recipe, whereas by 1992 this was only permissible for occasional ancillary items. This certainly, in retrospect, produced some proposals that might upset persons of delicate sensibility or disposition: ten ways to make a meal out of a packet of dried mashed potato – potato wedges, potato turnovers, thatched cottage pie and potato pizza among them – was one of the more striking (*PF*, 11 May 1968). Third, the distance separating the domestic from the professional cook apparently still remained considerable, if readers' favourite recipes indicated their current practices and preferences.

In Britain, wine used to be a product identified with expense, mystery and snobbery. Hence, *She*'s supplement could simply equate the use of wine with extravagance. The promotion of the recipes contained copious didactic information about wines and alcohol. Like other magazines of the period it assumed some need to teach readers about fundamentally unfamiliar items and ingredients, a necessity which has apparently subsided. But *She* was alone in 1968 in attending to wine in this fashion. Since then the amount of wine consumed in Britain has increased very considerably. Wine columns have become common in newspapers and, though to a much lesser degree, commentary has been introduced in the women's magazines. Nevertheless, the proportion of recipes suggesting particular alcoholic accompaniments to dishes remained constant between 1968 and 1992. However, by the later date it was almost universally wine, rather than cider or punch, that was recommended. Moreover, it was likely that a specific bottle of wine, replete with price and the name of the chain or supermarket where it could be purchased, would be identified rather than just a generic regional type. Yet while wine has become a more popular drink it still retains some of its former associations with connoisseurship and style and is most extensively consumed by the professional fraction of the middle class. A knowledge of wine remains a sign of distinction.

It is interesting to speculate why reference to extravagance as a quality of dishes or recipes in the magazines had almost disappeared by 1992. One strong possibility is that it is hard for private households to display rank or social position through food purchasing and that extravagance in the field of food is now more readily associated with eating out. In the absence of extensive domestic entertaining, it is hard to demonstrate pecuniary power through domestic provision of food. The emphasis on economical entertaining may be an indication of the continued decline of the expensive and elaborate dinner parties that characterized the British bourgeoisie at the beginning of the century. Affirmation of both opulence and culinary taste is perhaps now more easily and more decisively achieved by dining out on commercial premises.

Since the 1960s, increasing publicity has been given to all forms of eating out. Some has concentrated on pretentious, gourmet cuisine. Attempts have been made to define standards of fine food through food guides, newspaper columns, systems for scoring quality which facilitate comparison, etc.; long the case in France, but recent in the UK, innovative chefs have emerged as personalities, particularly through television exposure but also by publication of glossy volumes of their recipes; and a body of consumers has emerged who consider themselves expert in discriminating among restaurants, ingredients and culinary experiences. The latter, predominantly from the middle class, were caricatured in the 1980s as 'foodies', such was the extent of their enthusiasm. Certainly it is members of the professional middle-class households who spend distinctively large proportions of their food budgets on eating out in restaurants (see p. 117 below).

Given the price of dinner in highly regarded restaurants they are unlikely to attract all sections of the population. The price of dinner for one person, including half a bottle of house wine, at the Sharrow Bay Hotel, Ullswater, one of the more expensive, well-regarded Lake District restaurants, in 1992 was, at £44, almost exactly equal to the average household's weekly food expenditure (*FES*, 1992; *GFG*, 1992). That figure was 25 per cent greater than the amount spent weekly by households containing a lone parent with two or more children. In 1968, dinner at the same place was from 35 shillings, half a bottle of wine was 10s. 6d., so with other courses and a 12.5 per cent service charge dinner would probably have cost about £3 per head. In that year the average household spend £6 11s. 9d. (£6.59) on food, making the cost relative to total food expenditure much lower in the 1960s, a feature common to others of the dozen restaurants that, like Sharrow Bay, have had an entry in the *Good Food Guide* continuously since the 1960s. (*FES*, 1968; *GFG*, 1969–70).

There is evidence that the habit of talking about food and its qualities, or evaluating it in aesthetic terms, is predominantly a trait of the professional and managerial middle-class fractions. DeVault, in her study of Chicago, detected very considerable class differences in this respect. Professional and managerial households drew on written texts and expert advice about what to eat, and were concerned that even their everyday meals should be interesting, entertaining and pleasurable. Moreover, 'the requirement for their social gatherings is that the meal should be interesting enough to serve as a focus for conversation and sociability' (1991: 210). Lower-class households, by contrast, drew on experience, custom and their local connections, especially with kin, for culinary inspiration and did not share in the food-related 'common code that can mediate relations among professional and managerial couples' (ibid.). Some knowledge and a capacity to make small talk about food and restaurants is an aspect of cultural capital, being a practice presumably most useful among those who entertain clients, travel frequently, or eat out regularly with colleagues. This capacity does not, necessarily, as some Canadian research showed, entail that participants are particularly enthused by food, it is merely required in professional inter-action (Erickson, 1991). Nevertheless, such accomplishments have to be acquired and can only be attained through exposure to restaurants and to information about canons of good or fashionable taste.

When Raymond Postgate set up the Good Food Club in 1950, he anticipated that, given sufficient affluence and a modicum of knowledge, most people would come to appreciate the joys of excellent fare.[2] Perhaps his expectation was mistaken. Consumer culture fosters the illusion that coveted items are universally available and accessible, while simultaneously promising purchasers the capacity, through proper choice, to render themselves superior to others. One important feature of this pretence can be understood in terms of Hirsch's (1978) concept of positional goods, which identifies the contradiction between these two statements. In the pursuit of exclusivity, people will tend to adopt innovative and often fashionable practices which, so long as they are exclusive, serve the functions of enhancing self-esteem and giving satisfaction. Once these practices are adopted by a large number of people they become less attractive, sometimes because of congestion (as with driving private motor cars), and sometimes because they no longer confer any special distinction on their consumers. Universal availability misses a key aspect of the logic of consumer society, which is that its most appealing items must be elusive in order to function as a social marker of distinction. The logic of the accumulation of cultural capital probably requires that the aesthetic orientation to food be limited to an exclusive section of the population. It is doubtful if the aspirations of Postgate for the extension of good taste, and an associated demand for improved standards of catering, has permeated much beyond an enthusiastic and specialist section of the middle class. The combination of the very high prices charged by acclaimed restaurants and the knowledge and confidence required to enjoy such meals keeps this sphere of eating a zone of exclusivity.

Women's magazines show little interest in, or concern for educating their readership about, eating out. Reviews of restaurants are very infrequent; the faces of celebrity chefs are, even in the 1992 magazines, conspicuously sparse and rarely are recipes or ideas for dishes attributed to them; the resident food editor is the principal named journalist, and recipes are mostly anonymous. Indeed, despite the expansion of eating out since 1968, attention paid to it has probably declined. There were few recipes in the 1992 tranche for dishes simultaneously fashionable in the restaurant guides. This is consistent with the principally domestic and personal focus of the magazines. It may also be associated with the emergence of more specialized food magazines and the proliferation of television programmes which feature professional chefs demonstrating how to make the more complex and stylish dishes. But in the end, if extravagance is now primarily associated with eating out, then the notion will be less commonly alluded to in the recipe columns directed towards domestic food provision.[3]

A taste for luxurious or expensive food is not simply a function of size of income and the cost of ingredients or services, as might be suggested by a simple economic explanation. There are more subtle social and normative processes at work. Different social groups have different preferences. In the past this variation has arisen between groups with religious and ethical commitments, between ethnic groups, and, perhaps most importantly, between social classes.

6.3 Class differences over time

Sociology has always been more interested in the group differentiation arising from social norms and relationships than that arising simply from money income. The best-established sociological accounts of consumption began from the premise that consumption practices were themselves, in advanced capitalist societies, a clear reflection of class position. Class position always provides some basis for different patterns of consumption behaviour because it is ineluctably associated with the unequal distribution of income and wealth. But in the past it was always seen as more than that. While Veblen was impressed by a simple effect of opulence, Bourdieu maintained that consumption reflected complicated class distinctions and the transmission of cultural capital. To a significant extent, poor workers came to like those things that they could afford while the more affluent middle class developed extravagant tastes. Social hierarchies were expressed through display of commodities and engagement in activities which were attributed different degrees of honour. It has been widely accepted that in the United Kingdom class cultures existed as a result not only of financial power, but of learned tastes that were deeply ingrained in, and consistent with, other aspects of daily life. Accounts depicting patterns of class differentiation in modern British history are numerous, and have involved descriptions of coherent and mutually exclusive class cultures (e.g. Benson, 1994; Burnett, 1989; Cronin, 1984).

Few deny that some class differences still exist, and for analysts of nutrition and health this remains a basic datum (e.g. Townsend et al., 1988; Calnan, 1990). But the currently popular belief is that class differences have been declining, at a particularly fast rate since the 1970s. However, the evidence for this thesis, at least in the field of food, is not strong. Even though my evidence is unable to offer a highly refined indication of symbolic significance, the data exhibits considerable continuity over time. This is apparent to some extent in terms of the kinds of foodstuffs purchased and also, more significantly, in the persistence of social distance between classes.

Expenditure differences between socio-economic groups

The existence of class variation in food consumption is demonstrated by Table 6.2, which describes simply some differences in household expenditure on strategic items in 1988. The table distinguishes households headed by small industrial and commercial employers, the more affluent self-employed professionals, routine white-collar workers, the *petite bourgeoisie* and skilled manual workers.

Households headed by a self-employed professional (group 5) spent the largest amounts of money on food, the routine white-collar workers the least. This partly reflects household size. Examining the percentage of food expenditure on particular items shows strong similarities between skilled manual and *petit bourgeois* households and the strongest contrast between them and professionals. The professionals spent proportionately most on beef, fish, fresh vegetables and fresh fruit; and proportionately least on sausages, cooked meats, fish and chips, fresh milk, canned vegetables, potatoes and tea. Of all groups, the professional had the diet that would be most strongly endorsed by nutritionists, avoiding fresh milk, sugar, potato

Table 6.2 *Expenditure (£s) per week and percentage of food expenditure, by socio-economic group of heads of household, for selected food items, 1988*

	Socio-economic group*									
	3		5		9		15		12	
	£	%	£	%	£	%	£	%	£	%
Bread, rolls	2.11	3.7	1.58	2.6	1.59	4.0	1.89	4.0	2.05	4.5
Cereals	0.99	1.7	1.25	2.0	0.86	2.2	0.79	1.6	0.83	1.8
Beef & veal	3.62	6.3	4.02	6.6	1.58	4.0	2.16	4.5	2.35	5.2
Bacon & ham	0.79	1.4	0.78	1.3	0.62	1.6	0.84	1.8	0.84	1.8
Sausages	0.39	0.7	0.35	0.6	0.28	0.7	0.37	0.8	0.45	1.0
Cooked & canned meat	1.10	1.9	1.01	1.6	0.88	2.2	1.18	2.5	1.35	3.0
Poultry & game	2.27	4.0	2.37	3.9	1.50	3.8	1.65	3.4	1.57	3.5
Fish	1.39	2.4	1.50	2.5	0.93	2.4	1.00	2.1	0.90	2.0
Fish & chips	0.65	1.1	0.38	0.6	0.42	1.1	0.58	1.2	0.53	1.2
Milk – fresh	3.10	5.4	2.74	4.5	2.02	5.1	2.68	5.6	2.62	5.8
Fresh veg.	2.16	3.8	2.85	4.6	1.50	3.8	1.66	3.5	1.37	3.0
Canned veg.	0.51	0.9	0.39	0.6	0.44	1.1	0.56	1.2	0.60	1.3
Potato products	0.90	1.6	0.53	0.9	0.70	1.8	0.86	1.8	0.94	2.1
Potatoes	0.76	1.3	0.51	0.8	0.52	1.3	0.67	1.4	0.71	1.6
Fruit – fresh	1.95	3.4	2.56	4.2	1.44	3.6	1.40	2.9	1.29	2.9
Tea	0.60	1.0	0.32	0.5	0.38	1.0	0.53	1.1	0.47	1.0
Coffee	0.68	1.2	0.87	1.4	0.49	1.5	0.61	1.3	0.61	1.4
Sugar	0.32	0.6	0.26	0.4	0.20	0.5	0.30	0.6	0.32	0.7
Eating out	12.70		17.87		8.95		11.04		9.03	
		22.1		29.1		22.6		23.1		20.0
All food expenditure (£)		57.47		61.42		39.58		47.80		45.17
Total expenditure (£)		297.00		370.05		233.44		244.93		
Food as % all expenditure		19.4		16.6		17.7		19.5		
N households		152		81		395		349		733

* Socio-economic groups: 3. Small industrial and commercial employers; 5. Professionals, self-employed; 15. *Petite bourgeoisie*; 9. Routine white-collar workers; 12. Skilled manual workers.

products, sausages and the like. The professionals spent the highest proportion, and much the largest absolute amount, on eating out.

Perhaps the most interesting feature of this table is precisely the distinctiveness of the eating habits of independent professionals. This is probably the class with the highest cultural capital and with income sufficiently substantial to express its cultural knowledge and judgment. Eating out in stylish restaurants, experimenting with domestic cuisine and eating more healthily probably are features of the food experiences of this class. But they constitute a small proportion of the British population and their experience is probably not widely shared.

The household expenditure of the small employers and the routine white-collar workers were less distinctive. Socio-economic group 3, small employers, spends a much larger proportion of its food budget on eating at home and spends more absolutely on some items than any other of these groups – bread, fresh milk, potatoes and potato products, fish and chips, tea and sugar. These are some of the staples of recent British working-class diet and make their culinary habits appear generally conservative. This suggests that it is professionals rather than the bourgeoisie that are the cultural innovators, at least in the sphere of food. The foodways of the *petite bourgeoisie* (self-employed without employees) bear more similarities to those of the skilled working class than to the professional classes.

There are, then, differences in spending patterns between socio-economic groups, but it is not clear whether these are properly class differences. To be meaningfully described as class differences entails that socio-economic groups can be amalgamated into some kind of meaningful larger entities (classes) and that there is some homogeneity within, and differences between, classes in food purchasing patterns. The purpose of the discriminant analysis exercise was to see whether such patterns exist.

The working class and the middle class

There was a considerable degree of difference between working-class and middle-class patterns of food consumption and this persisted from 1968 through to 1988. Using a model that contained only households whose head was an employee currently in employment, and distinguishing professionals, managers, routine white-collar workers and blue-collar workers, it was possible to classify successfully 55 per cent of households in 1968 and 47 per cent in 1988. In 1968 (see Table 6.3b), there was a very clear division at the manual/white-collar boundary and the successful identification of the large number of manual workers (63 per cent) is the main reason for the power of the model. The inaccurate allocation of working-class households was 9 per cent to each of the professional and managerial groups and 18 per cent to the routine white-collar workers, indicating a considerable social distance from the two higher social class groupings.

The equivalent model for 1988 (see Table 6.3a) had a lower, though still fair, success rate of 47 per cent. A declining capacity to predict membership of white-collar groups, which constituted a much larger proportion of households, resulted in a poorer model overall. However, an even higher proportion of working-class households (65 per cent) were correctly identified in 1988. This strongly suggests the maintenance and consolidation of a distinctive working-class diet but with the weakening of patterns, based on occupational divisions, within the middle class.

The food items which distinguished working-class people were very similar in both years: expenditure was comparatively high on bread,

Table 6.3   *Class differences in household food expenditure, per capita (households with head in employment), 1968 and 1988 (discriminant analysis)*

(a) Classification results: 1988

Actual group*	No. of cases	Predicted group membership			
		1	2	3	4
Group 1:	808	307	167	165	169
professional					
& auxiliary		38.0%	20.7%	20.4%	20.9%
Group 2:	771	191	213	176	191
managerial		24.8%	27.6%	22.8%	24.8%
Group 3:	530	121	77	166	166
routine white					
collar		22.8%	14.5%	31.3%	31.3%
Group 4:	1713	173	119	308	1113
working class		10.1%	6.9%	18.0%	65.0%

Percentage of 'grouped' cases correctly classified: 47.07.

* Classes: 1. Professional and auxiliary workers (socio-economic groups 5, 6, 7); 2. Managerial (socio-economic groups 2, 4); 3. Routine white collar (socio-economic groups 8, 9); 4. manual working class (socio-economic groups 10, 11, 12, 13, 14, 18).

(b) Classification results: 1968

Actual group*	No. of cases	Predicted group membership			
		1	2	3	4
Group 1:	628	229	120	168	111
professional					
& auxiliary		36.5%	19.1%	26.8%	17.7%
Group 2:	353	72	127	73	81
managerial		20.4%	36.0%	20.7%	22.9%
Group 3:	501	94	83	189	135
clerical		18.8%	16.6%	37.7%	26.9%
Group 4:	3296	314	299	599	2084
manual		9.5%	9.1%	18.2%	63.2%

Percentage of 'grouped' cases correctly classified: 55.02.

* Classes: 1. Professional and auxiliary (socio-economic groups 2, 4); 2. Managerial (socio-economic group 3); 3. Clerical (socio-economic group 5); 4. Manual (socio-economic groups 8, 9, 10).

sausages, cooked meats, beer, fish and chips, sugar, tea and canned vegetables, and relatively low on fresh vegetables, processed fruit, wine, meals out and fresh fruit. The only item that was typically middle class in 1968 that became common in all household budgets twenty years later was coffee. That differences are not just due to income is confirmed by a comparison of spending on different categories of food by professional and manual households with similar levels of income. Table 6.4 shows that there are statistically significant variations, irrespective of income and

Table 6.4 *Expenditure per capita (£s per week) on selected food items by households with a disposable income of £125–175 per capita, headed by manual and professional workers, 1988*

	Manual	Professional
Food expenditure per capita	20.74	21.12
Meals out	2.99	3.44
Take-ways meals	0.75	0.41**
Beer drunk away from home	4.63	2.50**
Wine taken home	0.47	1.28**
Coffee	0.29	0.37
Cooked meats	0.6	0.38**
Poultry	0.76	0.84
Fish	0.43	0.62*
Milk products	0.26	0.37*
Fruit juice	0.18	0.37**
Bread	0.70	0.70
Cereal	0.29	0.47**
Fresh vegetables	0.61	0.93**
Fresh fruit	0.61	0.90**
Sugar	0.11	0.07*
Total household disposable income	305.94	375.44
Per capita disposable income	142.50	150.30
N	187	108

Significant differences (t-test):* > 0.05, ** > 0.01.

Source: calculated from Family Expenditure Survey for 1988

household composition, with manual working-class households spending more on take-away meals, beer, cooked meats and sugar, and less on wine, fish, fresh fruit, vegetables and cereal. The implications for present purposes are that the manual working class, though smaller now than in the 1960s, retains distinctive dietary practices, suggesting the persistence of class taste, class culture and a firm class boundary with higher classes.[4] However, at first glance, the expanding middle class appears to be becoming more heterogeneous, raising the question of whether it is possible to identify its component parts.

6.4 The middle class and distinction

The greatest sense of refinement of taste might be expected among the middle and upper classes. Historically, the social prestige of these strata has been associated not just with their greater financial power, but with their claims to be cultured. Education, the cultivation of aesthetic sensibilities and the promotion of civilized modes of conduct have been elements of the self-image of the higher classes of western societies. This is the basis of

Bourdieu's notion of cultural capital, the process whereby those with other bases of power have attempted to legitimize their own taste as good taste, and thereby further justify their own superiority by proclaiming themselves deserving and worthy of respect. From the 16th century the struggle over good taste was perceived as, essentially, between the aristocracy and the bourgeoisie, because extravagance, expensive tastes, and the jockeying for status were available most obviously to that minority section of the population whose incomes were far above subsistence level. However, such behaviour had spread to the urban working class by, at latest, the Victorian era, causing lower white-collar households to struggle to exhibit a respectable distance from manual worker households. Consumption practices have, then, long been symbolically significant among the middle class in Britain.

Divisions within the middle class, 1968–88

Mere difference from the working class does not entail the existence of a middle class which is internally coherent in its consumption practices. Indeed, the sharp growth of the white-collar workforce, the different levels of remuneration for those with authority compared to those doing routine jobs, and the difference between the conditions of men and women, might imply rather the opposite. Whether the upper echelons of the British middle class are becoming more homogeneous in their values and aspirations is subject to debate (see Butler & Savage, 1995). Goldthorpe (1982, 1995), for instance, anticipates that the 'service class' of professional and managerial workers, who fill higher positions in the bureaucratic organizations and who deploy similar strategies to transmit their privileges to their offspring, will become more coherent and more conservative over time. Savage et al. (1992), by contrast, argue that there are three quite distinct 'fractions' of the middle class. Based on their possession of different kinds of 'assets' – property, organizational position and cultural capital – owners, managers and professionals adopt different strategies for economic security and for transmitting their privileges to their children. Savage et al. show some differences in the consumption habits of these different groups: managers are generally fairly undistinguished; there is an ascetic, often public sector, professional group with preferences for health and exercise, particularly individual pursuits like hiking, climbing, skating and yoga; and there is what they ironically describe as a 'champagne and jogging' group of younger, private sector, professionals, who have considerable incomes and who, *par excellence*, exhibit the antinomy between health and indulgence. Although there is an imperfect correspondence between consumption and asset-holding, cultural practices are central to the creation and reproduction of these fractions.

   Within the middle class food expenditure provides some evidence of the fragmentation of taste. In those calculations designed to ensure strict comparability on categories of food items, a number of patterns emerged.

Taken as a whole, the employed middle class, compared with other large groupings, became less easy to identify. Distinctions between the intermediate and the service classes remained quite stable. This did not, however, have the effect of creating a more homogeneous and distinguished service class, as was anticipated by Goldthorpe (1982). Most apparent was the increasing heterogeneity of managerial workers. As Table 6.3a showed, by 1988 managerial workers seemed to have almost nothing in common, being distributed almost evenly across all four classifying groups. This was the case throughout the discriminant analysis. It is just possible that this might indicate that they systematically exhibit a tendency to individual diversity and that the absence of a coherent collective pattern to their behaviour disguises high-level capacities for personal and individualized discrimination in food taste. But it seems much more likely that they are, as Savage et al. (1992) claimed, 'inconspicuous consumers'. Lack of shared taste can be explained by the varied jobs that come under the label of manager, the great variety of career trajectories involved, and the absence of channels for developing shared cultural capital that arise from common educational experiences. Overall, even though the contemporary middle classes might be thought structurally most susceptible to informalization and individualization (see Warde, 1991), patterns of shared cultural behaviour based in occupational position have not disappeared. With the exception of those in managerial occupations, the evidence does not suggest a rapid dilution of class-based consumption patterns, nor their replacement by unregulated individual choice.

Core middle-class groups

This chapter, so far, has used the 'collapsed' set of food items which was designed to make the comparison between 1968 and 1988 more exact (see section 3.2 and Appendix). However, when using the full range of categories for itemizing food expenditure in 1988, stronger evidence of well-developed, significant internal differentiation within the middle class appeared. Apart from managers, other middle-class fractions maintained their distinctiveness. The model that most successfully discriminated between middle-class groups was one that distinguished between 'employers', 'professionals', 'routine white-collar workers' and 'the *petite bourgeoisie*'. This model hence excluded from consideration the more heterogeneous middle-class socioeconomic groups, including managers and supervisory workers. It was especially powerful when applied only to single person households, where it suggested considerable nuanced variation. One problem with the analysis of households containing more than one person is that it is never entirely clear whose tastes are reflected in food purchasing. There is little scope for ambiguity with single person households, where people buy what they themselves consume. Unsurprisingly, models for single person households give higher scores using the technique of discriminant analysis. The extent to which models are improved is very striking.

Table 6.5 *Differences in household food expenditure, single-person households, in the middle class (households with head in employment), 1968 and 1988 (discriminant analysis)*

(a) Classification results: 1988

Actual group*	No. of cases	Predicted group membership			
		1	2	3	4
Group 1:	8	5	1	1	1
employers		62.5%	12.5%	12.5%	12.5%
Group 2:	64	0	43	9	12
professionals		0.0%	67.2%	14.1%	18.8%
Group 3:	28	1	5	18	4
petit bourgeois		3.6%	17.9%	64.3%	14.3%
Group 4:	139	4	29	12	94
routine white collar		2.9%	20.9%	8.6%	67.6%

Percentage of 'grouped' cases correctly classified: 66.95.

* Classes: 1. Industrial and commercial employers (socio-economic groups 1 & 3); 2. Professionals and auxiliaries (socio-economic groups 5 & 6); 3. *Petit bourgeois* (socio-economic groups 15 & 17); 4. Supervisory and routine white collar (socio-economic groups 8 & 9).

(b) Classification results: 1968

Actual group*	No. of cases	Predicted group membership			
		1	2	3	4
Group 1:	27	17	1	3	6
self-employed					
white collar		63.0%	3.7%	11.1%	22.2%
Group 2:	57	4	36	3	14
professional		7.0%	63.2%	5.3%	24.6%
Group 3:	18	1	2	11	4
self-employed,					
manual		5.6%	11.1%	61.1%	22.2%
Group 4:	75	6	11	14	44
clerical		8.0%	14.7%	18.7%	58.7%

Percentage of 'grouped' cases correctly classified: 61.02.

* Classes: 1. Employer and self-employed, white collar (socio-economic group 1); 2. Professional and auxiliary (socio-economic groups 2, 4); 3. Self-employed, manual (socio-economic group 7); 4. Clerical employees (socio-economic group 5).

Table 6.5a shows that 67 per cent of middle-class single person households were classified correctly in 1988. (With multiply occupied houses the success rate for an equivalent model was only 46 per cent.) In Table 6.5a the significance levels of the F statistic are all 0.001 or better, indicating that the small number of cases in each group is not responsible for the findings. This offers strong evidence for the existence of formed and differentiated tastes within the contemporary middle class. The patterns of food preferences are similar to those in multiply occupied households, but are expressed more strongly. In 1988, the *petite bourgeoisie* shared working-class tastes for buying beef, bacon, margarine and potatoes, and for drinking beer away from home. Routine white-collar workers avoided eating in restaurants and drinking in pubs, but otherwise shared preferences with professionals for cereals, poultry, fish and fruit juice. Table 6.5a shows that it is possible to identify the occupational class category of two middle-class individuals out of every three by reading their weekly grocery bills. Given difficulties of measurement, the still high levels of aggregation of the food items used, and especially the fact that the indicator of class position used is no more sophisticated than current occupation, the strength of this model is remarkable. There were some very coherent tastes among middle-class occupational groups in 1988.

Though comparison was inexact because of altered class categories, the closest model for 1968 was less accurate, explaining only 61 per cent of the variance (see Table 6.5b). Because the social characteristics of employed people who live alone changed significantly between 1968 and 1988, it would be hazardous to interpret the comparison in detail. But it is possible that the distinctive tastes of identifiable, 'core' fractions of the middle class have increased rather than diminished since the 1960s. Such a trend is perceived in the USA, for instance by Levenstein (1993: 222), who argued that 'food again became an important sign of distinction' during the 1960s and that 'the widening of the class gap seemed to accelerate in the aftermath of the 1973–5 oil shock, the spread of the Rust Belt, and other industrial woes'.

Significantly, it was the incorporation in the discriminant models of detailed evidence, previously muffled by the collapsed spending categories, about expenditure on eating out and on alcohol, that disclosed strong internal striations within the middle class. As Table 6.2 showed, professional workers spend large sums, and a comparatively large part of their food expenditure, on eating out. In the discriminant analysis it was particularly their tendency to use restaurants, rather than take-aways, cafés and so forth, that make them easy to identify. They were also distinguished by their propensity to spend disproportionately on wine. If, then, eating out and a taste for wine are contemporary symbols of extravagance, then the professionals are deploying them most extensively. It is also significant that, in 1988, those items which are consumed visibly and in public were best able to discriminate between fractions. Hence, the discriminant analyses give some genuine support to Savage et al.'s view of internal differentiation within the service class by suggesting the existence of some 'core' styles of food consumption sported by different occupational fractions.

Gender differences among the middle class

Analysis of the middle class can be further developed by taking account of gender differences in behaviour. Gender operates partly independently of occupation. Men and women in the same occupational classes do not always have the same tastes. Moreover, the items which differentiate between classes are not the same for men and women separately, as was shown by examining models for middle-class men and women separately. Interestingly, the differences among middle-class men, which were as strong as for women in 1968, had much abated by 1988. Intra-class distinction among women living alone and employed in non-manual occupations, however, persisted. Perhaps most remarkable was the coherence of taste among professional women workers, who in 1988 were correctly allocated in no less than 80 per cent of cases (see Table 6.6; for further details of this model and its implications see Warde & Tomlinson, 1995). It may be that, overall, it is women who principally inherit and reproduce the class taste which underpins class-based patterns of consumption. Speculatively, the persistently strong class differences among women in middle-class occupations is perhaps a function of their comparatively recent incorporation into these sections of the labour market and their having had fewer opportunities for social mobility than men, for improvement in access to higher education has been slow. It would be consistent with the limited available evidence (McRae, 1990; Goldthorpe, 1987) to imagine that women currently in professional positions are particularly likely to have originated from professional households. By comparison, the much larger group of female routine white-collar workers, whose tastes, while still very distinct, are less homogeneous, originate from more diverse class backgrounds.

Overall, the models indicate that the food expenditure of middle-class socio-economic groups shows quite considerable, yet still patterned, variance. This was the case in both 1968 and 1988. The idea that class, as a function of occupation, inheritance and education, is no longer significant, or is in precipitate decline, should be rejected. Change since the 1960s is fairly negligible. Indeed, given the escalation of market discipline in the UK in many areas of life under successive Conservative governments, sociologists might predict *increasing* class inequalities.

6.5 Lifestyle and class

Extrapolating from spending to issues of style or taste is difficult. Evidence of expenditure tells of preferences, in the economists' sense of what category of item is purchased, but not of the grounds for making aesthetic judgments. The evidence is sufficient to maintain that the distance between classes has not dissolved, but is not enough to determine conclusively whether class differences in Britain operate in the ways described by DeVault or Levenstein in the USA. Nor does expenditure data release many clues about whether differentiation within the middle class should be attributed to greater concern with style and distinction. For some people, undoubtedly, what and where they eat is a very conscious expression of their personal identities and style of life. But it is hard to decide whether

Table 6.6 *Single person households, by gender, middle-class occupations, 1988 (discriminant analysis)*

(a) Classification results: men, 1988

		Predicted group membership			
Actual group*	No. of cases	1	2	3	4
Group 1: self-employed	34	21 62%	4 12%	6 18%	3 9%
Group 2: professional	49	4 8%	23 47%	9 18%	13 27%
Group 3: managerial	51	12 24%	12 24%	16 31%	11 22%
Group 4: routine white collar	97	21 22%	25 26%	14 14%	37 38%

Percentage of 'grouped' cases correctly classified: 41.99.

* Classes: 1. Self-employed (socio-economic groups 1, 3, 15, 16, 17); 2. Professional (socio-economic groups 5, 6); 3. Managers (socio-economic groups 2, 4); 4. Routine white collar (socio-economic groups 7, 8, 9, 10).

(b) Classification results: women, 1988

		Predicted group membership			
Actual group*	No. of cases	1	2	3	4
Group 1: self-employed	7	3 43%	0 0%	1 14%	3 43%
Group 2: professional	15	0 0%	12 80%	1 7%	2 13%
Group 3: managerial	37	0 0%	5 14%	21 57%	11 30%
Group 4: routine white collar	181	2 1%	24 13%	40 22%	115 64%

Percentage of 'grouped' cases correctly classified: 62.92.

* Classes: 1. Self-employed (socio-economic groups 1, 3, 15, 16, 17); 2. Professional (socio-economic groups 5, 6); 3. Managers (socio-economic groups 2, 4); 4. Routine white collar (socio-economic groups 7, 8, 9, 10).

this is evidence of a general trend toward the stylization of everyday life or just the behaviour of another enthusiastic minority. Existing literature is speculative and indeterminate. Obtaining such information systematically is extremely difficult, but asking people about their tastes using survey techniques is an option, one that Bourdieu exercised and which was incorporated in the survey in Greater Manchester.

Food and lifestyle

As will be clear from occasional references above, our survey asked respondents to pick from lists of adjectives those that best described their

Table 6.7   *Style of meal served to guests (number of times a particular type was chosen)*, 1990*

	Number of choices
Healthy	84
Simple	55
Delicate	13
Plentiful	154
Economical	47
Exotic	31
Traditional	113
Whatever is going	29
Well presented	169
Don't entertain	31
N = 323	

* 'When you have guests for a meal, what kind of meals do you prefer to serve? (Choose no more than three.)'

Respondents were asked to choose up to three alternatives, but we have not weighted responses where fewer than three were chosen. 757 options out of a potential 969 were selected.

preferences for a variety of items. Thus they were asked, 'When you have guests for a meal, what kind of meals do you prefer to serve? (Choose no more than three.)' Preferences for the kind of meal that our respondents would serve to guests is in Table 6.7.

Despite reservations about the validity of this sort of question, the answers to this and other similar ones, about domestic interiors, clothes and books, suggest that the sample, despite being drawn disprortionately from affluent middle-class households, was not especially devoted to flamboyantly tasteful lifestyles. There is little distinctively 'expressive' in these answers. As regards cuisine, the frequency with which the traditional and plentiful were chosen instead of the exotic and delicate would appear to a 'foodie' as unimaginative. In terms of current culinary practice, the category 'well presented' might have been an indicator expressive of fashionable taste. However, looking at the way choices grouped, preference for well-presented food was five times less likely to be linked with the delicate and the exotic than with plenty, economy and tradition.

The answers to this question exhibited some social pattern when subjected to simple cross-tabulation with social and demographic variables.[5] Measures of the class position of the respondent and of the principal female adult in the household most regularly predicted varying taste. Women from the professional and managerial occupations were likely to express a preference for healthy, delicate, exotic and well-presented meals, and to avoid simple and traditional ones. In only two instances did a man's social class register a statistically significant correlation, with the professional and managerial men and the *petit bourgeoisie* expressing a strong preference for well-presented food and showing a high likelihood of entertaining.

Household income also made some difference, with richer households choosing plentiful and well-presented meals, and disliking simple, economic or pot luck ones. Lone parents were unlikely to choose plentiful meals and did expect to offer 'whatever was going'. This, to a minor degree, confirms Bourdieu's argument that preferences often tend to be the institutionalization of the necessary: 'resignation to necessity is the basis of the taste of necessity' (1984: 380). The poor 'choose' to give their guests cheap, simple or makeshift meals, suggesting that they have come to prefer, due to lack of resources, the inevitable. Households with children under 5 years old also opted for economical food.

Women respondents opted for healthy, economic and well-presented meals, but generally the gender of the respondent was less important than might have been expected. Older respondents opted for traditional fare, while younger respondents selected delicate meals and also would happily offer 'whatever was going'. Increasing levels of education resulted in the choice of exotic and healthy meals.

It is also possible to express these statistical relationships from another angle: what sorts of household would select a particular kind of meal? Healthy meals would be offered by women, households of higher social class and respondents with more educational qualifications. Traditional meals were most likely to be preferred by older respondents, of lower social class, where the principal woman household member was not in full-time employment and where there were no children under 15 in the household. Some of the strongest statistical predictions of all were associated with the preference for well-presented meals, with women respondents, men and women of higher social classes, owner-occupiers and richer households all considering appearances important.

One other aspect of food taste that might be considered a lifestyle choice is vegetarianism. In the sample 22 per cent of households claimed to contain a vegetarian, the total number of vegetarians present being 84. The total number of adults in our 323 households was 1,092 and there were another 234 children under 15, making a total of 1,326 in all. Of all persons, 6 per cent were vegetarian. Most households, however, had only one person so described. Since every household in the sample contained at least two people, an absolute maximum of 11 households could have been entirely vegetarian. This suggests that vegetarianism is a personal or individual commitment rather than a family style of life. The consequence for most households is, presumably, to increase the amount of work involved in food preparation since different kinds of meals are being provided for just one family member. Both these features imply that becoming and remaining a vegetarian may be difficult or contentious within families. The identity of vegetarians may, as a result, be rather volatile.

The evidence from the survey cannot, strictly speaking, address questions of change over time, for it generated only cross-sectional data. There is no way of precisely matching the current materials to earlier inquiries. But the evidence does suggest the persistence of conventional food taste. Responses to questions about preferences for styles of meal produced answers that emphasized traditional rather than novel or stylish tastes. The data tends to confirm Charles and Kerr's (1988) findings that food habits in northern England remain conservative. Nevertheless there are some signs of changing taste. The preference, by middle-class women especially, for healthy meals, may indicate some fresh emphases in home cooking. This choice, which is also related to level of education, suggests that state advice about nutrition is having an impact in some quarters. The widely stated preferences among middle class fractions for well-presented food may simply mark the persistence of concerns with appearance, but equally may reflect more fashionable approaches to food disseminated in the media in the 1990s. Additionally, the proportion claiming to be vegetarian is almost certainly higher than it would have been in a comparable sample twenty-five years earlier.

The concept of lifestyle

The recent popularity of the concept of lifestyle has been premised on the assumption that people's enthusiasms, their ways of spending their money and their spare time, are freely chosen, elective rather than socially constrained, with expression of individuality through style the principal trait. There are some powerful theoretical reasons for resisting such a view of consumer behaviour, not least that the concept of lifestyle is ill-defined, there being several different senses of the term in use, with substantially different implications for an understanding of the operation of consumption (see Warde, 1994b: 68–70). While there is no doubt that style is important and that food is a vehicle for its expression, the evidence from both the *FES* and the Greater Manchester survey suggests that collective styles of consumption persist and that these continue to be grounded socially. Thus, the success with which models – especially the single person household models – predict food taste gives good grounds for thinking that occupational differences continue to be powerful and widespread. Differentiation by gender and generation also remains significant and can be identified because these groups exhibit some coherent joint expressions of preference and taste. The same is probably true of ethnic groups too, but none of my data sources offered an opportunity to explore such differences. If these findings were generalizable to other forms of consumption, then it would suggest that there remains a fairly strong, and certainly a persistent, relationship between socio-demographic characteristics and purchasing patterns. Methodologically, then, it seems justified to continue to operate with a concept of lifestyle, bequeathed by the line of inquiry running from Veblen to Bourdieu, which assumes that lifestyles are the property of social collectivites whose boundaries are marked by shared patterns of consumption. This conceptualization at least provides a basis upon which to test whether consumption practices remain coherent and whether there is any collapse in the coincidence of social position and consumption practices.

While consumption patterns do distinguish between classes, and between fractions within the middle class, it might nevertheless be doubted whether in contemporary Britain these can be ranked hierarchically. In Bourdieu's account there was a clear hierarchy of lifestyles. It was not simply a matter of each class fraction having different symbolic insignia to express membership. Rather, the commercial and industrial bourgeoisie were at the top of a social hierarchy: this elite owns economic capital, is economically dominant, and has a style of life which outsiders recognize as superior, worthy of emulation and the arbiter of good taste. Consequently those excluded might seek to share in that lifestyle. Alternatively, the lower echelons of the middle class, the intellectuals and the new *petite bourgeoisie*, struggling to combat their inferiority, might try to usurp social honour by redefining, or inventing anew, styles of life which deserve acclamation. Whether a hierarchy of lifestyles exists in the UK cannot be decided on the evidence available. Though some individual foods and some eating places are widely accepted as luxurious, and are correspondingly expensive, large parts of the population probably do not aspire to their use. While reasonable to assume that people in all classes would welcome more resources, it is not obvious that they would then seek to alter their fundamental patterns of consumption in order to emulate members of another class. Even while behaviour continues to exhibit significant degrees of class distance, such styles of consumption may act as expressions of class identity without entailing a widely agreed calibration of aesthetic superiority and inferiority. Only further research targeted at the ways in which some groups of people classify and evaluate other groups in terms of taste can resolve this question.

6.6 Summary

The principles of economy and extravagance are rarely invoked simultaneously, their inconsistency being too obvious to disguise. The more interesting sociological aspects of this antinomy arise in the general context of the unequal distribution of material resources and the ways in which wealth and poverty are created, constructed and displayed. Differences in consumption patterns among households of varied composition, ethnic origin and class background remain significant, but pass unnoticed by the magazines. Differences between single person and family households are not associated with, or represented in terms of, different levels of wealth. While ethnic cuisine is represented, the audience is addressed as if it were uniformly white and British.

The magazines valued economy to much the same degree in 1988 as in 1968 but had eliminated recommendations in terms of extravagance. This may be partly because the main fields in which expensive and exclusive conspicuous food consumption takes place now are eating out and drinking, neither of which is a staple topic for discussion in the magazines.[6]

Their concerns with food remain centred on its domestic provision, whether for family or guests.

While processes of distinction almost always depend upon excluding others, and though this is largely achieved in complicated ways by symbolic means, cost still remains one of the ways of denying access and achieving the distinction of exclusivity. In the realm of eating because, taken item by item, food is relatively cheap, cost has played little role in the sociological analysis of foodways. Yet a good deal of social difference even in the UK can be appreciated simply in terms of income and expenditure. Richer households spend much more money in absolute terms than do poorer households, while that constitutes a significantly smaller proportion of their total expenditure. But still it is class differentiation, and especially its persistence, which is more significant sociologically.

All the data suggests the continued existence of class differentiation. The working class was at least as distinct from the middle class at the end of the 1980s as it had been in the 1960s. The middle class exhibited internal differentiation, the data for households suggesting blurred boundaries, but that for individuals suggesting quite powerfully formed 'core' communities of taste within the middle class. Models including managerial workers as a category are always comparatively unsuccessful, suggesting that they are a rather undistinguished category of consumers. Professionals were distinctive, particularly as a result of their patterns of public consumption, including their preferences for restaurant meals and wine. As regards their purchases of food for consumption at home, they seem to have learned health messages most thoroughly, their diets conforming most closely to the recommendations of nutritionists. Routine white-collar workers, whose habits have many echoes of professional employees, though at lower levels of expenditure, have also absorbed the messages about healthy eating. The *petite bourgeoisie* proper, the self-employed person without employees, has an expenditure pattern very similar to that of skilled sections of the manual working class, from which many of its members will have originated. The employers are also rather undistinguished, sharing some more expensive tastes with the professionals, but having generally fairly traditional tastes with affinities to those of the *petite bourgeoisie*. It seems, therefore, that projections derived from Bourdieu are supported by this evidence, while Mennell's anticipation of diminishing contrasts between classes is not.

Less clear is whether these class differences constitute the elements of a hierarchical system of taste that intrinsically exhibits social prestige. At the most general level, it might be argued that many differences are in the quality of items, rather than the fact that large groups of people are entirely excluded or deprived of the same commodities. Some households eat more expensive versions of the same items – better cuts of meat, or wine; and some households have more cosmopolitan tastes than others, which they share with their perceived peers and in which they may invest considerable identity value – though this arises only indirectly, if at all, as a result of cost. It is not so much what can be afforded, more a matter of normative agreements about good or proper taste. This suggests the prevalence of concern with intra-group conformity. Food preferences exhibit a person's membership of a particular group, rather than their making strong statements about either individuality (personal taste) or social superiority (inter-group distinction).

This might appear to offer support to a very weak version of the neo-tribalist thesis, suggesting a harmonious pluralism which accepts the coexistence, and rough equivalence, of different tastes. However, group tastes are not matters of elective shifting identities, but remain embedded in socio-demographic collectivities. Any pluralism operates within the parameters and constraints of the class and gender systems rather than by dismantling them. There remain powerful mechanisms for the social regulation of food tastes.

While differences exist, they seem not generally likely to cause social conflict, nor to pose a threat to social order or social integration. In the absence of a propensity to emulate elites, for which there is very little evidence, cultural differentiation in the field of food is unlikely to cause resentment. Even if the professional classes may seem patronizing and the advice of the state and its cadre of experts might be unwelcome, differences in diet are not a major source of perceived social injustice in Britain. This, of course, is not the case at the global level, nor is it to deny the enforced inadequacy of the diets of the poorest households in the UK. Food practices may symbolize group attachment without becoming a focus for conflict over material inequality.

7
Convenience and Care

7.1 Commodification: production and consumption

The contribution of domestic production to consumption, through the provision of services like cooking and cleaning within the household, frequently goes unrecognized. Many accounts deriving from mainstream economics, for example, discount such labour, because consumption is equated with purchase; what happens to goods after they leave the shop is inconsequential because preference is expressed at the point of sale. Such a view is rendered partly plausible because some of the more spectacular changes in British consumption are associated with the further extension of commodification, increased variety of available foods being one of the most obvious examples. Also, in historical perspective, the contemporary house-hold possesses more kitchen machinery and buys more part-prepared or ready-made foods, while growing, gathering and preserving less produce than before. Nevertheless, although almost all household foodstuffs are now bought, the transformation of groceries into meals often requires considerable time, effort and skill on the part of household members. What is not clear is whether the greater availability of part-prepared foods and kitchen technology has reduced the amount of domestic labour required or has altered attitudes to the provision of food to families.

Rosalind Schwartz Cowan's book *More Work for Mother* (1983) gives clearest expression to an irony about household organization: despite enormous application of technology to the home, the amount of domestic work that women have to do seems not to decrease. Her book attempts to explain why 'a woman's work is never done!' She examines the transition in the USA from a situation in the early 19th century, where households did most of the necessary work of subsistence by applying its own labour to raw materials, to that of the late 20th century when a vast number of goods and services are purchased for domestic use. She notes, however, that although this removes some onerous tasks, it creates others. She identifies eight technological systems that bear directly upon the household:

> 20th century household technology consists of not one, but of eight, interlocking technological systems: the systems that supply us with food, clothing, health care, transportation, water, gas, electricity, and petroleum products. Some of these systems have followed the conventional model – moving production out of the home and into the factories; but (and this is the crucial point) some of them have not. (Cowan, 1983: 71)

An instance of the latter is transportation, where there are now few deliveries, no pedlars, and most people use private rather than public transport. Consequently women drive cars to go shopping and to deliver children to school or to the doctor's surgery with the result that they spend much more time on these activities than previously. The energy systems had equally ambiguous consequences for women:

> the modern fuel-supply systems did not necessarily lighten the work of individual housewives, although they certainly did reorganize it. Some of the work that was eliminated by modernization was work that men and children – not women – had previously done: carrying coal, carrying water, chopping wood, removing ashes, stoking furnaces, cleaning lamps, beating rugs. Some of the work was made easier, but the volume increased: sheets and underwear were changed more frequently, so there was more laundry to be done; diets became more varied, so cooking was more complex; houses grew larger so there were more surfaces to be cleaned. Additionally, some of the work that, when done by hand had been done by servants, came to be done by the housewife herself when done by machine; indeed, many people purchased appliances precisely so that they could dispense with servants. It is not, consequently, accidental that the proportion of servants to households in the nation dropped (1 servant to every 15 households in 1900; 1 to 42 in 1950) just when washing machines, dishwashers, vacuum cleaners, and refrigerators were increasing just as markedly. Finally, some of the work that had previously been allocated to commercial agencies actually returned to the domain of the housewife – laundry, rug cleaning, drapery cleaning, floor polishing – as new appliances were invented to make the work feasible for the average house-wife, and the costs of labor (all labor, that is, except the labor of the housewife) continued to escalate in the postwar years. (Cowan, 1983: 98–9)

Cowan's most general claim, though contested, is that despite alterations in the technologies for, and organization of, household work, the overall burden remains constant. As regards the supply of household food, however, Cowan tends to accept that commodification has reduced labour, mentioning food processing and commercial brewing as examples of the way that industry has reduced tasks in the long term. Precise data is not available, but in the last thirty years in the UK it seems likely that, of the time spent on food-related tasks, shopping will have increased, while preparation has reduced.

The number of shopping trips has probably declined with the advent of the weekly supermarket visit to buy a wide variety of items at a single shop. But longer journeys, and the greater distance travelled for the purchase of other and supplementary fresh foods, given the closure of neighbourhood shops, offsets any time saving in this field. Households without access to cars probably devote considerably more time than previously.

Time involved in the preparation of food, by contrast, probably has declined. Startlingly, one study of meal patterns within households on Tyneside is reported to have found that:

> Some 94 per cent of meals involved less than ten minutes' preparation time, and 51 per cent no time at all. Some 61 per cent of all meals involved no cooking time and only 7 per cent more then 20 minutes' cooking time. (Ritson & Hutchins, 1990: 44)

An overall reduction in time spent in the kitchen may be less the effect of the availability of pre-prepared ingredients and whole dishes, more a consequence of the demise of cooked breakfasts and of midday meals served in the home. Again, age, household composition and degree of commitment to the labour market are bases for considerable variation within the population. Nonetheless, even if reduced, the amount of labour time still devoted to feeding is very substantial and, moreover, most of it falls to women. That discussion of food provision should pay attention to the amount of time involved is unsurprising, particularly given the rather peculiar late modern attitude to time use.

Schwartz Cowan's conundrum is one of many reflections on an apparent shortage of time in contemporary society. Linder (1970), reflecting on change since Veblen's era, pronounced the contemporary leisure class 'harried', and observed, enigmatically, that time had become increasingly scarce. Against the background of a goods-intensive society and from the premises of the model of rational economic behaviour, he advances three reasons for extensive pressure on time. First, as productivity and wages rise, it becomes increasingly less rational to take time off; the opportunity cost is such that we cannot sensibly decline paid work. Second, goods require time to make use of them. Third, the maintenance of goods takes yet more time. Hence, economic growth implies that workers will have less free time than before.

Cross, in *Time and Money* (1993) explored this scenario further, coining the concept of the 'work and spend' culture. It used to be the case that there was a shortage of goods: people had insufficient to eat, they got cold because they lived in draughty dwellings, they slept on grasses on the floor because they did not have feather mattresses. It was imagined, for centuries, that economic growth and the expansion of available goods would permit greater comfort *and* less work, because economic growth increased productivity. People would be able to spend spare time in spiritual, self-developing, intellectual or sociable activities.

Cross shows that in the 19th century most theorists assumed, and most employers feared, this would happen if productivity rose and workers were paid higher wages. Industrial workers would simply not bother to work for any longer than was necessary to satisfy a set of fixed, traditional needs. However, this did not transpire. Instead workers chose the 'work and spend' resolution to the opportunities offered by increasing productivity. Rather than take more time off, those who can obtain employment work longer hours and thus increase their purchasing power. One implication is that the desire for goods and services is highly elastic, if not insatiable. There is no evidence as yet that people will run out of new things that they want to possess. Hence the further intensification of the logic identified by Linder.

Working hours are only a little shorter than they were a hundred years ago. Indeed according to Schor, they have increased significantly in the US since 1969. Gershuny's (1992: 79) calculations for the UK between 1974 and 1987 show a slight decline in total time in paid work for couple households, the increased hours women spend in paid work having not quite offset the reduction for men, but an overall increase in the sum of paid work plus housework. Certainly, compared to increases in industrial productivity, reduction in work time is trivial. The complex interrelationship of money, time and goods that besets the consumer society as a whole surfaces conspicuously in the kitchen. Much effort is devoted to saving time at home. While many new machines are advertised for their time-saving capacities, housework is not highly rationalized. Indeed, it is doubtful if it could be, given the current preference for independent, single family living. As households get smaller, even more time in total must be being devoted to domestic work.

Social scientists have often used time-budget techniques to explore such matters. Household members are asked to keep detailed diaries recording the time spent on each of their daily activities. There are many reservations about accurate measurement and the adequacy of interpretation in such studies. Particularly relevant here is the fact that domestic labour is tightly connected with the management and reproduction of family relationships. Time budgets can never reveal the meaning of the emotional or caring dimensions of domestic work. Because there is a technical dimension to housework, it might in principle be rationalized and the amount of time devoted to it decreased. However, it is less clear that a similar process of rationalization would make any sense in respect of the emotional and caring aspects of family management. The notion of 'quality time' for family members at home, which emerged in the 1980s, and the reason given by some of the respondents in Gregson and Lowe's (1994) inquiry to explain middle-class households' decisions once again to employ domestic servants, is perhaps an attempt to apply industrial rationalization techniques to human relationships. Whether it is possible to achieve better relationships in fewer and shorter, but more intense, episodes is uncertain. More striking, perhaps, is that people even think of trying. This peculiar obsession with the saving, disciplining and regulation of time has become even stronger, for certain sections of the population, at the end of the 20th century.

More scholarly attention has been devoted to the technical than to the caring aspects of the domestic division of labour, probably because of ease of measurement. It is comparatively straightforward to discover who does what tasks in the household and which mechanical aids are available. It is rather more difficult to tease out the meanings associated with care. Charles and Kerr (1988) found their interviewees acutely conscious of the symbolic and comforting role played by wives and mothers through supplying family meals. Wilson (1989: 180), discussing poorer urban British households, was able to conclude that 'food as love meant providing the family with the meals they liked in so far as the budget allowed. When it conflicted with the message of health educators women did not give priority to health.' But perhaps the most insightful and detailed appreciation of the caring aspect of domestic food provision is DeVault's *Feeding the Family* (1991).

DeVault is exceptional in the attention she pays to the detail of the coordination, and particularly the social and emotional coordination, involved in food provisioning. While we might recognize the various tasks of shopping, preparation, cooking and cleaning up as work, the complexity of their coordination, with potential as a source of anxiety or failure, is obscured by simple counts of the frequency of each stage. DeVault is particularly keen to recognize the way that food provisioning, almost always by women, involves 'the skill that produces group life, the effort of being constantly attentive, or the subtle pressures that pull women into relations of subordination and deference produced by this work' (1991: 228). One important effect is that through the family meal, women produce the family itself. As DeVault puts it, 'the feeding work traditionally under-taken by women is both produced by and produces "family" as we have known it – the work itself "feeds" not only household members but also "the family" as ideological construct' (1991: 236). The fact is that

> 'feeding a family' involves not just the physical care and maintenance of house-hold members but also the day-to-day production of connection and sociability. The physical tasks of food preparation – essential as they are – combine with equally important coordinative work that produces group life within a complex market society. (1991: 230)

Women face these obligations with different perspectives, some willing and wholehearted, some with resignation. But they all tend to combine a certain degree of deferential personal service to their families with their expression of caring for them. Caring has two aspects: caring for someone, tending to their needs, and caring about them, which concern is manifest in the process of pleasing them. As DeVault puts it:

> The principles and skills of attention to others are built into the work of feeding, and more generally, of care. The work is directed towards pleasing others as well as serving their more material needs for sustenance and comfort. . . . [I]t is clear that food does provide an important symbolic terrain, used expressively by family members in a variety of ways, and not easily dismissed as trivial. (1991: 233)

Providing food that is rejected is disheartening, disappointing, and ulti-mately fruitless. To avoid this, women have to subordinate their own preferences to those of other family members, sometimes men, sometimes children. Often they do not perceive this as a problem, and usually not as a form of personal deprivation. Yet it is one of the subtle ways that women become effectively subordinated and deferential, in relation to their obligation, and desire, to please others.

DeVault's analysis relates to households in Chicago, yet there is nothing in the available evidence about the UK that would suggest that the conditions she describes are not equally pertinent. The work of Charles and Kerr (1988) largely corroborates her interpretation, though DeVault is, rightly, at pains to stress that it is the very work itself, rather than some extraneous gender ideology, that has the effect described. The power of DeVault's account arises, above all, from the success with which the nature of the work of food provisioning is related in the words, and from the perspective, of those actually doing it, which exposes its ambivalent social and emotional facets. The association of care, love, family and provision is intricate and inextricable, and serves largely to confirm the subordination of women in society more widely.

Food preparation, then, involves both technical and emotional dimensions. Means exist for reducing time spent on domestic food production. A diet of raw food would be perfectly nourishing and very economical of preparation time. A diet exclusively comprised of packaged and pre-prepared foods from the supermarket similarly would save time and effort. At a price, all meals could be purchased ready-made in restaurants, sandwich shops and take-away outlets: the early feminist vision of the kitchenless house, where meals would be prepared collectively and delivered to people's homes, is now a viable commercial alternative. However, it is unlikely that such alternatives, though technically efficient in terms of time use, would be generally acceptable. Hence the amount of time devoted to household labour, particularly given its unequal distribution among family members, plays a large part in any understanding of the organization of food provisioning. It appears in various guises in the magazines, prominently as an antinomy between convenience and care.

7.2 Convenience or care: advertising the antinomy

The tension between viewing household cooking as an instrumental and technical activity, as opposed to a labour of love, was graphically symbolized by an advert for Stork frozen pastry products, which might stand as the condensation of this fourth antinomy.[1] A two-page ad, the first side is devoted to tips about how to make good pastry from scratch, the second side to the availability and characteristics of some pre-prepared pastry products – frozen croissants, apple turnovers, vol-au-vent cases and short pastry tarts (ready to fill).

Side one contains emotion-laden and housewifely homilies. The headline is 'Cold hands, warm heart. It's not about love, it's about pastry.' it starts by noting that 'They say "The way to a man's heart is through his stomach".' It notes that 'there are few loves stronger than the cupboard variety'. A large ginger-biscuit Cupid fills in the middle of the page. Some technical advice about pastry-making is offered: 'you must never "stretch" it too far by rolling too vigorously'; 'people with naturally warm hands may have to resort to dunking their fingers in iced water'; use of marble slabs and glass rolling pins is recommended. It also considers some of the difficulties of making rough, flaky and puff pastry. Finally it displays a tiny motto: 'Pastry-making is definitely a labour of love.'

The second page starts by announcing, 'You don't always have to roll your own.' Circumstances don't always permit making pastry from scratch. However, 'Thanks to new ready-to-bake shortcrust pastry tarts and vol-au-vents from the Stork Bakery, you don't have to. You can still enjoy the smell of fresh baking wafting from the kitchen. You can still experience the taste of crisp pastry eaten hot from the oven. You just miss out on the hassle.' The ad then talks about the pre-prepared goods, gives a few recipes for the fillings, gives instructions about how to cook your vol-au-vents, and suggests that they will emerge from the oven 'crispy and delicious'.

This in many ways epitomizes the dilemma of convenience against care. Home cooking is declared the way to a man's heart. It is the proper way to cherish a family. Food is an expression of love, and a sacrifice too – a labour of love. You can do it, and indeed would do it, if only you had the time – how could you not, given what it means. But of course you are sometimes busy! You would not choose easy ways out just because you are insufficiently skilled, but because there are other demands upon you. Then you can use the made-up version. This contains Stork ingredients, a branded guarantee of good quality. The commodity is a perfect substitute. Or, if not quite perfect, it will still perform the function of expressing love and care. It is simultaneously the same thing and the next-best thing. The outcome will be perfect and, though the advertisement does not say so, it implies that nobody will be able to tell the difference.

This advert might be read as an invitation to feel less uneasy about not expressing love properly. However, it confirms that home-made is best while trying to compensate for the fact that we do not live in a perfect world. The manufactured product offers the nearest thing to authenticity, much more quickly. It is make-believe; it is inauthentic; but you avoid hassle. Not quite that you should feel good about this; rather that you can get away with it. It is counterfeit food; it fulfils some requirements – expressing love, smelling of fresh, real baking – so it is certainly worth buying. But, really you are cheating. However, since you will do-it-yourself properly on other occasions, using the helpful tips, it can be condoned.

This advertisement is instructive for several reasons. Though appearing light-hearted, it plays on potential guilt associated with giving insufficient attention to emotionally significant aspects of cooking for families. It affirms an association between traditional home baking and a mother's love. It promises a short-cut to everlasting familial commitment. The wish to save time is condoned and treated sympathetically, but it is still questionable. In this vein, the convenient is always suspect, second best, perhaps necessary, but to be regretted. While convenient food can be made in the home, it does not have the same emotional impact as home-made items.[2] This range of frozen pastries failed and was withdrawn from the market within the year. There may be many reasons for this, not least that most new food products fail, but it might be that the stark exposure of a symbolic contradiction repelled readers. Advertisements generally avoid linking care and convenience. Lien's (1995) analysis of Norwegian adverts observes that those for children's food almost never invoke convenience as a selling point, despite the fact that many are for baby foods which come pre-prepared in jars or tins. It is not appropriate to suggest restricting the time involved in nourishing children. Interestingly, Lien's content analysis indicated that foreign foods were more likely to be marketed as convenient, implying that manufacturers would find it easier to sell convenience goods if people were relatively uncertain about the proper taste of a dish.

Advertisements suggest some opposition between commodities and labours of love. Simply to purchase food is less satisfactory than if mingled with womanly labour, thereby providing a food that is emotionally, if not necessarily technically, superior. There are many other oppositions, different by subtle nuance, that build up the power of this antinomy. Antitheses include personalized provision against commodified product; lavishing care against saving time; expressive against instrumental work; particularistic attention against mass provision; and so forth. In each case, the first element of the antithesis conjures up familiar and homely love, the second the cold and impersonal world of capitalist rationalization. Tensions identical to those in the adverts appear also in the food columns, where both principles are frequently invoked.

7.3 Convenience and care in the magazines

Convenience

Gofton and Ness (1991: 20–1) point out that there are many senses in which a food item might be, or be perceived as, convenient:

> The idea of convenience refers, for many people, to the ease with which a product may be prepared, served and eaten. Even this, of course, may involve different aspects – simplicity in the cooking process, or speedy cooking, or being able to cook a product without special utensils, or being able to serve without cooking, or without special tableware, or being able to use the product in combination with many different things, or being able to serve it to different sorts of people on different kinds of meal occasions.
>
> Convenience may involve a large number of other characteristics, however – ease of acquisition through being available at a large number of retail outlets, being easily stored and so available for use at any time, or suitable for use as a lap or TV meal.

Very few of these senses are appealed to in the recipe columns. The values promoted are primarily speed of preparation, simplicity in cooking and ease of storage.

Manufactured convenience foods, those at least partly prepared before sale so as to be ready, or almost ready, for the table, items that the food industry finds most profitable, are not ones generally referred to in the columns: there could be no recipe for those – only taste tests, which now occur occasionally, or advertisements. The recipe columns distance themselves from such products. Significantly, they almost never, in either year, used the actual term 'convenient' to recommend a dish. They prefer synonyms. However, the notion and value of convenience is never far from the surface. The ways in which this concern is represented are complex and intriguing.

Speed   Time is important. Recipes considered convenient are those which are time-saving; their appeal is that the housewife-cook does not have to devote too much precious time to domestic food preparation. The circumstance is one of time scarcity, largely caused by increased involvement in paid work and other perceived priorities regarding time use. But it was no more important in 1992 than in 1968: in 1968, 14 per cent of recipes were recommended as quick, in 1992 it was only 15 per cent of cases. Clearly, the need for foods that required limited preparation time existed twenty-five years ago too. However, there were some differences in the circumstances in which quick foods were to be served.

In the 1960s the magazines were much less circumspect about the attractions of convenience foods. Recipes occasionally openly encouraged use of tinned foods or frozen foods. For instance, *People's Friend* (May 1968) in an article 'Potatoes from a packet' said:

> One of the most useful food products that has ever been devised to help the busy housewife is packaged mashed potatoes. In a matter of seconds they are ready to serve with a meat course, or for use in making any dish for which they are required.

Such celebration of convenience foods in the 1960s showed signs of an equation between the convenient, the modern, the exciting and the good. There was an anticipation that new, advanced, manufactured foods would eliminate work without loss of quality and would thereby break oppressive routines which absorbed women's time. In the 1960s, convenience foods were associated with novelty and invention and there was a certain openness to the incorporation of such time- and labour-saving items into domestic cookery. 'Angel Delight', a powder to which milk was added to make a pseudo-mousse, was recommended as 'packed magic . . . something new . . . try this quick, convenient, package sweet' (*WH*, Aug. 1968). More likely, ways would be suggested to 'customize' manufactured products. Thus, various recipes were provided for the use of instant mashed potatoes. This might be understood as the personalizing of the commodity, bringing it back into the domestic circuit by adding things to it.

Of the recipes coded as 'quick' in the monthlies in 1968, four involved using commercially packaged, pre-prepared products, three of which required a little extra work; six were for extra-routine domestic events like parties and holidays. It seemed to be taken for granted that considerable but fixed amounts of time would be spent in routine cooking. This use of time is not regretted. But on some exceptional occasions speed in preparation would be helpful. This is not to say that time-saving was irrelevant in all other situations. Two regular columns 'Jiffy Dishes' and 'Quickie Cook Recipes' appeared in the 1968 magazines.

By 1992, the term 'quick' was used in a matter-of-fact and descriptive way: length of time became a technical property of every dish, a normal concern associated with everyday cooking. Markedly, more reference is made to preparation and/or cooking times of featured recipes. In 1968 only 8 per cent of recipes contained such information, but by 1992, 44 per cent did. This is the strongest evidence that concern with time-saving and time management had become a more widespread concern by 1992. It reflects an increase in the force and complexity of time constraints on women. It also indicates the general trend towards more explicit calculation and greater precision in advice about food. It is another sign of rationalization, the imperative of precise measurement being entailed when expert advice is codified as rules for successful practice.

Recipes denoted 'quick' in 1992 rarely took longer than ten minutes to prepare and cook. Stir-fry dishes, salads, 'ultra quick puds' and marinated olives were among the recipes. There were also a number of suggestions about how to entertain without spending much time in preparation. As regards use of new technology, the monthlies in 1992 do not suggest use of the microwave, though the weeklies do so more frequently.

Ease of preparation   A second aspect of convenience altered more substantially between 1968 and 1992. Twenty-two per cent of recipes were deemed 'easy' in 1992, compared to 11 per cent in 1968.

In 1968, 7 per cent of recipes were described as *technically* easy and some 4 per cent are labour-saving because they use short-cut ingredients. Thus in total 11 per cent of recipes could be classified as easy. A further 4 per cent were described as simple, but in the very different sense of unfussy or plain.

In 1968 it was generally items required in exceptional circumstances that were addressed in terms of ease. Living alone was one such exceptional circumstance:

> There may not be many people who'd actually choose to cook for themselves –
> but the fact remains, there are thousands, particularly hard-working 'bed-sit' girls
> who do! And that's why we're giving these recipes – recipes that take the chore
> out of 'cook-for-yourself' and turn it into fun. (*MW*, 11 May 1968)

These recipes are 'quick to make, easy to wash up afterwards': they are easy not with respect to technical difficulty, but because of the limited amount of energy required. Another exceptional situation was where advantage might be gained by advance preparation. Food that could be taken away from home, on picnics for instance, might be made the day before. The theme of the dishes referred to in *Ideal Home*'s (Aug. 1968) 'At the Ready' is 'spreading the load. They can be prepared when life is leisurely and put in the fridge. When needed they are simply reheated or served chilled.' It is not that they require less work, rather that they save time at a critical juncture. They can be prepared in advance by the housewife, not by the industrialist.

If more than one recipe in five was recommended as easy in 1992, there were various meanings of 'easy'. The most common was that a dish was technically easy to prepare; eleven recipes (9 per cent) conveyed this message. A further five had reduced the complexity of a dish for the readers. Three were recommended because they saved effort. Five were easy because of the nature of the ingredients. Six were deemed easy primarily because they were quick to prepare. For a further seven, the description 'easy' appeared to act as a form of reassurance, since the recipes were relatively complex and would take a significant amount of time to prepare. Only one recipe appealed to simple or plain tastes.

Somewhat anomalously, in the recipes in the 1992 magazines, dishes deemed quick are always made of basic ingredients, built up from scratch, never identifying use of pre-packaged produce as a time-saving feature. One article in *Cosmopolitan* specifically compared manufactured convenience meals (Marks and Spencer's cook-chill dishes, which were highly recommended for some occasions) with recipes for dishes cooked from scratch but requiring limited preparation time which, though more work, were ultimately preferable. The message increasingly was to prepare home-made food, but in a way economical of time and effort, thus suggesting that care and convenience might be reconciled. It was implied, in addition, that rather less culinary skill, if not knowledge, was expected of readers at the later date, the vocabulary associated with simplicity having changed significantly. Thus did reasoning about convenience change.

Storage   A third direct indicator of increasing concern with convenience was the extent and nature of reference to the capacity for certain dishes to be stored for future use. In 1968 only 6 per cent of recipes made any reference to keeping foods. It was occasionally noted that a cooked item could be kept in the fridge or stored in an airtight jar, and one article observed that pancakes froze well. But generally such knowledge was either assumed or considered irrelevant. By 1992 this consideration was more transparent: 30 per cent of all recipes contained some instruction about interrupting the cooking sequence by storage, freezing, or similar processes. A small part of this increase reflects the wider availability of freezers, but there are strong hints of other issues regarding time management. Information includes how long items can remain in the fridge, extensive planning ahead, most notably for Christmas, and frequently the identification of preliminary processes to be done 24 or 48 hours ahead. This gives the opportunity to save time on another day, when entertaining people or when otherwise short of time, rather than to eliminate its need.

The information is much more varied and sophisticated by 1992. This suggests time congestion, reflecting the key shift in working women's lives, from having the time flexibility associated with being a full-time housewife, where it was possible to have some control over the organization of time, to a situation where the time devoted to paid work takes priority in the organization of daily life. More external constraints mean more domestic pre-planning.

Care

By contrast, a *declining* value is placed upon care. In 1968 *explicit* reference to family food and home-made food was made in 20 per cent of cases. A number of others appealed to the nostalgic (4 per cent) and emotion-supporting (3 per cent) aspects of home cooking. By 1992, only 8 per cent explicitly recommended a dish because it was home-made, and the proportion of references to nostalgia subsided to 2 per cent.

In 1968, frequently, and somewhat gratuitously, it was the family to whom dishes were said to appeal: 'for the hearty eaters of the family' (*FC*, Nov. 1967); 'The cries of delight from the family also make it rewarding' (*IH*, Nov. 1967); 'family menus' (*WW*, Nov. 1967). Reference back to the family was repetitive and unspecific, reminder of an assumption that it was family members who would be the beneficiaries of whatever was cooked. Recurrently families are identified as justifying cooking, because they will be pleased by the resulting meals. Dishes, especially cakes and puddings, are recommended because children like them: the term 'home-made' is most frequently deployed in respect of buns and cakes, evidence of the particular significance in the 1960s of home baking as a symbol of traditional housewifery. There is also some explicit reference to nostalgia which again tends to be related back to the family, especially to grandmothers. For example, the article about British cookery, quoted above, which began: 'most of us have a nostalgia for those plain, but perfectly cooked dishes granny served' (*WR*, Aug. 1968), offered a recipe for 'Nan's bread pudding'. The columnist specifically mused about cooking skills: 'How many young housewives know how to make bread pudding? We have given a really authentic recipe.' This was, however, the only occasion when the cooking skill of the readership was impugned. Overall, the 1968 magazines offer numerous instances of family sentiment, locating food and its production firmly, and almost exclusively, in the ambit of co-resident family. The impression of the central importance of the family meal, one prepared by housewife and mother, runs powerfully through the food journalism of the period. Significantly, only the most 'progressive' magazine in the sample, *She*, fails to register any reference to family care, as recorded in the categories of the content analysis.

By 1992 there were still references to the family, but they were fewer and of a more varied and matter-of-fact kind. Co-resident family no longer provides the quintessential legitimation for home cooking. Several of the references to family are to the possibility of making food presents to extended kin. Guests for whom home-made food is appropriate are more readily envisaged as its recipients. Cooking becomes more a technical matter, the food stands for itself, the result of effective performance, a demonstration of culinary expertise or knowledge about food. By the same token it is less an emotional expression of familial care and concern.

By 1992 little nostalgia is expressed for home-made food; indeed scarcely any explicit reference is made to the value 'home-made'. In the 1992 sample, the terms 'home-made' and 'home-cooked' occurred on only three occasions: once regarding presents, of home-made sweeties for family and friends; once as 'how to turn a shop-bought cake into "home made"' (*FC*, Nov. 1991); and once 'Take Christmas in your stride by filling the freezer with lots of delicious home-cooked food. You'll be relaxed, and unexpected guests will be welcome' (*GH*, Dec. 1991). While reaffirming that to be home-made is a positive feature, none were concerned with pleasing or cajoling the immediate family. Family *meanings* have, apparently, escaped from home-made food. Ironically, in the 1990s, the term 'home-made' is more likely to be seen on advertisements for meals in restaurants and pubs.

The reduction in reference to the familial and the home-made is remarkable, though it should be put in the context of the fact that all recipe columns are directed towards the reader preparing the dishes listed. The presumption is that preparation will be in the domestic kitchen. Nevertheless this is no longer trumpeted as a virtue in itself. It suggests, by default, the importance of the various aspects of convenience to food preparation now, and a desire on the part of the magazines to avoid being disparaging about saving time. The implication is always that women should, if they wish, be excused the obligation to perform the domestic role of carer. And the magazines are careful not to expose women who make this choice to unnecessary guilt. Their readers' time pressures are taken seriously. There is less emphasis on family and housewifery than in the 1960s.

One further indication of the extent to which food preparation is family centred, is found by examining the number of servings that a particular dish is supposed to provide. Average household size in Britain has declined. In 1992, 27 per cent of households contained only one person, and a further 35 per cent contained two persons (including single parents with one child). However, in the 1992 magazines there were very few recipes for one or two persons: only 3 per cent of the recipes sampled. This compared with 14 per cent in 1968. In both years just under half of the recipes where number of servings was mentioned were for four persons, and about a quarter were for six. Recipes for larger groups were much more common in 1992, with 29 per cent being for eight or more people, compared with 11 per cent in 1968 (see Table 7.1).

One reason for this increase is that a significant number of recipes in the sample in 1992 were specifically directed towards Christmas festivities where one might expect parties to be larger. In both years, about a quarter of all recipes were designated for a special event of some sort. Of those, in 1968, recipes were suggested for a wider range of special occasions: entertaining guests to various meals, parties and picnics were mentioned regularly. In 1992, in 59 per cent of instances, the occasion was Christmas,

Table 7.1   *The number of servings expected per recipe, 1968 and 1992 (percentages)*

	1968	1992
1	6	2
2	8	1
3–4	49	47
5–6	25	21
7–9	8	21
10+	3	8
	99	100
N cases =	63	96

and a further 24 per cent of mentions was entertaining guests to a meal. In 1967 Christmas was the subject of just one sampled recipe. Quite why this was the case is hard to determine. It is only partly attributable to changed scheduling of content by the magazine editors: in 1967 Christmas items appeared in December rather than November. Even taking this into account, little space was devoted in the food columns to Christmas. Magazines assumed that roast turkey, with a variety of stuffings, accompanied by sprouts, would constitute Christmas dinner for almost everyone and that readers would mostly know how to prepare it.[3] More attention was paid to supplementary foods – like cakes, mince pies and sausage rolls, which might be offered to guests or children – than to Christmas dinner itself.

The addition of vegetarian alternatives to Christmas dinner encouraged greater variety on that festive occasion in 1991. The increase in volume of Christmas dishes might alternatively suggest that greater nostalgia developed for Christmas as a family occasion. It might also suggest a decline in customary knowledge among readers of what is suitable for cooking at Christmas.

The sharp decline in the number of dishes specified for celebrations other than Christmas could indicate that domestic entertaining has itself become less frequent. The magazines of the 1990s presume so. Perhaps entertaining is also less formal. Specifying dishes for particular occasions would be in retreat if those occasions no longer occur. Alternatively it may be that greater flexibility is expected of recipes, it being more important to suggest dishes that can be adapted to any eventuality. If we no longer know what is appropriate to any occasion, the columnists are less likely to dare to make apparently prescriptive suggestions.

The overall impression is that there is slightly less formality about special occasions, which no longer call for particular kinds of dishes, and that there is slightly less emphasis on routine and practical daily cooking, as indicated by the loss of interest in dishes for one or two people. In this, taking into account the extra attention paid to guests, the magazines have, to some minor degree, begun to sever the link between the amount of time a woman spends in her own kitchen and the degree to which she cares for her family. This is partly because food comes to have value outside and beyond family situations. Though there is no necessary reason why home-produced food should have so high a symbolic value, it currently does have, a fact probably evidenced by the relative amounts of space given to cooking as opposed to shopping features. Recipes are recommended because they are quick and easy to prepare, but manufactured products are increasingly shunned. It is assumed that readers will prepare fresh foods, but in a manner economical with time.

There have, then, been some significant shifts in the way that this antinomy has been handled in the period since the 1960s, as the claims of convenience have been accorded greater legitimacy and the obligation to express care through domestic labour has become less explicit. Overall, in the magazine sample, recipes making some reference to one or other aspect of convenience increased sharply, from 28 to 67 per cent of recipes, though the principal reason was the new tendency to record preparation and cooking times. More significant, and almost certainly not an artefact of the coding scheme, was the fact that reference to the virtues of home-made food reduced in this period. One interesting question is whether these representations in the magazines coincided with actual changes in domestic behaviour.

7.4   Domestic divisions of labour[4]

The antinomy of convenience and care epitomizes gender inequalities in the household. Balancing the demands of her time use against her family obligations appears, in the magazines, to be a problem that a woman must solve for herself. It is her responsibility to manage such matters without fuss or conflict. If magazines are beginning to dissociate care from cookery, some change in the organization of domestic food provisioning might be anticipated. Understanding of the practical impact of the trade-off between care and convenience can also be illuminated by examining household divisions of labour.

Whether the division of labour within the household has altered in recent decades is a matter of controversy. Some studies undertaken in the 1980s argued that appreciable change has taken place. Tendencies identified include: a spread of egalitarian ideology; equalization of the *total* work done by each partner in couple households; greater resistance among women to traditional allocations of tasks; more diversity in the ways that different households organize their work; and that households are strategically purchasing services to substitute for their own labour (for detail of these arguments, see Warde & Hetherington, 1993: 26–9). Empirical evidence to adjudicate these claims is still insufficient.

When the project team conducted a survey in Greater Manchester, in the autumn of 1990, 323 households were interviewed to investigate divisions of labour within the household (Warde et al., 1991). Questions were asked about many aspects of domestic work, including about a range of food-related tasks, with particular attention being paid to the social influences on patterns of food provision. I first recount some general findings about the domestic divisions of labour and then address specifically food-related matters.

Household organization: patterns and trends

The study was organized as a partial replication of Pahl's (1984) investigation of household arrangements on the Isle of Sheppey. A number of the general issues with which he was concerned are essential background to the understanding of changing food practices. Pahl was particularly interested in how households obtained services, whether from the market, from informal local arrangements or by household members doing the work themselves. Change in the balance between these different channels, or *modes*, of consumption has implications for the analysis of commodification. Pahl also explored the gender division of labour in the household, the distribution of tasks between partners. Both topics are germane to issues of convenience and care.

Self-servicing The Greater Manchester sample indicated that households do a great deal of work in the domestic sector. Despite the existence of informal paid work and some neighbourly cooperation, most people obtain the labour to reproduce their households either from the purchase of marketed services or by using their own labour. Where domestic labour is used, women do a disproportionate share of tasks.

Life-cycle stage and the involvement of women in paid employment were generally critical determinants of which households obtained what sources of labour. One major issue of interpretation revolves around whether we believe that households, when they can afford to, will purchase services rather than do the work themselves. Advocates of the self-service economy (e.g. Gershuny, 1978; Gorz, 1985; Pahl, 1984) imply that the pleasure or satisfaction obtained from self-servicing are rewards in themselves: people prefer to do things themselves. The alternative view is that there is a certain set of services that most households want, or are constrained to want, and that they make some, probably unarticulated, decisions about how to deploy their available resources to obtain all or most of those services. They might prefer to purchase all services, from washing-up to cooking, but they have to prioritize shifts of tasks from one sector to another. In this view, households gradually withdraw their own labour as the financial possibility arises.

Given the social characteristics of the respondents in the sample, Pahl's argument would imply considerably higher levels of domestic provisioning in Greater Manchester than in Sheppey, for affluent householders between the ages of 30 and 60 are precisely the ones who should be exceptionally busy in the domestic economy. In fact they were not, being much more inclined to purchase services. There was not the cumulation of self-servicing in 'work-rich' households that Pahl anticipated.[5] This renders Silver's (1987) argument, that the exigencies of employment for women are in the long run likely to increase demand for formally provided services, more plausible.

However, the actual connections between a woman's employment status and the domestic provisioning of the household is fairly complicated. In households where women worked the longest hours there was a tendency for fewer of the tasks investigated ever to be undertaken. Presumably they had insufficient time not only to do things at home but even to organize the purchasing of services. It was households containing a woman in part-time employment that tended to obtain the most services overall. Far more often than on Sheppey the employment status of women, or the combination of employment statuses of all household members, best discriminated statistically between households.

Social class position was quite powerfully associated with use of marketed services and use of different modes of consumption. There was evidence that our relatively affluent households (those with higher incomes, or higher occupational social class) were likely to withdraw from domestic provisioning and pay for services in the formal sector. Of course, they still did many tasks within the household (for further detail see Warde et al., 1991; Warde & Hetherington, 1993).

Changing domestic divisions of labour   Patterns of domestic divisions of labour within couple households were much as previous studies have demonstrated. There is a strongly gendered division of tasks, with women doing routine household and childcare jobs far more often than their male partners. Women do more work than men within the household. The actual amount done by partners in households is a function of household size and of the socio-economic status of the wife. In large households, where there is more to do, women do a bigger share. This supports the argument that men's contribution tends to be inelastic: they do the same amount regardless of circumstances. Where a wife is in full-time employment, or has an occupation of higher social class, she will do a rather smaller share. This may partly be the result of having greater authority due to a better position in the labour market, but also seems to entail that fewer tasks are done in the household overall, again corroborating the observation that men's domestic labour contribution is inflexible.

Questions about which tasks the respondent enjoyed and which he or she preferred to do him/herself, confirmed the persistence of a very strong sense of what are men's, what women's tasks, even though they are sometimes done by persons of the 'wrong' sex. The data demonstrated a continuing and pervasive conventional division of labour between men and women in couple households. The division of tasks has not remained entirely rigid: a minority of men and women had, on the last occasion, done tasks that were

Table 7.2   *Perceptions of fairness in distribution of some routine domestic tasks (percentages), 1990*

	More than share	Fair share	Less than share	%	n
Husband respondent	8	59	33	100	114
Wife respondent	65	33	3	101	160
All respondents	41	43	15	99	274

N = 274

stereotyped as more befitting their partners. However, these exceptions seemed to be essentially haphazard and probably the result of circumstantial pressures. A constructed index of unconventional behaviour indicated that scarcely any households practised a sustained role reversal of domestic tasks.[6] When compared with earlier accounts, and though some generational differences were detected, the sample showed the persistence of rigidity in the gender divisions in housework.

The analysis of both domestic divisions of labour and lifestyles suggests that the rate of change in household arrangements is slow. In the absence of comparable data for earlier years, a systematic analysis of change since the 1960s is impossible. However, inference is possible largely because the patterns exhibited by household arrangements were so apparently 'traditional' that there seemed to be little room for change to have occurred. There was little evidence in this sample of role reversals in households, or of decline in gender stereotyping of the responsibility for tasks. It might be concluded that some sociological and marketing scenarios of rapid and fundamental social change during the 1980s are overstated. Nevertheless there was some sign of change in popular ideas and values concerning domestic divisions.

Respondents were asked, with respect to five routine tasks (washing dishes, tidying up, hoovering, cleaning outside windows and cleaning toilets) whether they felt they did a fair share, more than a fair share, or less that a fair share. There were clear differences between men and women in terms of their impressions of fair distributions (see Table 7.2). Most men thought they did a fair share (59 per cent). Their partners were likely to disagree: a third of women thought that their own share was fair. However, almost a third of men thought that they did too little, which is some indication of a degree of guilt among men about their insufficient contribution to housework. But there is clearly a considerable degree of dissensus about what is fair. That 65 per cent of wives thought that they did more than their fair share (while only 33 per cent of husbands thought their own contribution too little) shows lack of agreement.

Men as well as women appear to pay lip service to the ideals of equality but their behaviour has not changed correspondingly. People think they should share; the inequities of conventional marital arrangements for domestic work are now widely recognized. But there is a difference between ideals and practice; a hard-pressed housewife might get little comfort from the fact that her husband now feels guilty about his limited contribution. Nevertheless it confirms that the stereotypical response of an earlier generation of men, that housework is and should be the total responsibility of wives, is now very much a minority opinion. Sense of fairness was directly and quite powerfully related to the actual distribution of tasks between husbands and wives. Thus the idea that caring should be shared between partners is one that seemed to be widely current in 1990.

Food in the domestic division of labour

Detailed studies of how households go about organizing food preparation and using food products have been rare. Sociological inquiries in the 1950s and 1960s looking for changes in the division of labour between spouses when they touched on food provision usually inquired only about who did the washing up: there was little chance that a husband would be involved in the other activities (e.g. Young & Willmott, 1973). It has been popularly assumed that in the period since then divisions of labour in the kitchen have become less rigid.

Tasks   Table 7.3 indicates who was recorded last having done some specific tasks, including some non-food-related ones for comparative purposes. It distinguishes between male partners, female partners, other sources of labour and jobs that were said to be shared. 'Other' sources of labour include work done in the formal and informal sectors as well as work done by household members other than the adult partners. As regards jobs said to be shared, it is not possible to determine who they were shared between, so it is not necessarily the case that they were shared between husbands and wives. Most surveys have inquired who 'usually' does particular tasks. However, having previously shown that this underestimated women's actual contribution (Warde et al., 1989), we preferred to ask who did the task last, which means that the answer 'shared' occurs relatively less frequently than in most accounts. In Table 7.3 responses were analysed only for the 278 couple households in our sample, as the debate about changing gender divisions makes sense mostly with respect to people married or living as married.

The distribution of tasks between men and women runs along very predictable gendered lines, with women undertaking routine household tasks and men involved most in house and car maintenance. Food preparation tasks were predominantly done by women. A woman was seven times more likely to have cooked the last main meal, twelve times more likely to have baked a cake. The only such task that men had done more frequently than their partners was cooking a barbecue, corroborating the observed tendency for men to be more willing to do special (and in this case relatively unskilled) cooking. The tendency for women to be

Table 7.3 *Person last doing particular task in households containing a couple (percentages), 1990*

	Man	Woman	Other	Shared	n
1. Food-related tasks					
Cake baking	5	61	31	4	243
Jam making	6	63	28	3	68
Cooking meals	11	79	5	5	271
Bread making	9	57	27	7	89
Preparing packed lunches	13	64	20	3	234
Main shopping	14	54	2	30	272
Doing the dishes	23	46	20	10	274
Take-away meals	42	21	26	10	242
Beer or wine making	64	12	11	14	94
Cooked barbecue	59	9	22	11	153
2. Other selected tasks*					
Washing clothes	3	87	4	7	277
Ironing clothes	5	68	13	14	276
Nursing sick children	6	80	5	9	132
Tidying up	8	72	12	8	277
Hoovering	12	65	17	6	277
Washing car	60	13	22	5	263
Plastering	62	3	34	1	251

N = 278

* We inquired about 45 tasks in all. This table includes all the food-related questions.

responsible for routine food preparation was also evident, as they were five times more likely to prepare a packed lunch. Men had more often fetched take-away meals and made alcoholic drinks. Men did the washing up on only half as many occasions as their partners. The only task to be shared fairly frequently was the main food shopping (30 per cent of households), but it was more often done by a woman alone (54 per cent of occasions). A man prepared the meal in 11 per cent of households and shared in its preparation in up to 5 per cent of others. This is more extensive involvement than was recorded by Charles and Kerr, due probably to the different composition of the two samples. The Greater Manchester households contained both a larger proportion of professional and managerial men, whom Charles and Kerr had found to participate more often, and more women in paid employment.[7]

A second feature of Table 7.3 is that it shows how many households ever do particular tasks. Thus, the final column shows that only 68 households (21 per cent) ever made jam at home, while almost all households prepared packed lunches. It is also noticeable that the tasks that were most likely to be done by men, making alcohol and cooking barbecues, were uncommon.

Our evidence suggests that life-course stage is highly significant in determining patterns of behaviour. The vast majority of the women (81 per cent) were in paid employment. Having a woman in full-time employment was by far the most important factor inducing men to have last cooked the family meal. Among couple households it was almost exclusively in those where a woman was in full-time employment that male partners prepared meals on their own. In 25 per cent of cases where the woman partner was in full-time employment a man had last made the family meal; the figure was only 5 per cent where the principal female household member was employed part-time or not in paid employment. That women's full-time employment affects men's participation is consistent with the hypothesis of England and Farkas regarding the gendered division of household labour.

> Men's participation in housework seems to be little affected by their earnings relative to their wives' or by their sex role ideologies. Rather, they increase their housework primarily in response to situational factors such as a wife who works through the dinner hour and simply cannot cook dinner. (England & Farkas, 1986: 100)

Providing meals is the prototypical occasion; for whereas some routine household tasks can be stored up until a woman finds time to do them (at the weekend, for instance), meals cannot sensibly be delayed for more than an hour or two.

There was a weaker statistical relationship between the class positions of the partners and the frequency with which men cooked. Men in white-collar employment, particularly in routine white-collar rather than professional and managerial jobs, were more likely to cook than their manual worker equivalents. More significant was the occupational class of the woman. Where a woman was a member of the salariat or self-employed her partner was more likely than other men to cook. If men's and women's class positions are considered together, there is a yet stronger statistical relationship. A fivefold variable for household class (a contracted form of Goldthorpe's, 1987 categories) was computed, distinguishing five situations: both partners were members of the salariat; both were intermediate; both were working class; the woman was in a higher class than her partner; and the man was in a higher class than his partner. Table 7.4 shows that household class discriminated rather well, with women in 'pure' manual households doing the most cooking, while those in 'pure' intermediate class did the least.

Cooking: pleasure of chore?

Cooking can be considered as drudgery or as intrinsically enjoyable and pleasing. Cookery programmes on television seem to have increased in number and popularity: around three hours per week on air time on the four main British channels are devoted to cookery. Cookery books constitute one of the largest sections of the publishing market: indeed, 25 per cent of the sample, when asked to select three favourite genres of book, chose cookery books.

Cooking is necessary work in the domestic economy but, in certain circumstances, can also be a source of enjoyment. The evidence presented

Table 7.4 *Whether male or female partner last cooked a family meal by household class (percentage by row), 1990*

Household class*	Who last cooked		n
	man	woman	
Both intermediate	24	76	21
Both salariat	17	83	69
Woman higher class	14	86	50
Man higher class	9	91	58
Both manual	-	100	19
N = 217			

* Missing data reduced the size of the effective sample to 217 households.

by Charles and Kerr was ambivalent. They showed that some women would have liked their husbands to be more involved, but that by and large women did not detest cooking. The emphasis put on their evidence was to say that 'the greatest pleasure in cooking lay in the relish with which it was consumed by others' (Charles & Kerr, 1988: 230). Among our sample, when asked whether they enjoyed doing particular domestic tasks, cooking was pronounced the most widely preferred after shopping for clothes (see Table 7.5). Cooking for special occasions and baking were enjoyed 'usually' or 'always' by over half the respondents who ever did them, and regular cooking and shopping for food were almost as popular. Other routine domestic tasks, including washing up, were much less frequently described as enjoyable. Other of our data showed that women were more likely than men to claim to enjoy all the tasks listed in Table 7.5, except for beer making, painting and washing cars, indicating a continuing, strong gender stereotyping of domestic tasks.

Compared to tasks that can be done with little experience and require mostly toil for their accomplishment, cooking is creative, involves knowledge and practical skill and can, moreover, be constructed as a form of gift-giving. This might seem to explain why it is preferred, but not *per se* why it might be enjoyed. Our evidence may reflect a rise in the status of the activity of meal preparation, perhaps associated with an increased interest in culinary matters in Britain. Such a shift in status may be confirmed by recalling the higher proportion of occasions on which men in households prepared family meals, for since it has been remarked that occupations are usually held in higher esteem if men do them, perhaps a similar situation holds for domestic tasks. On the other hand, the rising status of cooking does not appear to encourage people to invest much of their effort in self-provisioning tasks like baking. Only 3 per cent of households regularly made jam or baked bread. Those households that did make jam sometimes were also more likely to bake their own bread and to brew wines and beer. These data, and those in Table 7.3, give no support to the self-service

Table 7.5   *Respondents' enjoyment of household tasks (percentages)*, 1990*

	Always	Usually	Sometimes	Never	Not applicable	n
Regular cooking	15	29	31	18	7	321
Special cooking	35	18	19	19	8	321
Baking	22	20	21	22	15	319
Food shopping	15	21	31	29	4	322
Wine/beer making	6	5	8	26	55	320
Washing dishes	6	17	32	41	5	321
Tidying up	11	20	33	34	3	322
Hoovering	10	19	35	32	5	321
Clothes shopping	39	21	29	9	2	320
Washing clothes	11	16	20	42	11	320
Ironing	4	10	21	53	11	322
Washing car	8	11	27	28	27	322
Nursing children	20	11	11	15	44	320

N = 323

* 'I now want to ask about your feelings/attitudes to tasks that you do and whether you would rather someone else did them. . . . Which of the following activities do you *enjoy* doing?'

economy thesis, which maintains that households choose to produce for home consumption because of the pleasure or satisfaction that arises from self-provisioning.

Interestingly, baking was thought to be a rather pleasant task, wine and beer making was not, yet each was done with the same frequency. Possibly home-made bread and cake is considered a treat and preferable in taste to its shop-bought equivalents, whereas home brew is deemed an inferior substitute for manufactured products and resorted to only when faced by a shortage of spare funds or inability to get out of the house. Equally likely, however, the difference arises from a common-sense, gender-based, symbolic association connecting women with domestic products and the expression of care for the family while linking men with public space, manufactured items and efficiency. One reason why the antinomy of convenience and care is difficult to resolve is that its two elements represent idealizations of feminine and masculine virtues.

Commercial sources of food   It is now often popularly remarked that the family meal is in decline as 'snacking' and eating out become more frequent. Both these growing trends have important implications for understanding household organization. The first will affect amounts of domestic labour and probably who in the household works on food preparation, for the normal (but uncorroborated) understanding of 'snacking' is that the person who eats the food also prepares or collects it. The spread of eating out is also important because it almost inevitably reduces domestic labour and shifts work from the household to the formal, market sector of the economy. More meals eaten out is also diametrically opposed to the trends identified in the self-service economy thesis, for eating out involves buying a service rather than using family labour. It might nevertheless be the case, such are the ironies of calculations about domestic labour, that the time taken to produce clean and ironed clothes suitable for a public expedition and then to drive to a restaurant entails more self-servicing than would eating at home!

The growth of fast-food outlets, microwave ovens, TV dinners, etc. makes it relatively easy for anyone, regardless of culinary skill, to get a meal, or a substitute for a meal, at irregular times. This has led to speculation in debates on the sociology of food about the increasing prevalence of the habit of 'snacking' or 'grazing'. This has been said to reduce the importance of household meals in several ways. First it makes them less significant in collective time discipline: whereas for many households daily routines used to be organized around meal times, snacking allows greater flexibility. Some authors bemoan the demise of the family meal as it becomes more easily possible for individuals to prepare and eat their food alone at a time, or in the place, of their choice (e.g. Fischler, 1980). This may be seen to have effects either on the quality of food consumed or on the social relationships of the household. Some evidence of such a trend may be gleaned from the answers to the question about how often a family meal is cooked: 85 per cent of our households recorded a daily family meal, 13 per cent had several a week and 2 per cent had less frequent joint meals. Considering that all households contained teenage members this is remarkably high.

Nevertheless, a great many eating events occur outside households. Restaurants, pubs, cafés and take-away food outlets absorb a significant proportion of household expenditure on food. In 1991, 3.6 per cent of total household expenditure was on meals out (see Table 7.6). Within our sample there was considerable variation in the frequency with which households reported using commercial food outlets. The frequency and location of meals out is recorded in Table 7.7, which indicates that almost everyone eats out sometimes, though the number who do so very regularly is quite small. Compared, for instance, to the USA, visits to restaurants and fast-food outlets are still sporadic.

If we consider together all the indications in our questionnaire of sources of food either prepared or eaten outside the household, it is considerable. Thus packed lunches are prepared at least several times a week in 65 per cent of households and take-away meals are bought at least weekly by 34 per cent. Sandwiches or take aways are purchased at least several times a week by 21 per cent of our individual respondents; restaurants, pub meals and cafés are used at least weekly by 12, 9 and 12 per cent respectively. As household spending on food purchased and consumed away from home increases, the overall pattern of domestic organization will alter. It does not of course follow that gender divisions will thereby be reduced.

Food in household perspective   In many respects our findings corroborate those of Charles and Kerr (1988), the most authoritative existing study of

Table 7.6   *UK households' expenditure per week: in total, on food, and on eating out, £s and as percentages of expenditure, 1959–91*

	1959–61	1965	1970	1975	1980	1985	1991
All expenditure (£)	16.40	21.25	28.57	54.58	102.55	161.87	259.04
Food expenditure (£)	5.04	5.93	7.35	13.52	23.52	32.70	46.13
as % of total	31.0	27.9	25.7	24.8	22.9	20.2	17.8
Eating out (£)	0.50	0.66	1.00	1.85	3.95	5.71	9.39
as % of food	9.8	11.1	13.6	13.7	16.8	17.5	20.4
as % of total	3.0	3.1	3.5	3.4	3.9	3.5	3.6

Source: Family Expenditure Survey (various years)

Table 7.7   *Frequency of meals taken by respondents from different kinds of catering establishment (percentages)*

	Several per week	Weekly	Monthly	Less often	Never	Total %
Restaurant	3	9	30	53	5	100
Pub meal	1	8	26	49	16	100
Café	2	10	17	48	23	100
Sandwich/take aways	21	26	17	27	8	99

family food preparation in the UK. Domestic divisions of labour result in women doing a vast proportion of food preparation work; in northern England households are predominantly conservative in their collective tastes; and styles and patterns differ to some degree by class. However, food organization in our sample was rather less burdensome to women than in Charles and Kerr's inquiry, primarily because their respondents were mothers with a child under school age of whom scarcely any were in full-time paid employment. In such households women almost certainly do a larger proportion of all housework tasks than at other stages of the life-course (see also Oakley, 1974). In our households, which were at a later stage of the life course, men did more cooking, though primarily if their partners were in full-time employment. Also, in our survey, class differences were not very pronounced, though we discovered quite important differences in domestic divisions of labour and in food tastes.

7.5   Intensification, commodification and domestic life

Among the most significant and sustained of social trends in the last century has been the decline of the full-time housewife. In Britain at the 1911 Census, only one married woman in ten was recorded as being in employment; by 1991 more than half were. Much of the increase occurred in the period since 1961, with significant increases in both full-time and part-time employment for wives. The difficulties posed for women combining career and motherhood, the marital conflicts arising, and the persistence of women's responsibility for domestic matters have been extensively documented in terms of their being forced to juggle 'two roles' and manage 'the second shift'. In terms of time involved in paid and unpaid work, women have experienced an increased load. The debate about domestic divisions of labour currently revolves around whether relevant social institutions – the household and the family – are adapting in response to these new circumstances. At best such adaptation is slow and the willingness of men to accept a substantially greater share of domestic work and responsibility is minimal. Had our survey been administered fifty years ago, the evidence regarding the gender stereotyping of household tasks would probably have been very similar. In the absence of concessions and compromises by men, the consequence has been the need for women to seek their own personal solutions to the intensified time pressure to which they have been subject.

Evidence of this intensification of time pressure in the food columns appears in several ways. The recording of time required for different stages in the preparation of a dish increases, as does advice about the storage of food. Because cooking times were generally not recorded in 1968, it is difficult to make a systematic comparison that would establish whether twenty-five years later readers were being advised to attempt meals which *actually* took less preparation time. But it seems likely. Another indication of time pressure is its recognition in the context of entertaining. The expectation that a hostess will cook freshly for her guests remains, but consideration is given to containing the effort involved, not only by preparing some items in advance but by choosing quickly prepared dishes. Thus an article in *Good Housekeeping* (Sept. 1992) announced 'New Fast Food: 30-minute entertaining', a variety of eight main course dishes that required no more than 10 minutes to prepare and 20 minutes to cook.

One possible response to increased time pressure is to substitute commercially purchased products or services for the labour that would otherwise be expended in domestic production. The general exercise of this option is the defining characteristic of modern industrial societies. Now almost all raw foodstuffs are purchased rather than grown; goods like bread, cake and beer are bought rather than made at home; more ready prepared meals are available in shops and can be stored frozen so that there is no need to do anything except warm the food through at home; and increasingly there are commercial options for eating out or for home delivery that remove the need to make any modification to the purchased item – all that is required is that it be eaten. Some degree of com- modification of food is thus taken for granted, but its appropriate extent remains contentious. As yet, the last two options are not acceptable as the primary mode of provisioning. One reason is probably the implicit appreciation of DeVault's observations about the role that food provi- sioning, and the orchestration of food events, plays in the construction and reproduction of families. Women providers in part defend that role because it gives them some personal satisfaction and domestic control, though equally it constitutes a burden and a constraint. Women are ambivalent and, no doubt with strong encouragement from men and children, resist the latest stage of commodification.

From the point of view of rational action theories perhaps most surprising is the reluctance of women to turn to the market as a source of solutions to their predicament. There is something suspicious or improper about convenience food. The image of 'the lazy housewife' makes women apologize for and be reluctant to admit its use (see Gofton, 1995). The peculiarity is that it is less reprehensible for single people, men, and perhaps the elderly, to make use of such labour-saving strategies. This indicates the still strong expectation that women who live in family households will provide personally prepared meals for their co-residents. The emotional significance of food provision within the family might suggest a site of resistance to commodification itself. People believe, for moral or practical reasons, that certain things should not be bought. The provision of household meals is a practice at the edge of this prohibited zone.

We can only speculate on the reasons why women might be uncomfortable with the prospect of further commodification of food provision. Sometimes it will be because it simplifies the task of food provision and threatens to de-skill them, a situation that most artisanal workers resist: almost anyone can heat a frozen meal in a microwave oven. There is probably a sense of nostalgia for things that were provided for them, and which earlier conveyed precisely those emotional comforts represented by home-made cakes or bread. Probably regrets are only in regard to changes that occurred during the last generation: most would be averse to having to buy corn and take it to the miller!

One way the sharp edge of this antinomy could be blunted is by recognizing the way in which mass-production commodities can be customized, that is appropriated for personal and private purposes (see Miller, 1987). Defenders of consumer culture have often argued this with respect to clothing, motor scooters and hot rods, for example (see Hebdige, 1988; Moorhouse, 1983). Groups of people buy a common commercial product then work on it, adapt it, convert it into something that is symbolically representative of personal or collective identity. That it was once a mass-produced commodity becomes irrelevant after its incorporation into a person's household, hobby or life. In one sense all cookery is of this nature; labour is added, and by transforming groceries into meals social and symbolic value is created. That is the currently legitimate labour of love. The Stork advertisement tried to suggest that heavily processed, pre-prepared, manufactured products could effectively act as substitute for that domestic transformation process. Though a rational solution to the bitter antinomy between convenience and care, a solution which recognizes that shopping for such items requires skill, putting them in the oven requires time, and serving them on household crockery entails customizing products for family use, it was probably unpersuasive. Women surely do get some credit for keeping the fridge full of instantly edible items (e.g. see DeVault, 1991: esp. 63–6) and for producing baked beans on toast. Yet such ways to minimize labour still meet with remarkable resistance. So, while the ability to purchase goods or services is restricted by income, there are also powerful normative obstacles to seeking commercial solutions to the problems of domestic provisioning.

The magazines are understandably very cagey about the issue. After all, they themselves are commodities; and their principal sources of revenue are the advertisers of commodities. They could hardly be overtly hostile to the commodity *per se*. Indeed, it is surprising how ambivalent they are with respect to manufactured convenience food. They seem to have reduced their emphasis on the value of home-made food, concomitant with a decline in presentation of a certain kind of familialism. Nevertheless they are unable to commend outright the virtues of quick and convenient food. They implicitly and intuitively grasp a point which DeVault fails to appreciate, that care *for* and care *about* are inextricably linked in sustained personal relationships like those within families. It is emotionally difficult privately to care effectively for someone without caring about them (compare the situation in commercial operations, e.g. Hochschild, 1983).

The magazines apply less pressure than before in favour of the familial rationale for provision; that pressure is applicable or relevant to fewer of their readers as household forms change. Home-made food is not applauded explicitly; presumably since this would make many readers uneasy because they lack the time, and perhaps the inclination in the light of other more interesting activities, to spend long hours preparing family meals. But there is still a dogged underlying conviction that this is to be in some way negligent in the proper conduct of familial relationships. Hence, recipe columns refuse to use the term 'convenient' lest it offend by implying insufficient care.

Magazines seek to give guidance about customizing food, not just to make it edible but to render it socially appropriate. The latter involves adding labour, in different degrees, depending upon the occasion. The operative rule remains that the more formal or significant the occasion, the more labour should be added. The suggestion to buy ready-made Sunday lunch or food for a dinner party is rare, and in the latter case instruction will be given about how to disguise the fact.

7.6 Summary

Overall, in the magazine sample, recipes making some reference to aspects of convenience increased sharply, from 28 to 67 per cent, though the principal reason for this was the new tendency to record preparation and cooking times. Direct reference to the value of home-made food declined significantly. This reflects an awareness that the organizational problems faced by the harried wife and mother have become more pressing. In this instance the balance between competing demands has resulted in an intelligible trade-off between convenience and care. Over time, as one element becomes more prominent, the other recedes. Both cannot currently be maximized simultaneously, though for cultural rather than practical reasons.

Of all antinomies, this is probably the most complicated for the magazines to handle, given their female audience. Tensions surrounding the definition of ideals of womanhood, between wife-mother and autonomous person, make this a touchy subject. On the one hand the devotion of time to food preparation symbolizes caring for others in the household partly in proportion to the amount of value added by personal labour. On the other hand, time is restricted and the reward for, say, baking croissants, is uncertain and limited.

The history of consumption might be written as a process whereby activities shift between spheres – from the household to the market, and sometimes back again, from the market to the state, and sometimes back again. In such transformations and substitutions the texture of everyday social relationships is affected. Diligence in the arduous tasks of food provisioning, as a demonstration of caring for the recipients, has been, as DeVault argued, a principal prop for family relationships. As households become less and less organized in accordance with the logic of the male breadwinner wage, the preconditions for the maintenance of this means of symbolizing familial commitment are gradually being removed. The magazines are beginning to register this, if slowly and implicitly: they shrink from advocating the further commodification of domestic food provision as, one suspects, would many of their readers. There is some popular resistance to the commercialization of domestic activity; there is virtue in expressing care for people, though it would be more worthwhile if it were better appreciated; there is hesitancy about paying for domestic assistance; there is some intrinsic satisfaction to be gained from household activities like cooking. But at present, to judge from the evidence about who does what in households, these are considerations that occur mostly to women, since the domestic division of labour has changed relatively little in recent decades.

PART III
Interpretations of Taste

In the final part of the book I review and interpret the accumulated evidence about change in British food habits and consider its implications for different theories of consumption. The antinomies in discourse and the differences in practice in the field of food are associated with some of the structural anxieties of contemporary societies. Following consideration of the specificity of the case of food, I argue that consumption is now best generally characterized as an exhibition of undistinguished difference, a condition brought about by an obsession on the part of consumers with variety which matches the capacity of industry to provide mildly differentiated products in considerable volume.

Many aspects of British food practice in the late 1960s had changed by the end of the 1980s, but there were strong continuities also, more perhaps than might have been expected. In Chapter 8 I summarize the evidence and offer an overall assessment of changing British food habits. Section 8.1 summarizes key themes in the representation of what it is good to eat, consolidating the interpretations offered in Part II. Section 8.2 briefly discusses changes in actual food habits since the Second World War. I maintain that most of the trends in the popularity of particular foodstuffs began before the mid-1960s and that shifts in food consumption do not corroborate arguments for a social transition in the 1970s. In section 8.3 I review the evidence about socio-demographic variation in expenditure on food which suggests very little movement since the 1960s. On this basis I contest Mennell's thesis about diminished contrasts and question accounts of the decline of social embeddedness and class differentiation. In section 8.4 I reflect on the nature of the antinomies which I claim are central to contemporary understandings of food.

Chapter 9 begins by reflecting on the specific features of the field of food, which may render generalization to other areas of consumption hazardous. It then examines the way that the evidence about food reflects the general social processes of individualization, informalization, stylization and communification. The implications of the empirical material for theoretical arguments about contemporary consumption trends are drawn out in the third section. Section 9.4 argues that the increase in the variety of the products of the food industries encourages a form of consumption which corresponds to the logic of neo-Fordist production. The final section reflects on some general implications of the case study of food for the development of a sociological theory of consumption.

8

The Reconstruction of Taste

8.1 Thematic trends in representation

Trends in recommendation

The study of the magazines has included an examination of both a systematic sample of recipes and a general overview of the themes isolated in food columns. Change in the relative importance of particular principles of recommendation in those recipes is schematically outlined in Figure 8.1.

The principles invoked when columnists introduced their recipes altered in relative importance between the 1960s and the 1990s. Perhaps surprisingly the appeal of novelty, while still very significant, reduced over time, as did reference to extravagance and caring. The attractions of economy remained more or less constant, those of tradition and indulgence augmented a little, while those of convenience and health increased considerably. While some of the shifts are minor and all claims are subject to methodological reservations about content analysis, the changed position of particularly health and convenience in the hierarchy of values seems confirmed by other aspects of the food columns. They are, probably not coincidentally, also two themes that grew markedly in prominence in food advertisements.

Calculation and rationalization

One of the key features of food recommendations in the 1991–2 sample was its much stronger emphasis on calculation. Recipes have become steadily more precise over the last 200 years. Information is now given fairly routinely not only about precise quantities of ingredients and cooking times, but also about preparation time, nutrient contents, sometimes shopping instructions too. In other contexts, this would be acknowledged as a process of rationalization, of the pursuit of greater precision, control and predictability. Science, measurement, the use of information derived from experiment, rather than trial-and-error and *ad hoc* judgment, appear more frequently now in the food columns. Food is, to some degree, being drawn into expert discourses (of medicine, lifestyle, fashion and gastronomy) that present cookery as a matter of technical rationality rather than of practical judgment. This may, to some extent, devalue the skills of domestic cooks by suggesting that simply to follow recipes is sufficient to achieve delicious meals; certainly it implies that cookery is less an art than a science.

novelty	–	tradition	+
health	++	indulgence	+
ecomony	=	extravagance	–
convenience	++	care	–

Figure 8.1   *Changes in frequency of appeals to principles of recommendation in recipes, 1968–92*

In the context of wider cultural trends, the concern with precision and exactitude is in part a technocratic obsession with control which is often understood as a key aspect of the project of modernity. To be able to achieve the same standardized and uniform effect or outcome, repeatedly, is an essential feature of Fordist mass production that has been transposed into other fields of social existence. Calculability is also bound up with the medicalization of eating and the emergence of regimes of self-maintenance that treat bodies as machines. Increasingly too, food has reappeared in the health columns, where it was often to be found before the Second World War, signifying a further link between planned nutrition and physical well-being. It has become an integral dimension of the recipe columns themselves, with increased counting of fats, fibre and calories. In addition, in the period since the 1960s, estimations of quantities of time needed for various stages in food preparation have become more common. This occurs largely in response to intensification of pressures of time on women, requiring them to plan their routine activities more precisely.

Saving time, saving money, and preserving an effectively functioning body all presuppose a capacity to calculate costs in order to optimize personal performance. All are elements of the continuation of the more general social process of rationalization which has affected so many areas of life in the modern period. These tendencies have intensified in representations of food since the 1960s.

Discipline

Many commentators have seen the period since the 1960s as one where duty and responsibility have become less important guides to action, and where narcissism and hedonism have become predominant. For instance, in Daniel Bell's (1976) formulation, the cultural contradictions of capitalism were identified in terms of the erosion of the work ethic and its replacement by an individualistic hedonism. There may be some truth to this, but the themes in the magazines do not straightforwardly corroborate his view. The more hedonistic themes of indulgence and extravagance are not the ones most emphasized. Rather the opposite: health and its associated discipline has increased most powerfully as a recommended value, while economy has remained a virtue. Furthermore, a hedonistic society would not induce anxiety and guilt over indulgence or extravagance in the area of food consumption. Yet manifestly the taking of too much food is one of the great fears of the epoch, though among the reasons for this is a narcissistic concern with physical attractiveness. Despite their awareness, many of those afraid nevertheless fail to take the proper precautions. There is a strong presumption in the magazines that self-discipline remains a virtue. A tendency towards more disciplined consumption accompanies rationalization as a key process in contemporary food mores.

Variety and personal choice

Despite the growing stress on calculation and disciplined behaviour, the value of freedom of choice is paramount. Food columns in the magazines, in offering an answer to the implicit question 'what shall we eat?', conspicuously wrap their advice in the ideology of individual choice. Readers are never directed to do things; there is no ultimate prescription; no direct instruction is given regarding the overall effect required. Expert advice maintains a distance until the reader has chosen among recipes. Whereas Mennell (1985: 245) commented that the British magazines in the inter-war period had some tendency to pronounce what comprised good or correct taste, this was not apparent in 1968 or 1992. Good taste was not prescribed. Rather, in Weber's terms, the choice of ultimate ends has become a personal matter, though once chosen very precise, technical means are prescribed to ensure achievement of the optimum outcome.

Expert discourses of this sort, throughout the magazines, currently offer a set of *restricted* choices, whereby a variety of options, which are more or less equivalent, are presented, leaving the reader to decide what is ultimately and personally preferable. This tendency to honour a principle of restricted choice is perhaps most apparent in the articles about slimming, where it is now normal to offer people a list of equivalent foods to choose from, rather than prescribing a single week's eating, and where allowance is made for, usually, one special treat per day – hence the diet for chocoholics that includes a daily dose of the favourite indulgence. The respect shown for choice indicates limited assurance in the magazine columns regarding legitimate, or good, taste.

While in neither year was there a firm statement of good or proper taste, the tone and nature of advice proferred changed perceptibly. In the 1960s food columnists were not prescriptive about what people should eat, but they seemed confident in the value of their proposals, adopting the tone of a teacher and an approach reminiscent of a comprehensive encyclopaedia of household cookery. For instance, in December 1967 *Woman's Realm* issued a 'Cooks' Calender for 1968' which suggested a two-course main meal for every single day of the new year. The columnists seemed to anticipate an audience competent, though not especially interested in ordinary British cooking. The challenge was to awaken curiosity in different cuisines without becoming outlandish. But the discourse of personal choice was absent. By the 1990s the style of address was more that of a salesperson in an emporium where neither vendor nor purchaser had any reason to be deeply committed to one item rather than another. Readers could be expected to recognize a huge number of ingredients and dishes as the range expanded. But there is no compelling reason to expect the reader to follow the columnists' advice. As opinions proliferate, selection becomes more arbitrary. Columnists cede authority as they affirm the readers' right, and desire, to choose for themselves. Such lack of assurance is also demonstrated by the wider range of alternative recipes for celebratory occasions and the sheer range of culinary traditions that are now represented.

The appearance of choice itself depends upon there being a variety of items from which to choose. The magazines, as do advertisers, make a point of emphasizing variety as a fundamental virtue in consumer culture. The most striking aspect of variety is the promotion of recipes from different cuisines across the world, to the point where the exotic itself has become routine. The dishes in a single magazine may derive from several continents and the ingredients required are so diverse that it is hard to imagine them being accessible to any but the most enthusiastic and energetic domestic cook. For instance, a single issue of the most popular monthly, *Prima* (Nov. 1991), contained 39 recipes which used 176 different ingredients. Savoury dishes ranged from a chicken curry requiring 23 separate ingredients, through paprika pork needing 14 to pepper beef stir-fry using 11. Sticky gingerbread employed 19 ingredients, Greek baklava 7 completely different ones. The 27 dried herbs and spices included garam masala, Chinese five-spice powder, chilli powder, cayenne pepper and garlic salt; bottled sauces included hoysin, soy, Worcestershire and gravy browning; almonds were required in five different states; three types of margarine, seven types of sugar and seven different fresh herbs were mentioned. Incidentally, an equivalent magazine in 1967, *Family Circle* (Nov.), contained 31 recipes but only 87 ingredients, many of which were fruit, nuts and sweet spices needed for baking cakes. Only three savoury herbs were called for, none fresh.

Presumably the significance of such variety differs between readers. It might be deduced that a week's food often is, or even should be, drawn from a wide mix of culinary traditions and that readers are expected to have the skills, resources and store cupboards to support such behaviour. Alternatively it could be interpreted as evidence that the magazines are manuals for information about style and fashion in foods, so that the reader will know something about culinary variety without ever needing to engage in the preparation of alien dishes. Again, readers might simply select and cook an occasional dish which is consistent with their existing repertoire, thereby introducing a minor variation to their normal pattern of meals. Or perhaps they might choose something quite foreign and treat cooking a new dish as an experiment. Or maybe they simply read the columns in a state of abstraction, to look at the pictures and daydream about meals that someone else might some day cook for them. But whichever it is, the fact of variety, an obsession with variation, lies at the core of the magazines' presentation of food in the 1990s.

Oddly, the variation is not presented or recommended in terms of novelty. Rather it is taken for granted, assumed that readers can appreciate, absorb and accept a heterogeneous range of foodstuffs. An amazing range of foreign food has become normalized. Such routinization is part of the flattening of experience in a globalized world. There is no suggestion that one culinary tradition is better than any other. There are no hints that choice of food might be symbolic of a social hierarchy, nor that some types of people might prefer or concentrate on one tradition rather than another. There are no clues about the means by which particular items might convey a particular sense of style or identity. Variety, and associated casualization of social events and relationships, is a key aspect of a normalization of aesthetic indifference. Adorno's (e.g. 1991: 85–92) description of mass culture as characterized by 'interchangeable sameness' which becomes an impediment to autonomous judgment is pertinent.

The glorification of variety is a primary vehicle of the intensification of commodity culture. Although nobody objects, variety may not always be a virtue. Most obviously, the year-round variety of products in the contemporary British diet is dependent upon a global division of labour which often works to the detriment of the health of populations in the Third World. But it might also be argued that the systematic promotion of dishes from around the world is detrimental to national and regional culinary excellence, compromising the development of a local culinary style. It may also compromise other values like economy and, ultimately, because it is a tool for the promotion of market mechanisms in general, it may undermine alternative modes of service provision.

Changing sources: magazines as shopping manuals

What have been examined through the magazines are *representations* of food; the content analysis refers to what editors publish, not to popular appreciation and evaluation of food. Change in the economic environment of magazine publishing – changes in corporate ownership and competition, the growth of alternative media and forms of entertainment, more personnel involved in producing and writing magazines, reconfiguration of audiences, and so forth – complicates the process of reading the food columns, potentially defying attempts at systematic comparison of their contents. The tendencies described might be the effect of changes in the media through which they are represented.

There were some changes in the contents of magazines and their markets between 1968 and 1992. More magazines are now published, so the circulation figures of the most popular have declined. The magazines are a little longer, which in principle provides opportunities for more varied content, but because layout is now less cramped the volume of text and illustration is not much increased. However, the amount of space devoted to food has increased overall (see Table A.3, p. 213): there are more recipes in the monthly magazines, more food articles and more food advertisements. There was considerable variation in the amount of attention paid to food by different magazines in 1968 and that has not changed.

Audiences have become slightly more specialized on the basis of age than in 1968, with for example *Cosmopolitan* having very much younger readers than *Woman and Home* (see Table A.2, p. 212). Class differentiation is the same at the two dates: the higher class readership of the monthly magazines is apparent at both dates, with the range of variation between magazines similar. In general these remain mass-circulation media, and are less differentiated by content than might be imagined.

Changes in a product, in this case magazines, tells us nothing definitive about how it is consumed. There is no single or simple answer to the question 'what role do women's magazines play for their readers?' For their audiences they are, at one and the same time, sources of practical advice, of information about commercial products, of guidance regarding style and taste, of amusement, entertainment, daydreams, fantasy and pleasure (see Winship, 1987; Ballaster et al., 1991). However, scholars have often ascribed to the magazines coherent social and ideological effects, typically the arbitration and transmission of models of femininity and familialism (e.g. Ferguson, 1982; Winship, 1987). Rather less frequently, but now more insistently, their role in supporting consumerism has been examined. McCracken (1993) makes the strongest case, arguing that we must appreciate both the extent to which the magazines themselves are commodities and that much of their content is covert advertising. She suggests that there is little difference between the explicit ads, consumer testing articles, advice columns, feature articles and even stories, for these also – sometimes explicitly, sometimes implicitly – recommend goods and services to readers.

McCracken is probably correct in postulating that the primary common feature of the magazines is their celebration of consumer culture. In other respects they seem diverse and fragmentary (compare Ballaster et al., 1991). The messages encoded in the magazines are themselves fragmentary and inconsistent, as the examination of contradictory food recommendations shows. The growing number of more specialized magazines leads one to doubt whether a single and unified model of femininity is portrayed. Nevertheless, McCracken probably overstates her case.

Magazines are more than mere shopping manuals. Indeed, McCracken reports that editors believe that too much commercial advertising is likely to repel readers, for readers' confidence in the journal would be jeopardized were there not a clear separation between the supposedly impartial advice delivered by the editorial staff and the commercial persuasion of overt advertisements. Readers, presuming greater objectivity, probably give more credibility to advice columns and feature articles.

In addition, the messages transmitted by advertisements and cookery columns are perceptibly different. Implicitly endorsing McCracken,

Mennell (1985) used ads and recipes as equivalent forms of evidence. If more or less the entire content of the magazines consists of advertising products of some sort, then this would be unobjectionable. However, there is a less than perfect match between recipe columns and adverts in the recommendations they make. Looking in extremely cursory fashion at changing messages in a sample of adverts in the autumn magazines of 1967 and 1991, reference to novelty increased from 10 to 27 per cent of cases, while it declined in the recipe columns, whereas reference to health increased much more slowly in the advertisements, from 16 to only 26 per cent. If the trends in the symbolism of advertising copy are not identical to the trends in food columns, we should be suspicious about using evidence from them interchangeably.

Finally, McCracken also fails to appreciate the internal contradictions of the magazines. In particular there is some significant resistance to commodification, apparent in the uncertainty about how women should deal with convenience foods. Recipes in the food columns almost universally in the 1990s employ generic ingredients, implying that they should be bought fresh. It is also implied that, when preparing food, excessive use of commodities is a dereliction of duty. Convenience food, in some important respects, is contrary to those ideals of womanhood associated with care. Readers are thus not *only* being encouraged to foster the consumer attitude.

Ultimately, it remains uncertain to what extent advice columns are a significant source of practical information and a means to assuage anxiety about personal decisions about style, appearance, taste, cuisine, etc. The precise impact of food columns and recipes on everyday practice is impossible to determine. McKie and Wood (1992), in a small-scale study in Edinburgh, found that magazines were a moderately important source of recipes, used less often than cookery books or friends' recommendations, but more than any other source: 62 per cent of respondents claimed sometimes to use recipes from magazines.[1] If the magazines are, in addition, 'low involvement media', then their vacillating recommendations probably will not have any profound personally unsettling effects on their readers. But, considered simply as texts, as in my account, they seem to reflect collective, structural anxiety about judgment.

8.2 Trends and official statistics

Much of the evidence reported in this book is about representations of food because available data on changes in the food tastes of consumers is sparse and inconclusive. For while there is plenty of evidence on the production of food and the quantities and prices at which it is sold, such data answers few questions relevant to a social or cultural theory of consumption. Official statistics deal mostly in descriptive, aggregate data. This is amenable to secondary analysis; some of the possibilities were demonstrated by the use of discriminant analysis in Part II. In addition, aggregate data, when looked at over time, is certainly relevant to attempts at refutation or corroboration of hypotheses about shifts in personal and group tastes. But at present it still remains difficult to identify how group consumption practices have changed in the last thirty years.

Official evidence is flawed and hard to interpret for the purposes of understanding changes in taste. For example the National Food Survey, though offering a fifty-year time series, concerns only foods purchased for domestic use, is overwhelmingly concerned with industrially defined categories of foodstuffs, concentrates on the weight and price of items purchased, and makes minimal attempts to differentiate between the behaviour of different social groups. The *Family Expenditure Survey* is slightly more useful for sociological purposes, but still limited. Although commentators often succumb to the temptation to read off consumer motivations from aggregate consumption statistics, these are not a reliable source for discovering the extent of change in social practice.

Nevertheless, given many apparent changes in practice, it would be foolish not to try to estimate and outline tendencies. Particularly relevant is the National Food Survey, first carried out in 1940, which on its fiftieth anniversary explicitly reviewed trends disclosed in its series of data. The most abrupt changes occurred in the early 1950s, when the policies of subsidy and rationing, imposed during the war, ceased: consumption of meat, white bread and butter all increased very sharply in this period. However, it observed that 'Over the last 50 years, the proportions of household food expenditure represented by the main food groups have remained remarkably stable' (NFS, 1991: 34). Looking at trends since 1955, there has been a steady increase in consumption of some product categories (cheese and fruit) and a steady decline in others (milk and cream, fish, eggs, fats, sugar and preserves, vegetables and cereals, and beverages) (NFS, 1991: 93, Table 1). The only category that oscillates over the period is meat, where quantities consumed peaked in 1980 and have fallen since.

However, as the report points out, *within* those groups there have been significant changes. Demand for poultry began its expansion in the 1960s; yoghurt and frozen vegetables increased in popularity in the 1970s; fruit juices, wholemeal bread and low-fat spreads augmented their market share in the 1980s. While some of these developments could be interpreted as a result of growing concern among consumers with healthy eating, they could equally be considered a consequence of changes in the capacity of the food industry to mass-produce new items. *Social Trends* (1989: Table 7.10), showing changes in quantity of selected foods purchased for home consumption between 1961 and 1989, broke down the general categories further. It indicated, for instance, a shift away from the staple use of standard white loaves and the substitution of other breads, and changing preferences between butter, margarine and other fats. Overall it suggested that the dietary advice of nutritionists is having some effect, for assorted items that are disapproved of (saturated fats, white bread, sugar and red meat) decline, while white meat, other fats, fruit products (actually fruit juices) are rising sharply, though, it should be appreciated, from comparatively small bases. Nonetheless, and ironically, the sources of energy of the British population shifted from carbohydrates to fats over the post-war period. Again, however, this data gives little support to the view that there was a significant change during the 1970s, trends for most products having persisted throughout that twenty-seven-year period, pork, 'other meats', fish and margarine being the exceptions.

Little can be learned from the examination of single products, as the meaning of such changes in food consumption is usually highly ambiguous. For example, Ritson and Hutchins (1990: 35), use this data in an attempt to establish that the 1980s saw a 'consumer revolution'. After describing shifts in expenditure on various commodities like butter, meat, cereals and vegetables, they seek to estimate the underlying trend in demand as a way of isolating the changes in taste that comprise the consumer revolution in food. They list ten products for which there is the highest growth in underlying demand (1990: 43): other fresh green vegetables (e.g. broccoli), wholewheat and wholemeal bread, frozen chips, other fats (e.g. low fat spreads), frozen convenience cereal foods (e.g. pizzas), other vegetable products (e.g. prepared salads), fruit juices, crisps and other potato products, exotic fresh fruits and shellfish. They comment: 'Two features of "star" products stand out: they seem to be associated either with convenience or healthy eating.' They then list, without comment, the ten products with the largest fall in underlying demand: unfilleted fresh white fish, fresh peas, unfilleted processed fat fish, soft fresh fruit, instant potato, offal other than liver, baby foods canned and bottled, canned and bottled fruit, canned potatoes, brussels sprouts. Ironically, what this demonstrates is that people are abandoning items equally healthy and convenient. Not only are such values insufficient to explain alterations in practice; their deduction from spending on single items is problematic.

Commodity culture itself creates an illusion of rapid change because of its preoccupation with new products, which by their nature tend to be, in the field of food, either specific ingredients or composed dishes. In this respect there is much flux, but that should be viewed in the context of more profound continuity in other areas of food behaviour. Items purchased and dishes preferred have been subject to greater change than have the structure of meals, the rituals of the table, the social meaning of companionship, the allocation of domestic food tasks, or the social classification of what it is appropriate to eat. Some, especially the social, practices in the field of food are more resistant to change than others.

Accounts written from a social-historical, rather than a nutritionist, perspective tend to offer more socially meaningful and less item-centred accounts. The difficulty of knowing what the consumer likes is acknowledged by Burnett, the most distinguished historian of British food trends: 'It is tempting to speculate, though very difficult to know, whether British food tastes have changed radically since the end of the war' (1989: 310). Reflecting on the period since 1945, he identified a number of significant tendencies. He suggests since the 1970s 'a growing taste for foreign dishes', citing a 1976 Gallup survey 'into people's knowledge of foreign dishes' which indicates that 'chow mein and sweet and sour pork were known by seven out of ten, pizza by eight out of ten, and ravioli by nearly as many; chilli con carne was familiar to only four out of ten, while moussaka, sole meunière, and wienerschnitzel had reached only one in three' (1989: 312). He suggests, when interpreting change, that there is a fairly clear sense of decline in items typical of the pre-war British diet, but that the new items coming to replace them seem to have no single, simple, overriding rationale for their acceptance. Neither health, nor convenience, nor aesthetics, nor cost is a satisfactory overarching explanation of innovations in diet. However, his suggestion that items need more than one such merit to achieve incorporation is not a convincing solution.

Thus we have little reliable direct knowledge about the process of food choice from the point of view of the consumer. Theoretical accounts of changing consumption patterns tend to isolate decades of transition. For example, informalization is associated with the cultural revolution in the 1960s, flexible production and niche consumption with response to the recession of the early 1970s, and individualization with both. Aggregate data about changes in food production and household expenditure of food fails to corroborate either argument. For while there have been many piecemeal changes in the quantity and items of food consumed in Britain since the Second World War, the evidence suggests that any identifiable trends are long term and that there was no reorientation, or sharp turning point, in the 1970s or 1980s. Of the long-term trends, the steadily enhanced availability of a wider variety of products, particularly of foreign provenance but also resulting from manufacturing innovations, is probably the most momentous.

8.3 Increased variety and diminishing contrasts?

In section 2.2 I suggested that Mennell's theoretical insistence that 'increased variety and diminishing contrasts' is a single process was dubious, that his projection was indeterminate, and that some of his empirical claims were suspect with respect to post-war Britain. On the basis of the results of both content and discriminant analysis, a re-evaluation of Mennell's thesis is possible.

Increased variety

It has to be conceded that a greater variety of foodstuffs is commonly available to the British shopper in the 1990s than at any time in the 20th century. This represents less an absolute increase in ingredients for sale in the UK, more the *wider availability* to ordinary people of the same foodstuffs, achieved particularly through the large supermarkets. For example, Driver (1983) reprinted a list of tinned foods available in London before the Second World War, which comprise an enormous range including obscure items like turtle meat, Hungarian goosebreast, sweetbreads with mushrooms, okra, samphire and sea kale. Also available in tins were many items, now routinely available fresh but which were recondite in the 1950s, like capsicums and tropical fruits. It seems likely, however, that a taste for such products, and access to them, would have been relatively restricted in the inter-war period. Surveys of ordinary diets (e.g. Crawford & Broadley, 1938) suggest that most households consumed a modest range of foods.[2] Exotic foreign food items were probably the preserve of a metropolitan social elite. Supermarkets have given the opportunity for variety to a much wider section of the population. To be sure, some of the appearance of increased variation is illusory. Some of that variety is created by offering alternative forms of packaging (brands) or storing (frozen, tinned, fresh) the same item; some by having many versions of the same item, as with different fruit flavours for yoghurt or sauces for chicken. But overall, this is perhaps the most significant change since the Second World War.

Greater variety of available items does not necessarily entail an expansion of the range of items that any individual person will eat. True, most Britons have had the opportunity to try new items, learn new tastes, and develop a liking for previously inaccessible foods. Many Britons now regularly eat items, dishes and meals that would have seemed strange to their grandparents: garlic, chilli, curry and pasta have become popular tastes in many sections of the population. Awareness of foreign cuisines is, as the magazines imply, much greater and in recent years many people will have enjoyed dishes in restaurants drawing on culinary traditions from the far corners of the earth. But whether such experiences have sedimented into greater diversity of taste remains a matter of speculation.

More varied products do not necessarily entail that any, or every, individual has now developed a more diverse set of preferences. It is tempting to assume that the sale of a greater range of products will result in most people increasing the number of different items that they regularly eat. This is probably the case, though there is no data to prove it. It remains possible that consumption of, say, exotic fruit and vegetables is restricted to a fraction of the middle class and ethnic minority groups. A substantial proportion of the population may have tasted and rejected, or avoided altogether, most of the novel items that have been brought to market in recent decades. There are sufficient reports of attachment to conservative tastes, and lack of interest in food, to suggest that many Britons will have added very few new products to their menus. Moreover, the evidence regarding generational change suggests that younger cohorts, while developing new tastes, have eliminated previously popular items from their diets. So as manufactured potato products, pizza and soft drinks increase, offal, mutton, processed meats and blancmange decline.

One general outstanding question is: how do people respond to the enormous diversity of goods available in, for instance, the supermarket? Do they routinely buy the same limited number of items each week; or do they purchase different sets of items week by week, thereby exploiting the diverse supplies? A second issue is whether increase in the number of items consumed is the most significant social development. This clearly matters to food producers estimating demand for their products and to nutritionists calculating dietary intake. But for sociologists the construction of meals and the social relations surrounding their preparation and consumption are probably more important, and these may be affected less by the diversity of ingredients and be less amenable to rapid change.

Variety can scarcely but be welcomed. It offers new opportunities for sensory stimulation. It may also solve some practical problems of domestic food provisioning which have particularly burdened women in the past. Yet it may compromise quality. Some evidence has suggested that a degree of de-skilling is occurring with respect to domestic cookery (e.g. Gofton, 1995: 169). The development of the world menu typical of international hotels and the general tendency to domesticate foreign cuisines produce diluted and hybrid meals. Despite constant introduction of new items and dishes, there is little sign of the emergence of a consolidated British culinary tradition or food culture, notwithstanding the efforts of some upmarket restaurateurs (see Wood, 1994). While Britons enjoy eating and find cooking one of the least unpleasant of recurrent domestic tasks, they appear to remain, in international terms, comparatively unappreciative and uninterested in the aesthetic and gustatory aspects of food consumption.

The commercial origins of variety

We should therefore be careful about assuming that the wider variety of food available in Britain in the 1990s indicates that most people have a more varied diet, or that greater variety results in diversification. Consider, for example, the effect of the growth of international food: while it has increased variety locally, it has standardized food across the world. Mennell (1985: 320), when considering notions of mass culture, noted evidence of standardization: diets in capitalist commodity culture include junk food and frozen 'gourmet dishes'; there are many mass manufactured foodstuffs and people now have the capacity to eat the same thing all year round. But he adduced even more illustration supportive of a pluralist thesis: people have much greater choice now than ever before given the importation of foreign produce, the expansion of the restaurant trade, the diversity of recipes in magazines, the capabilities of electric kitchen machinery.

Mennell documented changes in the food production process, but with little proof of changing individual or group taste. Increasing variation is almost entirely a result of commodification. New products and new channels of communication are the outcomes of capitalist industrial activity. Mennell's most persuasive evidence derives from purely commercial forces and practices, as with, for instance, overcoming the seasons, introducing new items from overseas, the manufacture of convenience foods, and the spread of restaurants specializing in exotic cuisines. Even in the British case of the popularity of Indian and Chinese take-away meals, or of their equivalents in cook-chill forms in supermarkets, the foundation of increased variation is the further commodification of food services. Possibly wider knowledge of domestic cookery is one source of variation which is not a pure corollary of commercial intervention, though as Mennell himself notes, there is a relationship between this and the proliferation of magazines and cookery books. Variation is almost entirely a function of the logic of capitalist enterprise. As so often, claims about consumption patterns are primarily speculative deductions from evidence about what is manufactured (see Warde, 1994a).

The persistence of class and other contrasts

Mennell makes the diminishing contrasts claim with limited justification. By his own admission, he cannot detect any strong, one-directional trends (Mennell, 1985: 259). I have contested the view that the most plausible and central sense of the term 'diminishing contrast' – that there is a continuation of a process well documented for the first half of the 20th century, the decline of class differentiation – is not apparent in the period after 1968 (see also Tomlinson & Warde, 1993). Indeed, in one of his few empirical references to changes in social differentiation Mennell quotes another authority, Marjorie Ferguson (1982), to the effect that the 1960s and 1970s saw not homogenization but differentiation in the consumption patterns of social classes (Mennell, 1985: 262). The evidence amassed by Mennell for reduced differentiation in the post-war period is paltry. He is correct to identify a decline in regional differences, but almost no other indicator of *social* differentiation gives any clear support to the claim.

Mennell's primary basis for claiming diminishing contrasts was the declining importance of class. The evidence arising from our discriminant analysis does not corroborate his view. If decline occurred it was in the period before, during or soon after the Second World War. This seems likely to have been the effect of the collapse of a gulf in consumption behaviour between, primarily, households with servants and those without, which occurred early in the 20th century. The nature of that change is suggestive.

Gershuny (1988: 586) showed that the disappearance of servants gave a misleading impression of stability in the number of hours of domestic labour devoted by British housewives to their tasks. In fact, the burdens of working-class women were alleviated by new domestic technologies which did save time and effort on washing clothes, preparing food and so forth. However, their middle-class counterparts had done few such tasks in the era of widespread domestic service. Because they then had to undertake their own housework it was their extra inputs that kept the average household time spent on domestic work constant. In this instance the homogenization of practice across classes was a function of the de-commodification of food preparation. Equalizing tendencies, among women, arose from removing some forms of provisioning from the market. By the same principle, it is surprising that further commodification in recent decades has not subsequently *increased* class differences.[3]

Evidence from the discriminant analysis suggests strongly that social contrasts have scarcely diminished in the period since the 1960s. Standard socio-demographic variables, like class, income, gender, life-course stage and household composition, all continue to influence food choice. Moreover, it would appear that all are of roughly comparable importance, though the application of more advanced multivariate statistical techniques than were employed in this study would be needed to estimate the interaction of the socio-demographic variables affecting food choice. Even more significant, the impact of these variables altered relatively little between 1968 and 1988. Reflection on class differences suggests little significant overall change.

The processes maintaining class distance are complex but compatible with new culinary opportunities for all classes. For example, during the period the working class began to eat out more frequently on commercial, as opposed to workplace, premises. Greater affluence meant the opportunity for expanding culinary knowledge, experience and enjoyment. Even the poorest sections of the population make use of commercial eating places and come to share in food fashions. But sections of the middle class became even more engrossed in the pleasures of eating out. Eating out, in 1988, was highly discriminating on the basis of class. Probably there are phases when working- and middle-class practices tend to converge, in the 1940s and 1950s for instance, but they never coincide, and they may subsequently diverge once again.

Not only is there little evidence of class contrasts diminishing; differences of gender and generation equally show no tendency to disappear. Indeed, if there was any abrupt transformation in the patterns of behaviour of social groups it was in a particular age cohort, born in the 1940s, whose innovative impact registered in the 1960s. Generation is a social division ignored by Mennell, though it could be damaging to his thesis of diminishing contrasts. Documentation of systematic generational differences could also dent post-Fordist accounts because it implies less the emergence of specialized niche taste, more a general cohort effect in the food culture as a whole. However, although there are indications, from the National Food Survey for example, of persistent age-related preferences, we currently lack adequate data to determine whether there was any significant generational shift during the 1970s.

Theoretical issues

Mennell under-theorizes his account, ultimately arguing on the basis of evidence about production rather than consumption, despite seeking to explain taste and preference.[4] Most of Mennell's evidence adds up to a demonstration of increased commodification and thus the wider availability of a greater number of products. There are two reasons for theoretic concern.

First, there is no *necessary* link between an increase in variety and a decline in social differentiation. Important trends run counter to Mennell's claim that increasing variety and diminishing contrasts go together and are part of the same process. If there were a necessary correspondence we would expect that reduced variety would produce greater inequality. However, the experience of the 1930s suggests that de-commodification, in the form of the disappearance of servants, reduced class differences. So probably did the rigours of wartime rationing, despite the black market. In both instances variety reduced hand in hand with social de-differentiation. By the same logic we might anticipate that increased commodification would re-establish class differences, but nor does the evidence support that. The relative distance between key social categories of person – class, gender, generation – appears to remain constant.

Second, increasing commercial variety is indeterminate with respect to competing theses about social change. More variety could allow the formation of distinctive style groups, it could permit the retrenchment of class differentiation, it could encourage individual idiosyncrasy if people select in increasingly random fashion, or it could result in everyone selecting more or less the same set of items. Increased variety has only contingent effects on social diversity. Indeed it is surprising, given increased variety, that there is not more blurring of social boundaries. But social group differentiation still exists, its persistence implying less individualization than might be anticipated.

To summarize my reflections on Mennell's argument, I acknowledge generally increased variation for the majority of British households, but contest the extent to which real contrasts have diminished in the last three decades. Class contrasts diminished in the early part of the 20th century, but probably not recently. Those contrasts that did diminish, regional and seasonal ones, must largely be attributed to developments in the production and distribution of food. While demand for new food products may have developed, they have not been adopted in such a way as to eliminate social differentiation. The social distance between groups has remained fairly constant.

The mechanism that best explains Mennell's description of the 20th century is commodification. We remain uncertain about the extent to which the *tastes* of the individual consumer have changed: as Burnett notes, this is largely a matter of speculation since it cannot be directly inferred, although it often is, from the statistics of industrial production. There is little in the evidence discussed to suggest any kind of linear trends in taste. But we have not witnessed random fluctuations. Rather, people are constantly exposed to *systematically* contradictory judgments and recommendations about food, expressed here as four antinomies. Where Mennell (1985: 261)

172 *Interpretations of Taste*

discerned only irregularity in the representations of food in the magazines, the evidence amassed in Part II suggests the contrary: that there are some definable tendencies in representations of good food, but they are best grasped as the playing out of antinomial principles.

8.4 Antinomies and the structural anxieties of late modernity

Antinomies and guilt

The discourses of food exhibit a structured set of evaluative categories, or principles of recommendation. The relative importance of each principle may change with time but together they persistently reflect four fundamental antinomies, novelty and tradition, health and indulgence, economy and extravagance, convenience and care, each offering contradictory recommendations guiding food selection. Perhaps alternative oppositions could be used, but the ones proposed, which were primarily derived inductively from the magazine columns, provide a good and economical fit when classifying judgments about British food in the second half of the 20th century. This is because these legitimizing principles are not specific to the field of food, being readily applicable to other fields of consumption and cultural practices. For instance, motor cars and consumer durables are advertised in terms of the first and fourth antinomy. Leisure pursuits, hobbies and enthusiasms are represented in terms of all but the third antinomy; one might think of a health farm as novel, healthy and extravagant, but going to the pub as traditional, indulgent and cheap. Sexual behaviour, like food, is discussed and evaluated in terms of all four.

These antinomies are widely applicable precisely because they are fundamental categories of contemporary culture. Because most are familiar, people can appreciate the attractions of both poles of each antinomy. But they are not always helpful in the process of decision-making. Often the opposite, as they might become a source of anxiety about the best course of action.

Bauman (1988) argued that consumerism was itself a principal source of anxiety. Whether such anxiety is experienced acutely by shoppers in their routine everyday transactions I am inclined to doubt. Nor am I convinced that these anxieties are felt most strongly (or solely) in the supermarket; I expect that they will have more impact in social and domestic situations. Bauman over-personalized the nature of anxiety, over-concentration on questions of self-identity leading him to believe that anxieties were associated solely with the maintenance of appearances. But some level of anxiety permeates the magazines' discussions of food choice. All four antinomies are capable of generating anxiety, in the sense of creating problems in decision-making and entailing the possibility of making mistakes which will be personally demeaning, by making one look naive, lacking in self-respect, penny-pinching, conceited or uncaring. Food choice may be prejudicial to the presentation of self. But in the field of food these antinomies also have powerful moral overtones. One will rarely feel guilty about a choice made between novel and traditional food, but the other antinomies are inherently more threatening.[5] Indulgence, extravagance and evading responsibilities for emotional care are highly charged moral categories and therefore potential sources of guilt. So while poor choice may compromise a person's identity and thus induce anxiety, it may also be detrimental in the field of social relations as a sign of moral turpitude or impropriety.

The structural bases of the four antinomies

The ambivalence of modernity   A spate of literature in the last decade has depicted the ambivalence of the modern condition. Though with different nuances, the ambivalence concerns the mutual incompatibility of the simultaneous desires for individual freedom and collective security. Modernity allows opportunities for self-determination absent in traditional societies. Beliefs, habits, careers, friendships and enthusiasms are not authoritatively allocated to an individual. This in turn permits a range of personal experimentation and the appreciation of new and different experiences. The modern world can be exciting and fulfilling. On the other hand, as Martin (1981) put it, 'natural rootedness and automatic structures of belonging' are destroyed. The embeddedness of the individual in familiar social contexts and collectivities is forgone. Denied is the sense of comfort and security that can be derived from knowing that our tastes and preferences, even in the humble field of food, are endorsed and shared by others, whom we respect and with whom we consider we belong. One frequent response to the perceived loss of belonging is to try to recreate shared norms, to instantiate some common standards of judgment and feeling that can sustain a sense of community. This surfaces on occasion as 'tradition', to which people pay homage.

The terms of the first antinomy reflect the ambivalence of the modern experience. The unceasing, restless search for the possibility of novelty and change coexists with an equally insistent quest for the security and certainty that can be derived from belonging and routine. The magazines re-present, discursively, the competing attractions of two contradictory guiding principles of the experience of everyday life in the 20th century. Most people want, or can be addressed as if they want, both excitement and comfort, both change and stability. Hence the possibility of anxiety when contemplating a course of action or making decisions.

Discipline and self-surveillance   The health–indulgence couple centres around enhanced cultural concern with the body – both with its use value, as an efficiently functioning organism which is the basis of all sensation, and with its identity value, as an object of the impersonal gaze of people and institutions. The care and preservation of the body has been presented increasingly as a personal responsibility and a social obligation. Governments, clients, colleagues and lovers expect well-tended bodies.

Food practices are a classic site for observing a shift towards self-discipline and self-surveillance. It is not a matter of external compulsion, by peers or the state, that persuades one to eat carefully, but an internalized and self-regarding regimenting of consumption. Consumption has become disciplined. No longer is it a matter of careless unconcern, or the habitual pursuit of pleasure. With the arrival of abundance comes a perceived imperative to resist indulgence. This sometimes extends to the apparent pursuit of pain, of buying discomfort at the gymnasium or subjecting the body to torturous exercise as a personal objective or commitment. The screw of self-discipline tightens its grip as people monitor their intake and expenditure of calories and fibre.

The history of bathroom furniture remains to be written, but the increasing role of mirrors, weighing scales and tape measures signifies the spread of bodily discipline. The satisfactory body is very regularly monitored, both for appearance and efficiency. Subduing the body is not just a matter of bodily integrity and physiological efficiency but also of personal identity. Exercise may serve both purposes, as perhaps with body-building where participants perceive gains in both fitness and attractiveness. Controlled dietary intake has, in the same way, both a use value and an identity value. The weight-loss diet, except in situations of obesity, is a matter of appearance, the manicuring of self-identity. To follow the government's nutritional guidelines might be considered more a matter of bodily efficiency, food acting as a use value. Ultimately, these cannot be divorced the one from the other: dieting may damage one's health, eating a nutritious diet may improve appearance. But in both instances the associated practices entail careful monitoring and calculation about the body.

Elements of rationalization are embedded in the personalization of surveillance. The body becomes a personal achievement, something for which one becomes responsible and which therefore entails self-governance. We reach the point where the individual's capacity for reflexivity inspires him/her to treat the body as a machine, and to apply the techniques of rational management not just to economic production but to the person. Amazingly, though in accordance with the logic specified by Elias (1982), social and political intervention to mould the person becomes less and less influential as the individual responds to the imperatives of the self-flagellating society.

However, counter-tendencies exist. The logic of indulgence appeals to contrary values: it registers a desire for unregimented and relaxed pleasures, a search for satisfaction of emotional needs, the love of comfort even in excess. Probably individuals are not as thoroughly self-reflexive as some recent theoretical accounts would claim. People eat in social situations where even the most self-disciplined feel bound to relax their abstemious personal regimens. Social interaction requires compromise. They then may feel intensely guilty. A quasi-moral conflict arises between the imperatives of asceticism and conviviality, tomorrow and today, control and abandon. Nor should it be inferred that indulgence is social, while self-surveillance is individual; the practices of the gym are collective and indulgence may be private. People are extremely conscious of the possibility of indulgence, the very notion being evidence of the complex ideology surrounding bodily integrity in the modern world.

Cash and class Explicit concern with the symbolic relative cost of food declined in the magazines, though the actual cost of dishes came to be recorded ever more frequently. Still money matters. The unrelenting pressure to commodification means that money necessarily plays a central role in the management of feeding. Concern with the symbolic aspects of consumption quite often diverts attention from issues of the material resources required for survival. In practice, the unequal distribution of income and wealth has a significant direct impact upon food provisioning. Though in Britain fewer people than in the past may 'wonder where the next meal is coming from', the money to achieve a basic sufficiency is still beyond the reach of parts of the population. Behind the antinomy of economy and extravagance is the cash nexus and an increasingly unequal distribution of income. The possibility of possessing insufficient money is a structural anxiety of a commodified world.

Concern with the symbolic relative cost of an item – whether expensive or cheap, economical or extravagant – typifies stratified and status-conscious societies. In Britain this dimension of social judgment has usually been expressed in the language of social class. Class is not just a matter of money, though one of its manifestations is the option open to some to purchase expensive foods and to eat in an exclusive fashion. Important findings of this study are that class differences in food preferences have not recently diminished. The pattern is complicated but it remains possible to discover which class a person belongs to by examining their food tastes. The working-class diet remains distinct from that of the middle class. Within the middle class there are systematic differences between the *petite bourgeoisie*, routine white-collar workers and professionals. Public aspects of consumption, especially eating and drinking away from home, particularly mark the distinction of the professionals. The capacity to display rank in a social hierarchy by consuming in accordance with the criteria of a symbolic representation of that hierarchy confirms the powerful and multifaceted link between class and consumption. Distinction persists.

Gender and time Money and time are, to the calculating mind, partially interchangeable. The 'increasing scarcity of time' affects everyone who might be gainfully employed, but its impact in recent years has been particularly great on women. The numbers of lone parents and married women compelled to join the labour market are much greater than fifty years ago. As a consequence, these categories of person are subjected to renewed and deeper experience of the fourth antinomy, the counter-demands of care and convenience.

Care and convenience represent, *par excellence*, the current contradictions of the gender order within households: there is a central, contested and unstable accommodation on the part of women between caring work and paid employment. Employment offers women many rewards besides an income: sociability in the workplace, greater independence in familial decision-making, escape from low-status housewifery, potential long-term security from a career. But as has been pointed out frequently, the responsibility for maintaining family relationships and for the day-to-day sustenance of household members still falls largely to adult women. The duty to care, even if willingly assumed, creates the need for the very difficult balancing act between the sentiments of emotion and personal sacrifice and the pressures on time that arise from doing paid work. Women fail to surmount the difficulties because of the structural and institutional environment in which they are situated and which, ultimately, defines gender. Thus in their food provisioning roles, women cannot be satisfied with maximizing either care or convenience, since both generate anxiety and guilt.

McCracken (1993) anticipated one means to overcome this contradiction when she suggested excellence in shopping is itself becoming a defining aspect of the ideal woman. Shopping is increasingly important to female identity: Ballaster et al. note also that for women 'Shopping is not only elevated to the status of being the ultimate leisure experience, it is also the ultimate form of self-expression' (1991: 149). Finding the right commodity has also become intrinsically laudable. Bauman describes 'the consumer attitude' as the conviction that all wants can be satisfied, all problems solved, through shopping wisely. In such fashion, commodities, accessed through the market, have become central to everyday life and social survival. However, while there is a good deal of truth to this observation, not all social and personal transactions are yet commodified.

The magazines implicitly acknowledge that certain things are not to be exchanged at all, or certainly not to be exchanged for money. Imagine a world where everyone always paid for meals, conversation and sexual gratification – notwithstanding that many people, some of the time, do just that. Kopytoff (1986) notes that friends are not paid for giving dinner, though a small gift may be appropriate because in this field a system of reciprocal exchange operates. There is also some significant aspect of familial relations that renders it inappropriate to pay for meals, though sometimes people pay other household members or kin for the provision of food on a regular basis, as when children pay 'board', though rarely at market rates. As Finch and Mason (1993) document, such rules are complicated, in part negotiated within households and not entirely pre-established, but there is, nevertheless, widespread unease about substituting commercial servicing for personal care.

Corresponding attitudes towards commodification are apparent in the magazines, one effect being a prejudice against convenience foods. Despite desires to economize on time and effort, making a meal from a packet, or drawing a manufactured meal from the freezer is, in some way, an abrogation of caring. Though people are less prepared to positively associate care with extensive domestic labour, there is no wholehearted embrace of the ready-prepared products of the food industry. Attachments to homemade food betray resistance to commodities, but it represents a rearguard action with limited prospect of success in the face of the forces of progressive commodification in the field.

The discursive institutionalization of anxiety

Individual articles in magazines are rarely ambivalent in their recommendations; they do not, for instance, simultaneously encourage discipline and indulgence. In practice, reference is made usually to only one side of an antinomy, temporarily denying or obscuring the existence of its opposing principle of recommendation. Most stories are designed to convince in one direction. Occasionally, however, two sides appear together, directly, as with the advertisement for Stork products or the *Cosmopolitan* article about comfort food (Chapters 7 and 5 respectively), making their contradictions starkly visible. In cases which include both poles of an antinomy, they are often in a joking format, though nevertheless serving to remind that decisions are risky and consequential.

It is debatable whether these antinomies can be resolved or eliminated in practice. One solution for the reader might be to follow a systematic set of preferences, whether conscious or unconscious, always regarding some principles above others. When asked in our survey what sort of meals they liked to serve to guests, most respondents answered readily enough, suggesting that they had some longstanding preferences. Also, the significant minority of people who follow rigorous diets exhibit a consistency in their preferences which could not be dismissed as anomic or unprincipled. If there is a dominant discourse of recommendation in any period, then it might offer guidance.

An alternative way to confront these antinomies might be to do one thing one day, another the next, much as the *Cosmopolitan* column suggested; indulge today and repent tomorrow. Such practice is described explicitly by Levenstein (1988: 209–10) as one aspect of behaviour in the USA:

> Perhaps as a result of confusing signals being emitted by the 'experts', few middle-class Americans seem to stick to one set pattern of eating. Buffeted from food scare to food scare, enticed by the convenience (and, let it be said, the taste) of fast foods, unable to resist snack foods and 'grazing', yet still relishing the occasional Julia Child-like triumph in the kitchen, *Homo Americanus* and family present a confused picture. As *Fortune* magazine notes, 'The same working mother who repairs to McDonald's three times a week may settle down on the weekend for a bout of gourmet cooking. Diet sodas with pizza, health food for lunch, and junk food for dinner – the trends in the market for food are precisely as consistent as the eating habits of Americans.'

There is no reason in principle why this should not become a dominant approach to provisioning. However, it reduces severely the opportunity to derive social meaning and emotional comfort from eating. It may thus be, as Levenstein goes on to argue, that this is merely 'the turbulent surface' beneath which are still 'calm steady currents originating from bygone eras, for, although confused and confusing, contemporary attitudes are still solidly grounded on ideas' formed a century ago.

To what degree people, when choosing and eating a meal, actually *feel* anxious is a moot point. The anxiety may be greater for the person providing and preparing a meal than for its other final consumers. The magazines probably try to reduce anxiety. Indeed, the recipe itself is an expert device, in part designed to give both technical and aesthetic confidence to the cook. But the columnists are probably not enormously successful, discursively, because they lack the conviction of established standards and are severely hampered in any attempt at defining good taste because they accept wholeheartedly the ultimate legitimacy of choice in consumer matters. Each, hence, usually writes at one pole of an antinomy, advocacy of which gives the appearance of a consistent standard. But collectively they express a structured and structural set of anxieties which arise from food choice.

Anxieties might be suppressed under a temporarily dominant resolution. Some principles – novelty, discipline, economy and convenience – are, currently, more prominent than others. These are the recommendations most frequently canvassed in the 1990s. We should eat international, healthy, unostentatious and easily prepared foods. These are the messages most frequently appealed to in the recipe columns, and are even more prominent in advertisements for food. The opposing principles, which call up emotion, responsibility to others, comfort and habit, are present, but less pronounced. These values are subordinated to a primarily rationalized and self-regarding discourse.

8.5 Conclusion: practice and representation

The most important change since the 1960s is, as Mennell claimed, 'increased variety'. This largely follows from the incessant, ever driving, logic of commodification, a corollary of the concerns and strategies of the producers of food, rather than being driven by changing taste on the part of consumers. Taste is, as many commentators on food have argued, slow to change; it is no longer glacial, in the metaphor of Braudel and the Annales School, but is still resistant to commercial manipulation. New products became available on a mass basis in rather unpredictable and uneven fashion from the early 1960s but their adoption was, for most people, a slow process. There are no signs of a sharp transformation after 1968. Nevertheless, Britons have learned new tastes in the post-war world and the mass of the population has acquired a tolerance, or positive liking for, items and dishes that their parents would have rejected, had they ever even experienced them. In particular, supermarket distribution, using its key competitive advantage of offering enormous variety, has made routinely available to ordinary people a range of foods previously only accessible to an elite.

The contemporary phase of consumer culture has become obsessed with variety; a new discourse of variety and choice, itself nurtured and legitimized by the dominant political ideology of the period, has become dominant and has tended to obscure underlying continuities in food practice. As regards other much-heralded processes of change, scarcely any began in the period under examination. As so often when looking for historical turning points, it is assumed that they occurred a generation ago, say thirty years, but when inspected carefully they have deeper roots. The evidence seriously challenges those accounts that argue for a major transformation in popular culture and consumption associated with a post-Fordist or postmodernist epoch emerging in the 1970s.

As regards consumer tastes in food, evidence of change remains inconclusive. While much is known about developments in production and the volumes of sales of different food items, whether there was any decisive change in the ways in which different groups of consumers made use of such products remains obscure. How people respond in practice to government advice or the food columns in popular magazines, and how they put their purchases together into meals, needs more research. We know for certain only how they were encouraged to alter their eating patterns. Ways of discussing and evaluating food did alter. Assuming that women's magazines can serve as a barometer for the prominence of shared classificatory categories, change in the ways that food is recommended gives some indication of shifts in popular understandings of taste. During the 1970s and 1980s greater prominence was given to a number of themes. The motif of health, conceived as the exercise of self-discipline over the body, grew in importance, but so did permission to indulge in treats. The need for convenience foods was increasingly acknowledged, but with considerable regret. Foreign foods were normalized, a routinization of the exotic apparently implying that readers had become more familiar with international cuisines. And the magazines included more detailed technical instructions about how to prepare dishes, part of a rationalization of information about foodstuffs. But these changes in mass media representations of food preparation were no more than tendential: it was a matter of some becoming more prominent, others receding to some degree, rather than any transformation in the cultural categories being used to evaluate food. The importance accorded to the poles of the antinomies of taste were adjusted, but the structural principles persisted.

9

Theories of Consumption
and the Case of Food

9.1 The specialness of food

It is becoming accepted that universal propositions about consumption practices are impossible to sustain because different areas of material culture and different types of commodity do not operate in accordance with a single rationale (e.g. Miller, 1987; Fine & Leopold, 1993). This raises a doubt about precisely how useful a case study of food is in the explanation of consumption behaviour more generally.

Food is a complex case. Its consumption is universal, mundane and polyvalent. Everyone eats; most eat several times a day without much reflection; yet the activity is integrally connected with many other highly meaningful aspects of living. It is meaningful because social; usually people eat in company and subject to inspection by others. Moreover, because people live in households, where food procurement and preparation are not equally shared, where decisions about what is to be eaten are usually collective, often vicarious, and only sometimes individual, it may be less open to individualizing tendencies than some other consumption fields. Also, in principle, it is markedly ephemeral. Once I have eaten the contents of my refrigerator, I could go and buy a completely different set of items. I could eat traditional Cantonese meals in May, junk food in June, and be vegetarian in July. There is little financial penalty for changing my mind; I am not constrained by last month's decision as I might be had I purchased an expensive car.

In these respects food is different from many of the fields used to explore consumption. Cultural studies has generally concentrated on the most sign-infested purchases – vehicles, clothes, and the artefacts of popular media. We can certainly learn much about consumption from the study of such beacons of self-identity. Analogues exist in the field of food: public display entailed in eating out or announcing a taboo amounts to disclosure. But these are exceptional in a mundane area of consumption practice. Much of the activity surrounding food is private and domestic. It concerns physical and emotional needs, is a site of domestic conflict and a key aspect of family formation. It is also, remember, a field which absorbs a considerable proportion of people's income, looming larger in family budgets than clothes or entertainment, for instance.

Food thus is a corrective to understandings of consumption which exaggerate identity-enhancing or status-symbolic aspects. However, because it is a complex field, its overall significance for theories of consumption is difficult to establish. Some evidence can be found to support every competing theory of consumption and every account of contemporary trends. The analytic problem is, then, to weigh the relative importance of the evidence reviewed.

9.2 Food trends and tendencies in consumption: undistinguished difference?

In Chapter 1 I identified four social forces influencing modern consumption. Individualization, 'communification' stylization, and informalization provide orientations to action among individual consumers as they go about making decisions. Evidence of all these tendencies exists in the field of food in the period examined.

Individualization

For many social theorists, individualization is the key social tendency of the current epoch. It is interpreted in terms of the detachment, or disembedding, of individuals from the institutional situations in which they were previously cocooned. For Beck (1992), the demise of class and the disintegration of the family are responsible for the new situation where self-identity becomes consciously chosen by the individual and expressed through consumption. For Giddens (1991: 5, 18), the emergence of 'reflexively organized life planning', or the choice of lifestyles by individuals, is concurrent with disembedding of social institutions, 'the "lifting out" of social relations from local contexts and their rearticulation across indefinite tracts of time-space' as individuals become obliged to trust in abstract expert systems for personal guidance.

To operationalize the concept of individualization is difficult. However, it might be said to occur if each individual member of a household eats in ways increasingly distinct from other household members, such that common patterns of behaviour within households diminish. It also happens if each individual becomes more distinct from those in otherwise similar households, implying that communally endorsed patterns of consumption have less influence on behaviour than previously.

Changes in the organization of food provisioning in households have encouraged individualization. An entrenched, gender-based, domestic division of labour persists, entailing that wives and female partners do a disproportionate amount of the work involved in food preparation. Nevertheless, revised domestic time schedules have put considerable pressure on such arrangements. A dual-earner household with longer distances to work and less regular working hours experiences greater difficulty in coordinating the time-space paths of household members. In households where women are in full-time employment the number of domestic tasks undertaken falls significantly. Where women are unavailable to prepare meals, which by

nature cannot be postponed, men and children may take over those tasks
on behalf of the household as a whole, but they may equally well come to
service themselves. New domestic technologies and new supermarket products have increased people's capacities to prepare a meal for themselves,
using tinned food and a microwave oven for instance. There has probably
been a commensurate decline in skill and time invested in food preparation
overall, which has somewhat reduced dependency on household members
with developed culinary skills.

There are more outlets selling ready-cooked food, further increasing the
independence of individual household members. Though people are reluctant to go out to eat alone, they may go more with friends. If alone,
recourse to a take-away or sandwich outlet is an option. Social circumstances throw people into more situations where they are making an
individual decision about what to eat. The increase in the number of
households containing only one adult is but one other factor that removes
many from the orbit of family decision-making about what should be
eaten. Food selection is becoming less a matter of making joint decisions.

The enforced growth of individual decision-making is profusely legitimized in terms of the ideology of choice. Personal choice, and personal
taste, become pre-eminent in an intensifying ideology of consumer individualism. The expectation that families will eat together is in decline, as,
probably, is the assumption that all will eat the same things when they are
together. Anecdotal evidence suggests that different meals may be being
eaten at the same table more than in the past. The menu at the commercial
outlets, which demands selection from a range of dishes, may be pene-
trating domestic practices, an aspect of the convergence of commercial and
domestic food provision identified by Mennell (1985).

However, food patterns probably appear more fragmentary than they
actually are, a false impression arising from the language of choice and
variety. One reason for its persuasiveness is its superimposition upon the
well-recognized phenomenon that personal tastes and preferences differ.
People have entirely personal aversions to some items, but they tend to be
fixed. In response, as Charles and Kerr (1988) show, women food providers
tailor their menus to the personal preferences of household members. While
occasionally highly eccentric diets are reported, usually among children,
they are rare. People are not generally known to their friends for their
eccentric eating habits. Only where people respect taboos like not eating
meat is their distinctiveness recognized and then they are described by
affiliation to a collective menu – vegetarian, kosher, traditional, etc. There
is little evidence of 'individualized' diets. Indeed, there is scarcely a
vocabulary, except in medical discourses (of allergies, disorders and
homoeopathy), for talking about individualized eating patterns. Diet,
though it offers opportunities, is a comparatively weak emblem of personal
self-identity.

The impression of personal choice in diet is probably enhanced by the
growing stress on self-discipline in dietary matters. The many regimes for

the management of the body are directed towards the individual, who, it would seem, is independently and personally responsible for his or her health and efficiency. Government reports and guidelines imply that people should take care of themselves and take steps to protect their bodies against illness and decay. Thus, primarily collective regulation – whether national, class or familial – is replaced by personal self-regulation. Adopting a specialized diet, whether for reasons of weight loss or good health, requires a level of self-discipline. Often, however, collective reinforcement or support is needed to maintain a regime, for dieting is a form of deprivation. Equally often, dietary management is accomplished vicariously, final consumption being shaped by the person who does the shopping and cooking. While these aspects of familial management limit the extent of individualization, recent change does imply some reduction in the extent to which families structure eating. The pragmatics of household organization, enhanced consciousness of choice and obedience to the call to be disciplined in the maintenance of the body all require more individual initiation and monitoring.

'Communification': identity and the imagined community

To be part of a community is an aspiration widely held in modern societies, in part because modernity is perceived to destroy the natural rootedness and uncomplicated sense of belonging which village life in traditional societies engendered. Community is a difficult concept to define. While its passing is bemoaned, it is not obvious that the reality of the small community of the past lived up to its image. Nor is it clear that 'communion', or the sense of community, necessarily or exclusively derives from dense face-to-face interaction in limited geographical areas. Nevertheless, the ideal of intense community life continues to inspire individuals, groups, neighbourhoods and state policy-makers. Attempts are constantly being made to restore, recreate or invent communities.

What fires the contemporary desire for community is debatable. Arguably it is a search for institutional patterns of action that will provide security and assurance in the management of everyday life. In the field of consumption it is comforting to know appropriate ways to act, to have aesthetic judgments affirmed by like-minded people, to share in a consensus on what comprises a decent and good life. However, such a communion cannot be stage-managed, but rather evolves piecemeal over time: thus the paradox of projects consciously designed to create community. Participation in community is less a matter of personal zeal, more the becoming immersed in a Bourdieuvian habitus – deep-rooted, subconscious, informal, given, persistent. Such spiritual unions have in the past been variously associated with place, with nation, with ethnic group and with social class. To the extent that people share a way of life their practical and aesthetic dispositions are likely to converge. However, most people touched by modern experience are inherently suspicious of the viability of primordial

community. They recognize the rapidity of change, expect mobility, anticipate diversity of opinion, search for novel experiences: they are fully aware
of the fleeting and contingent character of modernity which militates
against the fixity of community. Still, the desire for community life persists.
The aspiration to culinary communion is exhibited in the language of
tradition, the appeal of regional cuisines, the validation of home cooking,
nostalgia for high-quality locally produced ingredients, and endless reflection on the authenticity and coherence of national cuisines. Not only is
food rather more firmly socially embedded than many other items of
consumption, the attempts at its further re-embedding are particularly
marked. The recipe columns betray a search for some kind of coherent
meaning in culinary life; the role of meals in the maintenance of family life
is regularly commended; the lifestyle advertisement represents a commercial
equation of social membership and collective taste; attention to the
geographical origin of produce and recipes is part of the assurance that to
consume is to share in good taste.

Some social groups appear more 'communified' than others. The
working-class menu remains culturally distinct and strongly demarcated,
yet still provides the model of the majority national eating pattern.
Workers share their tastes with the *petite bourgeoisie*. The rest of the middle
class is more differentiated. There can be found the most strict adherents to
the scientifically defined diet prescribed by nutritionists and the state. There
too are the activists for the campaigns for real ale, real bread, regional
cheeses and so forth, which are in part trying to reinvent tradition.
Religious or ethnic groups exhibit some of the strongest distinctive eating
habits, a consequence of doctrine or communal taste. But above all it is the
family as a commensal unity which is the primary institutional vehicle for
providing the reassurance of confirmed and shared standards for culinary
judgment. The family is the bearer and reproducer of the embedded
dispositions which comprise the habitus. While individualization challenges
and disrupts its function, the practical experience and emotional significance of family cooking remain a preponderant force behind most people's
tastes for food.

Stylization

Style is a ubiquitous notion of consumer culture. Its precise character is
hard to fathom, its definition contested (see Ewen, 1988). But especially it is
visual appearances, of people and things, that are classified and analysed in
terms of style. Stylization involves use being made of styled items to
express, in a predominantly aesthetic manner, group membership. Such
expression implies the existence of a code of conduct or set of rules, usually
implicit, which presupposes the importance of appearance and performance
in maintaining group differentiation. Rules are obeyed fairly strictly
because it is the definitive system of aesthetic preferences or judgments
which symbolizes membership. There are many kinds of style group,

ranging from Weber's status group, which registers its members position in an established and long-lasting hierarchy of prestige, to Maffesoli's neo-tribes, impermanent, voluntary and small alliances of people with kindred tastes or values. Stylization, for the individual consumer, involves the adoption of an identifiable and admired set of practices which are perceived as common to a 'style group'.

The neo-tribe, considered by some (e.g. Bauman, 1990) to be an important mechanism explaining contemporary consumer behaviour, provides a possible template for understanding stylization in late modernity. Compared to the community, the neo-tribe requires more discipline with respect to taste and judgment. Because aesthetic rules are constitutive of the group they are prominent and restrictive; and the sanctions for breaking them greater. The habitual community has much more relaxed, because embedded, conventions, which will usually be readily obeyed; minor transgressions will be easily forgiven. The neo-tribe is self-conscious about its rules. Obedience is voluntary, a matter neither of necessity nor habit. Members can drop out at any time, but for so long as they voluntarily subscribe they obey the rules to the letter to confirm their membership. Though not a relaxed arrangement, the commitment is temporary and conditional.

Observance is the key to stylization. The need to appear to be a member suggests that confidence of acceptance is precarious, and that precautions, visible to other groups and to ourselves, are necessary to confirm allegiance. Observance often accompanies active participation. Stylization offers some of the same rewards as communification – social meaning, a known standard of behaviour, a sense of belonging – but lacks its permanent and unreflective character. Stylization occurs in many aspects of food practice, both in active membership of small groups with distinctive political or ethical commitments and in mass media circulation of symbols of style and fashion.

The objectives of active campaigning groups are diverse and include the protection of animal rights and fostering of humane standards of livestock management; the preservation of real ale and bread; the promotion of vegetarianism; the boycotting of items from some sources or privileging products from countries deemed worthy of aid; improvement of standards of commercial products, whether the quality of meals in restaurants or additives in manufactured foods; cultivation of taste, fashion, discretion and refinement, particularly prominent among some middle-class groups; mutual support for those on weight-watching diets; advocacy of specialized diets directed towards curing medical problems; and the promotion of organic foodstuffs with a view to environmental protection.

The published and broadcast images of food and its usage contribute enormously to stylization. Advertising, the ubiquitous accompaniment to urban life, plays heavily on the appeal of style; and the contexts in which products are put, most notably in the format of the lifestyle ad, are silent visual guides to expression of social identity. In parallel, exposure given to different styles of restaurants rises and falls, as if in a fashion cycle. Media exposure is a principal basis for the expanded knowledge of the alternative ethnic cuisines which have now become thoroughly familiar. Guides to eating out, the Sunday newspapers, television programmes hosted by celebrity chefs, and glossy cookery books purvey style. Standards of appearance, of presentation of food on the plate, are particularly important. So too is the transmission to the reader of the sense that he or she can read various culinary styles. In a world of styles, there is an obligation to become acquainted with the rudiments of many, even those one would never seek to engage with, because being acquainted with their variety is essential to deciphering those expressed and discussed by others.[1] Otherwise one may be puzzled, disconcerted, or appear ignorant. Some of what is learned thereby is reapplied in the domestic arena, altering standards of presentation and senses of authenticity. Cognitive and visual resources are widely available to allow food to become part of the universe of style that people might mobilize to express adherence to a group.

Recent generations have been brought up to have a sense, aspiration and notion of style, which is associated with shopping and selection among commodities. It has become a part of common sense that people make some statement of who they identify with through their appropriation and exhibition of style. Nevertheless, the extent of the spread of neo-tribalism remains in doubt, being restricted in its strong forms to youth and protest groups, though these have impacts greater than might be indicated by the size of their memberships. Less demanding forms of stylization are probably more common. The model of post-Fordist consumption suggests a weaker form, a world of discrete niches but without the intensity of commitment, or the volatility of attachment. Slightly less demanding still is the identification apparent in some fractions of the middle class, which undoubtedly contains style groups, and for whom food is a figure of distinction. Older forms of distinction share some similar characteristics; class distinction and cultural capital have to be actively displayed and deployed on occasion. Mannered behaviour, facility in conversation with aesthetic judgments about food and drink, an appreciation of fashion in cuisine and a respect for formal eating out are characteristic of the professional fraction. Class-based style survives.

Informalization

Many people remain little affected by stylization, its extent restricted by the power of the counter-tendency to informalization. Stylization increases social differentiation on the basis of specialized, symbolically expressed, aesthetic discrimination which, when observed closely, creates a plurality of identifiable, internally homogeneous, style groups. However, there are well-documented counter-tendencies which suggest that observance of social rules and conventions is less predictable, less widespread, and less enforceable than in the past. Greater informality in many spheres of everyday life has been attributed to the cultural revolution of the 1960s. Evidence might include: greater toleration of personal eccentricity in dress and entertainment; more legitimate scope accorded to feelings and emotions; greater freedom of sexual expression; less formal relationships between persons with different degrees of authority in bureaucratic organizations, schools and families; the decay of formal systems of etiquette. Social behaviour has become less authoritatively regulated.

The evidence of informalization in the British food system could be interpreted as enormous individual diversity in which there is a deficit of regulation. Nutritionists and officials despair about the irrationality of a population which ignores guidelines for healthy eating. Gastronomers bemoan the collapse of the conventions which maintain a valued national food culture. Both regret the lack of a universal and collective regulatory framework, and both attribute its absence to the perversity of individuals who abjure substantive guidance in aesthetics and the practice of everyday life. It is tempting to interpret the vacuum left by the demise of what Beardsworth and Keil (1990) called the traditional menu as causing a crisis of personal judgment and a crisis of social legitimation. The evidence suggests something less dramatic, but informalization nonetheless.

Some elements of informalization relate to the relaxation of rules governing behaviour at eating events. The conventions and courtesies associated with fast-food places are less formal and demanding than those of the restaurant, a reason young people in France, for instance, favour them (Fantasia, 1995). It is reported that people eat fewer meals around a dinner table, more in front of the television, where formal manners and rules of etiquette are not appropriate. There is also a greater element of irregularity in frequency, time and location of eating. Any very strong sense of there being a universal standard of good taste, an ideal menu, has gone into abeyance, with the magazines for instance purveying multiple styles rather than suggesting a preferred model. The hierarchical and ordered family meal where parents disciplined their children has become more relaxed as attention to the preferences of children has increased. There is a growing tolerance of diversity in food practice and a somewhat broader definition of what it is appropriate to eat. The definition of the proper meal as containing meat and two veg is losing ground: an opinion poll in 1995 reported only a bare majority of this opinion.

This does not, however, mean that 'anything goes', that all standards are removed, all regulatory devices suspended. Media industries transmit criteria of judgment, even if their recommendations are in some ways contradictory. They also transmit information about fashion, which serves to reduce the legitimation deficit consequent upon the demise of the traditional menu. Simply to respect the current fashion is partially effective as a response to uncertainty (Gronow, 1997). The mass fashion system is widely diffused and provides some general guidance that results in a sense of shared common practice. But at the same time it is permissive rather than prescriptive, so that it does not generate discrete and distinctive style groups. Rather, it portrays an image of diversity within a weak hegemonic endorsement of a mass food culture. There is significant differentiation within the national framework but it is aesthetically undistinguished. Informalization permits the popular culture of a flat world, where nobody and nothing is superior to any other.

Informality thrives on variety. In some respects, the more options there are, the less likely that relevant rules can be formulated or policed. For instance, vegetarians in Britain in the 1990s report decreasing hostility and greater toleration (Simms, 1994). Large quantities of information about alternatives, from innovations in food manufacture to foreign cuisines, undermine the legitimacy of any traditionally dominant set of rules. As Habermas (1976) argued, once the authority of a tradition is challenged and it is shown that practice could be otherwise, it is hard to substitute alternative authoritative injunctions which bind. There is an inevitable residue of scepticism and uncertainty. The state through its nutrition polices, the food industries through their advertising and the cultural intermediaries through the mass media all offer alternative guidance. But none has yet established a new hegemonic culinary code. Consequently, even informal regulation is unsustainable, since few sanctions can be imposed in the face of deviance. Even so, behaviour is not primarily anarchic, characterized by the peculiar tastes of discrete individuals, but is simply becoming more irregular.

Standard responses to expert advice on nutrition are instructive. When faced with contradictory advice, people in Britain frequently invoke the balanced diet as the appropriate basis for their dietary regime. According to common sense, this should include a variety of items, none to excess. But people have not the means to monitor their intake to ensure nutritional balance. Their attitude is casual; concern is expressed sometimes and some expert guidance is followed. But nothing is done systematically. Observance of rules is irregular and perhaps inconsistent. Some of the recommendations of the recipe columns will be followed on one occasion, others on the next. This may achieve balance, but only by accident. They may be no more likely to attain balance than the many who express indifference to what they eat.

9.3 Food and theories of consumption

The diversity of food practices and the contrary trends identified hinder definitive evaluation of theories of changing consumption. Difficulty is compounded by the imprecise specification of some of the theories in the first place. Nevertheless, the accumulated evidence permits some general conclusions.

Behaviour is not uniform in the way that a mass culture thesis might imply, nor is it idiosyncratically personal. People are selective and come to share identifiable patterns of diet with others. There is some evidence of neo-tribal behaviour. Some groups make a positive and conscious social, ethical or religious commitment by means of their dietary behaviour. Their behaviour can be understood in terms of their self-election to a social group maintained in part by its style of consumption. Some behave in accordance with the political logic of new social movements. Others are primarily style groups. Though drawn predominantly from certain sections of the population, being comparatively young and middle class, these are not their most significant sociological characteristic. Rather, it is their attachment to group cultural practice that is revealing. In their observance of a set of fairly strict rules which indicate their identification with a social group, they are better understood as an example of groups of enthusiasts than as occupants of a market niche. However, though a prominent and expanding section of the population, they comprise a minority of Britons and probably will remain so.

Combined tendencies towards individualization and informalization exist, though fears that consumption might become a terrain of egotistical and anomic decisions seem unfounded. The individualizing tendencies contribute sometimes towards greater stylization, which may be expressed personally through concern with the strict disciplining of the body in dietary regimes as well as by neo-tribal attachment. More often individualizing and informalizing pressures coincide. Food behaviour is probably more irregular, more casual and less determined by joint household conventions than in the past. The symbolic dominance of the traditional menu has passed away and there is acceptance of diversity and a greater awareness of alternative cuisines. This is partly a result of changes in household composition and organization. It is encouraged by the indecisiveness of the messages from experts and the media about what it is appropriate to eat. The language of the magazine columns promotes diversity in personal choice. But despite the ambiguities of their messages, their effect in fragmenting behaviour is still limited. There has been no revolution.

If informalization and individualization were overwhelmingly dominant we would expect a greater degree of interpersonal variation in diet than the evidence supports. In fact, expenditure on food is no less strongly socially structured now than in the late 1960s. The forces operating to restrain highly individualized selection include recommendations by the state about eating and health, the popular media circulation of information about the nutritional features of their recipes, and a current obsession with the body. Patterning is reinforced by the distribution and inter-generational communication of taste, a process which Bourdieu would call the transmission of cultural capital. Impressions that a shift has occurred towards heroic postmodern consumption may owe more to the enhanced prevalence of the discourse of choice than to newly adopted food practices.

Many forces operate together to provide collective orientations towards selecting food. Socio-cultural forces, media representations of taste, and socio-demographic circumstances predispose people to similar consumption patterns. The evidence about spending showed considerable persistence in patterns of social differentiation in food consumption. Gender, generational and class differences are much the same now as in the 1960s.

Most remarkable, the extent of class structuring of food consumption showed little change. Distances between classes were not reduced. There is some evidence of the polarization of employed and unemployed, and of the distance between the manual working class and other classes becoming even greater. However, the middle class seems to be becoming more internally heterogeneous. Some members are adopting government nutritional guidelines, caring for their body by carefully calculating the consequences of their food intake. Others are even developing stylish and gourmet pretensions. Both fractions thereby exhibit a degree of cultural capital. However, the social and political significance of variations between classes may now be different. Whereas once class cultures could be ranked hierarchically, with consumption reflecting social position and subordinate groups aspiring to the consumption patterns of those above them, this is probably no longer the case. Instead the hierarchical aspects of consumption are played down, in quasi-democratic fashion: the privileged seem to affirm a pluralist model of aesthetic variations with no one style pronounced superior.

Overall, the case of food provides some evidence in support of each of the general theoretical projections about changing consumption behaviour. Probably the dominant tendencies are individualization and informalization. But the counter-tendencies are nevertheless highly significant, so the total degree of change should not be overestimated. Perhaps the changes could be described as leading from a system of distinction to one of undistinguished difference. Differences in practice are structured along class, gender and generational lines, but without inspiring emulation or consciousness of inferiority and superiority. The 'neo-tribal' visible specialization of diet among some groups is a minority pursuit; the unpredictable, creative and inventive postmodern consumer of food is difficult to locate and may be a rare figure. In the field of food, claims about the decline of class and the dominance of postmodern culture seem much exaggerated.

9.4 Variety and commodification

The social processes that operate to affect consumer tastes are many and complex so it is difficult to reduce them to any simple mechanism or principle. Consumers have a wide range of tastes and preferences that arise from their individual and social differences. From the point of view of orientations to selection, few generalizations are possible: counteracting tendencies have resulted in a constant level of socio-demographic differentiation, and predictions about more stylish consumption patterns are not confirmed. We cannot strongly corroborate any of the alternative theories of change in the nature of consumer choice. However, if we consider what producers are doing, an interpretation of the current *form* of consumer choice suggests itself as a response to the increased variety of products routinely made available.

Between variety and difference: industrial logics

Food production industries in a country like the United Kingdom are faced by two significant problems. First, overall demand cannot increase much. There is a limit to how much any person can regularly eat, and that threshold has already been reached. Generally, if people are to eat a new product they will have to stop eating something else. Second, it is not highly profitable simply to sell people raw foodstuffs. Premium profits are gained from intervening in the chain of provision, thereby adding value. Typically, making something from cheap ingredients and selling with a significant mark-up after processing is commercially the most rewarding strategy. In general, these two restrictions induce competitors in the food industries to find new ways to persuade consumers to abandon some of the work done in the kitchen in favour of a commercial alternative. Commodification occurs as commercial organizations take over more stages in a provisioning process and thereby eliminate activities of a domestic or communal nature. Consequently, market exchanges become more frequent. As Lee (1993: 87) remarked, 'Throughout the twentieth century, capitalism has consistently raised the average standard of living and also extended the commodity-form into previously uncommodified areas of social life.'

Designing new products, apparently with some unique properties, is a principal means by which firms prosper. New or distinctive products are typically more profitable than those of which competitors have made copies. Most new products, in the nature of things, are minor adaptations of existing ones. It then relies on the skills of marketing departments and advertising agencies to create the impression that the items are valuably different or distinctive. This encourages the proliferation of variety. Inventing variety is a key strategy of the producers.

The extensive variety of available food can be explained largely in terms of the further intensification of commodification. This is happening, unevenly but rapidly, in the field of food and, recently, in two contrasting ways. First, the food manufacturing industries have extensively employed new ways of preserving part-prepared food, including freezing, cook-chill, pre-prepared meals, and part-processed ingredients. Second, the catering and hospitality industries deliver ever more food directly to customers. Both serve to reduce the time and effort spent in the kitchen. Food preparation absorbs less labour, shopping more. Increasingly the domestic kitchen is short-circuited.

Theoretically, what is occurring is a substitution between different modes of provisioning, from home to market. The substitution of practices between modes has great significance for understanding the social consequences of consumption. In contemporary society there are four common modes of provision, each characterized by distinctive ways of producing goods and gaining access to the fruits of labour. Market, state, domestic and communal provision are the main contemporary modes. Thus, I can buy a meal in a restaurant; I may prepare it myself or prevail on someone else in my household to cook it for me; if I could mount a successful political campaign, I might get the state to provide it free or subsidized in public restaurants, as did occur during the Second World War; or a friend might make me dinner. These are, in principle, alternative ways to meet my need for a meal. However, the social relations involved in *production* for the market, in the household, in the public sector and in the communal sphere are dissimilar in many important respects. Moreover, the criteria of *access* to goods and services provided in these different sectors are also analytically distinct: purchasing my meal, availing myself of the fruits of the labour of another household member, being in receipt of a state-provided service, or being invited to a friend's table, entail diverse relations of access. Usually these four kinds of processes of provisioning are governed, respectively, by relations of market exchange, familial obligation, citizenship right and reciprocity. It is because services are produced under distinctive conditions and access to them is regulated accordingly, and because this has consequences for their enjoyment, that the substitution of services between modes is so important socially and politically. Commodification involves precisely the increasing dominance of the social relations associated with production in the formal economy over those fostered by communal and domestic production.

Though all are engaged in commodity production, the commercial logics of the industries in the food system are complicated. Many industries are involved – farming, chemicals, food processing, wholesaling, distribution, retailing, catering, etc. They do not all operate in accordance with the same commercial imperatives. Three distinct logics operate in the contemporary industrial food chain, with some tendency for each to be concentrated in a particular sector.

The food manufacturing industries are classic examples of Fordist production. Using new forms of preservation they can obtain considerable economies of scale as the volume turnover required for mass production becomes feasible and they can make large quantities of identical items for increasingly international markets. By contrast, some elements of the system operate in accordance with a post-Fordist logic: the catering trades, especially in small establishments making intensive use of personal service, offer items tailored to the customer's specification; delicatessens with wide ranges of, for example, local farmhouse cheeses and cooked meats offer product differentiation that permits the kind of consumer experience characterized as post-Fordist. A third logic, 'neo-Fordism', has also been discussed in the debate about contemporary industrial change (e.g. Leborgne & Lipietz, 1988). The principal modification of mass production associated with neo-Fordism is the capacity, by the use of flexible machinery and appropriate organizational principles, to produce goods in comparatively small batches, the batches being fundamentally similar to each other but incorporating minor variations. The manufacture of automobiles follows this logic: on each model the manufacturer can offer multiple variations – of engine size, gadgets, upholstery, trim, etc. The purchaser acquires a car which is similar to very many others of the same series, but identical to few. In the food system the supermarket performs in this way. It offers a wide variety of items, mostly sourced through mass production techniques, delivered just-in-time to its branches throughout the country. The supermarket is the prototypical institution of the contemporary system of consumption. It multiplies the *variety* of goods and services available through market exchange. But it is a particular kind of *extensive* variety.

Supermarkets stock many thousands of different products, and a few brands or versions of each one. They routinely make available several different types of tomatoes, baked beans, beers, or whatever. To the customer this constitutes an opportunity to plump for pineapple rather than grapefruit or mango; and for cherry rather than beef tomatoes. There will also be choice between a few brands of most manufactured products. This variety is valued because it permits the appearance of choice. Nevertheless it is predominantly quantitative variety rather than qualitative differentiation. The delicatessen, by contrast, offers the latter: specialization in fewer sorts of products, but holding each in many forms, it delivers *intensive* variety. The aggregate consumer response to extensive variety helps explain the systematic generation of 'undistinguished differences' in the field of food.

Variety and the consumer

The variety of food products readily available is truly staggering. The expectation of this constantly available variety is reflected in the magazine recipe columns which utilize a huge number of products. It has become mandatory to appreciate variety. It is almost unthinkable to want less variety, fewer options. The desirability of variety, for its own sake, has become a central ideological precept.

The wider variety of commodities has no necessary consequences for substantive patterns of consumption. Logically it is perfectly compatible with more stylized and differentiated display and with greater individual expression. It is also compatible with a uniform national pattern, for everyone might consume, in small amounts, the full range of available products. Nevertheless, although greater variety could be used in many ways, there is a dominant orientation in late 20th-century Britain. It is inspired by the diffusion of the consumer attitude, nurtured by the commercial imperatives of product differentiation, and might be called the neo-Fordist manner of consumption.

Kopytoff (1986: 73), reflecting on different forms of exchange, noted that 'commoditization homogenizes value, while the essence of culture is discrimination'. Hence, he argues, all societies preclude some things from commodity exchange. Moreover, people make efforts to appropriate commodities so that they become personal. Since any object is a commodity not by virtue of its substantial properties but because it is destined for monetary exchange, it may cease to be a commodity. Religious relics, family heirlooms, coffins and muffins are among items typically withdrawn from commodity circulation. Kopytoff calls the process 'singularization'. The same process is described by Miller (1987) as re-contextualization, the reappropriation for personally meaningful activity of items that were previously available impersonally in the market-place. He welcomes the opportunities this offers for self-development and amusement in an abundant material culture.

Food has been singularized for centuries; that is to say, it is purchased as commodities and then transformed by often extensive domestic labour before being finally consumed. What is new is the extent of the industrial pre-preparation of a huge variety of foods, circulated particularly by supermarkets on a mass basis, such that identical produce is widely available without regard to place or season. The consumer response is primarily to select in a restricted way from the variety on offer, determining to add less domestic labour than before, and to singularize the commodities by re-combination. The very diverse contents of shopping trolleys become meals by juxtaposition on the dinner plate. Mass-produced commodities are arrayed together in, if not unique, at least very diverse ways. This confirms the impression of a choice having been exercised. It allows the possibility of highly stylized culinary behaviour, as in the model of neo-tribalism. But for most it is not approached in such a fashioned manner, even though the greater variety of products available is appreciated.

Supermarkets, where the majority of British households now do most of their food shopping, simplify selection and make possible a particular form of singularization. This is achieved largely through the *array* of products. To array commodities, in combination, is the basic means of achieving the individuality and singularization that is encouraged by neo-Fordism. For example, buying pasta and sauce from the supermarket, heating the two items and putting them together on a plate is singularization, but of a weak form. By comparison, cooking the same meal from raw ingredients allows more scope for personal intervention, for recontextualizing the materials by stamping them individually. The array is probably also the primary means to impose personal meaning with respect to many other products such as clothing or domestic interiors. People realign, or *permutate*, mass-produced items in personalized ways. But the effect is not highly distinctive. Extensive variety encourages undistinguished difference. This world of consumption is led less by great personal aesthetic imagination, more by the logic of the retailing of commodities.

The purpose of this critique is not to suggest that consumption should be a labour-intensive exercise in pursuit of connoisseurship. The supermarket and the food industries can be congratulated for democratizing access to an extensive variety of produce and reducing unwelcome expenditure of time on cooking. It is a strange, but common, argument that exhorts people to add more of their labour – regardless of the circumstances, their propensities, their time constraints – to purchased items. Given the domestic division of labour typical of contemporary Britain this still means consigning women to a large number of tasks which, despite giving some practical and emotional satisfaction, often constitute an unwelcome burden. Thus do industrial societies retain a romantic affection for the world of local and personal self-provisioning. But the inverse conceit is equally unsatisfactory. Celebration of commercial popular culture in the last twenty years has frequently overstated the extent to which people act to modify and adapt purchases to their own ends. Greater commodification has been justified because the active consumer transforms goods for purposes of identity formation, personal self-development and social membership. This is true of some fields of consumption, particularly of practical enthusiasms. But what the example of food indicates is that active participation may diminish because the commodity can be used in the same state in which it was bought. Shopping becomes a principal practical activity in this part of the lifeworld.

There remain vast areas of practice not yet commodified. The amount of domestic labour added to purchased foodstuffs is still enormous, even in the UK which seems to have moved further down the road of commodification than most other European societies. Mingione (1991), for example, chronicles legion counter-examples from Italian society which appears much less dependent on and much less suffused by commodity exchange. Explicit rejection of commodification is rare, but there are hidden depths of resistance to the reduction of the lifeworld to commodity exchange. Important values, of sacrifice, charity, service, personal reciprocity and gift exchange, resist the logic of the commodity. The survival of the recommendation to express care through food provisioning is limited evidence of the continued resistance to commodified 'convenience' foods. Other symbols of resistance include appeals to tradition, to nostalgic appreciation of the home-made, and to the expressive and deeply skilled aspect of good cooking. The messages emanating from the magazines are not monolithic in their endorsement of consumerism. Nevertheless, the commodity continues its remorseless colonization of other spheres of the lifeworld.

Despite its continued relevance, this is not the place to reiterate the intellectual critique of the commodity, which revived in the 1960s and 1970s before subsiding again. But it is worth remarking on one effect of the current obsession with variety. The expansion of market exchange into spheres of welfare, which characterized British experience since 1979, was sustained by the language of choice. Parents were deemed to be better served by choice of school for their children than by universal high standards of public educational provision. To purchase a house of one's own choice was superior to being allocated one by a local council. The opportunity to select from a variety of options was vaunted as appropriate to a much larger realm than previously – to welfare, security and learning – becoming a new legitimizing principle of social policy. The ideal of universal standards of excellent provision for all citizens in key spheres was abandoned on the grounds that it failed to offer the variety typical of the realm of commodities. Variety poses a challenge to both quality and justice.

In sum, in the quest to explain consumer behaviour the continuing attempts of industry to displace the household and other social spheres must not be ignored. The organization of industry in its pursuit of profit ultimately constrains food selection, although it is not omnipotent: we can grow vegetables, collect berries, make jam, keep chickens. For most people, however, this is impracticable and against the cultural grain of the consumer attitude. Nevertheless, industry has not conspicuously changed tastes or overcome the social determinations of preferences. Substantive tastes, despite exceptions, have not altered decisively. The food industries continue to sell familiar items to customers, but packaged differently and processed to a greater degree than before.

A theory of commodification cannot resolve problems about who buys what, for it tells little about individual preferences, but it does suggest a currently dominant guiding principle of selection – the 'array'. The items to be arrayed are mass-manufactured goods and commercial services. Combination furnishes individuals and groups with a means for distinctive expression, but largely as improvisation within the limits of a collective uniform. A neo-Fordist norm of consumption prepares ordinary people for variety. Thoughtful selection is encouraged: confronted by a vast range of products one can experience and enjoy some degree of deliberation, with the final selection permitting one to be differentiated without being uncomfortably different. Most people do not aspire to be connoisseurs; they do not espouse coherent and explicit culinary philosophies. Rather they make minor modifications, within the bounds of the norms of their own social group, which, in array, add 'a personal touch' colloquially conceived as the outcome of individual choice. Permutation makes the most characteristic link between production and consumption in the current period.

9.5 Towards a sociological analysis of consumption

Commodification is central to understanding consumption processes and, despite its current eclipse by more fashionable approaches in cultural studies, a critical political economy still has much to offer. Nevertheless, a theory of commodification is insufficient to resolve many questions about taste. The notion of the commodity is neutral with respect to what is actually selected, by whom and to what purpose.

Specifically sociological approaches to consumption are closely associated with the concept of distinction which, itself, has usually been understood as class distinction. Thus for commentators like Fine and Leopold (1993), Veblen and Bourdieu are the prototypical sociological analysts of consumption. Given the currently prevalent view that class has declined sharply in importance, sociological explanations might be thought disarmed by the extinction of distinction. I think not. Rather there is a need for a more sophisticated approach to the understanding of social identity. A sociological approach might also contribute to a better appreciation of the way in which commodities are supplemented by other resources as they are transformed for use.

Identity and other purposes of consumption

The analysis of identity has played a central role in social theory recently. In studies of consumption, enormous importance has been attributed to the deployment of goods to create a personal image and to express and sustain self-identity. Two problems have arisen. First, functions of consumption other than identity formation are overlooked. Second, self-identity, because examined with little reference to its inseparable counterpart, social identification, is partially misunderstood.

The concept of consumption has several meanings. Perhaps the easiest way to distinguish them is to consider the purposes of consumption. Broadly, three sorts of ends or 'values' guide consumption: exchange values, use values and identity values.

When orthodox economists talk of consumption they usually mean the purchase of a product and what concerns them is its *exchange value*, its price. The model is that of pure commodity exchange; goods and services are brought to market and equivalence in the exchange is established as a money value. There are other types of exchange, but this is the normal process of purchase in the market sector. *Use values* are, typically, achieved in the process of what is often called 'final consumption', as a good is demolished (eating ice-cream) or as a service is delivered (taking a taxi). This is the sort of consumption that the Marxist tradition had in mind when linking consumption to the reproduction of labour power. The 'pathological' tradition of sociological study of consumption was also concerned with use values, with needs, with what individuals or households achieved as 'final consumption'. Consumption patterns in this approach are the satisfaction of needs or wants.

Recent studies of consumption have problematized the concept of use value, its critique being a primary step in the development of cultural studies approaches. According to Lee (1993), the basis of Baudrillard's critique of Marx was his observation that Marx naturalized use values by assuming that the needs satisfied by consumption were fixed and unproblematic. However, we know that perceptions of need change over time, and that some of the needs (or wants) that are satisfied by possessing objects or purchasing goods are symbolic rather than physical.

The notion that goods and services have symbolic meanings gives a clue to a third kind of purpose to consumption, rarely captured in the economics literature, and that is to enhance one's *identity*. Style, status, group identification, etc. are aspects of identity value, where people choose to display commodities or engage in different spheres of consumption with a view to expressing their identity. Certain objects, and participation in certain activities, are coveted for their social-symbolic value, placing the consumer in a social circle.

If *identity value* is significant, then it is worth considering briefly what sociological processes are involved in its creation. There seem to me to be three general ways in which people concerned to gain identity value may orient their action. They are to be distinguished broadly in terms of their orientation toward different reference groups, the Other that the consumer seeks to impress. That Other may be: members of a different status group, members of the consumer's own status group, or the consumer him/herself. The first process implies the potential for *hierarchical distinction*, a distribution of 'honour' between different social groups. Conspicuous consumption, as Veblen (1925) described it, was a way in which an aristocratic group marked its existence, and its privilege, to other groups. The second process is concerned more with differentiation than with hierarchy. The consumer uses identity-enhancing symbols in order to stress *membership* of a group – perhaps of enthusiasts for whole foods, or as wine-lovers, etc. – but without that entailing any overt social hierarchy. Finally it might be considered that increasingly identity value is *narcissistic* in purpose. You can play identity games on your own, a feature well recognized by advertisers and documented by Lasch (1978) and Bell (1976), where your reference group in the identity game is self. Distinction, differentiation and narcissism are different forms of the enhancement of identity value. Recent accounts have tended to concentrate on the narcissistic themes, on daydreams, on strategies of individuals to seek confirmation of their own self-image, on the desires inspiring, and personal pleasures emanating from, consumption. That consumer behaviour is hugely significant as an expression of personal identity and a grounding for the self is undeniable. However, the other forms should not be ignored. It is impossible to understand modern consumerism without appreciating all three types.

Values and explanation of shifts in consumption: an application

There is a tendency to underestimate the extent of consumer concern with the functional aspect of use value. The claim that food has a use value of the functional sort, meeting the need for nourishment to sustain bodily health, is banal but undeniable. That this can be achieved using a myriad of quite different products is equally uncontestable, implying that there is plenty of room for the expressive use of food. Nevertheless many consumers' foremost criterion for selecting items is their functional effectiveness. Major themes emerging in the magazines were rationalization and calculation. That foods be convenient, health-sustaining and inexpensive were dominant principles in recommendations for dishes.

Practical considerations frequently outweigh ones of style in domestic situations and in institutional contexts. For instance, the Consumers' Association in Britain has a million members, most of whom it assumes are seeking information in order to make rational decisions about which among similar products to purchase. Consequently it concentrates on testing the performance of goods, in effect leaving aesthetic considerations to their readers. So even items with apparent symbolic value are probably being chosen by many people in the light of their practical and functional properties. Use value is not yet irrelevant, for a goodly proportion of consumption is still driven by functional calculations of economy and effectiveness.

Food clearly also sustains identity and it has been suggested that identity value has increased in importance recently. Some people present their patterns of food consumption as symbolic of self. The vegetarian and the gourmet make statements about themselves through their practice. The process of stylization has affected food behaviour and both level and quality of consumption can act as indicators of personal identity. Arguably, though, food is a comparatively marginal way of expressing personal identity and, in any case, operates in much the same way as it did in earlier periods. There are three significant reasons for thinking this.

First, food is one example of many, which might in fact be the rule, where identity formation is a minor aspect of consumption. Many acts of consumption carry no personal symbolic significance. Having refuse collected, attending hospital, using electricity and water, travelling by train and so forth are rarely considered as having kudos or symbolic significance. Interestingly they might have done in the 19th century when having electricity and running water probably were socially significant. It is likely that a great many people, on a great many occasions, eat and watch others eating without engaging in social classificatory judgments.

Second, analytic attention is monopolized by concern with visual identity associated with style, fashion and good taste. Yet food consumption is more an example of the formation of other aspects of self-identity. Certain foods often signify emotional security – comfort food is that associated with feelings of familiarity, childhood dependence and a sense of social belonging. Such sentiments, while essential and deeply ingrained as part of self-identity, do not operate in the visual and aesthetic realm. They are not matters of style and are not subject to judgments about good taste. Indeed, at least in the field of food, style remains a minority concern, a predominantly middle-class preserve. Most people do not aspire to be connoisseurs of food and wine, nor to follow current fashions in foreign cuisine or exotic produce.

Third, projecting self-identity requires a system of social understanding that makes the process of self-presentation seem less of an individual achievement than many accounts imply. The expression of identity requires that audiences can read signs accurately. It is doubtful whether the British population is sufficiently fluent in the symbolic meanings of food *per se* (as opposed to its meanings for social relationships within the family) to make them effective signifiers of personal identity. Simmel (1991), in his essay on style, demonstrated that to give the impression of individuality requires general recognition of the meaning of artefacts on display. Without a shared understanding of the symbolic significance of particular attributes of material possessions, one's attempts at self-presentation will fail. Levels of discriminatory skill of this sort are very variable. With specialized knowledge of particular fields judgments may be highly discriminating, but people generally command extensive knowledge of only a few fields. Most judgments therefore use very general classificatory schemes; people observed are allocated to a social type, essentially negating any attempt to convey a unique individuality. Thus, not many retired people are able to distinguish expressions of individuality within youth cultures. Discriminating perception requires finely tuned knowledge which is not widely distributed. In the field of food most people have difficulty in interpreting signs of distinction. It is therefore premature to conclude that more identity value is invested in, or derived from, food consumption in the 1990s than in earlier decades. There are limits to the capacity of food to express personal identity.

Consumption, practice and use

Most theories of consumption focus almost entirely on the commodity sector. Too little attention is paid to the way that consumers mingle their own labour with goods purchased. Fine and Leopold (1993: 100) argue that the women's clothing sector in the USA was slow to industrialize *because* women had needlework skills, which meant that they could make clothes and alter clothes to fit. Their skills, exercised in the domestic mode of provision, influenced and constrained purchases from the commodity sector. Cooking skills, aesthetic appreciation and sense of design, and a capacity to organize items for display, are all important in food preparation. The impression that satisfaction, not to mention self-identity, is gained directly from astute shopping is a gross oversimplification. Commodities convey meaning partly as a consequence of the way in which they are processed and arrayed. The combination of items is especially important in the neo-Fordist manner of consumption where meaning comes from the configuration and permutation of commodities.

It is equally misleading to ignore the manner in which commodities are *portrayed* to others: many objects and services require narrative to divulge the meanings that make them symbolically effective; so people recount the significance of the photograph, the ring, the sofa or the second-hand car.

Generally speaking, metaphors associated with the gaze, with glancing at the immediately visible, are overused at the expense of the meanings of objects stored and recounted by their owners. Purchasers draw on their cultural capital not just at the point of shopping, but in their capacity to deploy items with skill to create aesthetic and meaningful scenarios. To some extent the aesthetic quality of commodities is guaranteed by the very fact that they have subsequently been tended by a person of taste such that knowledge of the owner is part of the process by which an audience makes a judgment.

Objects as signs need to be put to use; they cannot simply be displayed. Indeed, their application is often a key part of both the impression created and the associated pleasure: for example looking at a piano is less pleasurable than playing it, though it may be better than listening to someone else playing badly! De-skilling reduces pleasure. Much recent cultural analysis of consumption, by focusing on images, has concentrated on items that can be deployed without much extra effort – on clothes, cars and television programmes. Enthusiasms, hospital treatment and food resonate with other rhythms.

Social processes of selection

Sociological inquiry and explanation typically begin from an exploration of collective behaviours, trying to find evidence of group-specific practice. The central variables of sociological analysis are, therefore, ethnicity, education, class, gender, locality and so forth. The presumption is that these social characteristics will both constrain and empower individuals; people learn, and learn to adapt, their behaviour in social groups, networks and associations. Such analysis is most challenged when applied to highly individual acts like consumer choice. In such cases sociology hopes to specify the probability of purchase with a view to identifying commonalities that correspond to social characteristics like age, class or gender. Of course many individuals in those social groups will not share the practical and aesthetic preferences and norms of the majority of the group. However, so long as there is a significant probability of some groups of people behaving differently to others there is *prima facie* ground for assuming some mechanisms inducing collective action that can explain outcomes.

Ultimately, socio-demographic position is not sufficient to explain why individuals buy particular items. This problem is magnified in the field of food because of the situational nature of food choice. What is eaten in any given instance depends upon who is there, what other household members are doing, the time of day, access to providers of food, and so forth. The single event is a poor indicator of taste. This is because reasoning is situationally specific. Whether one has a starter in a restaurant is likely to depend on what companions plan to do; some situations, like buying a sandwich for lunch in a sandwich shop, give little opportunity for exercising a socially significant decision; Tuesday's evening meal will depend on what is left in the fridge since the last shopping expedition; people are less fussy about what they will eat when a guest than when they are at home; people with strong food taboos will often suspend their rules for social purposes in order to reduce embarrassment. Context plays a strong role in the decision. If friends are all going to eat at McDonald's, this is likely to override your personal preference for a pizza. It is, in many ways, permitting oneself to be exposed to particular social situations, and the groups of people in them, that determines what will be consumed. Examining a single eating event is unlikely to give a very strong indication of a person's taste. Mere observation of a few successive eating events will usually suggest a high level of disorder, or lack of rules, because eating is a fragmentary activity.

The social significance of different types of eating situation is demonstrated neatly by Toivonen (1994) in a statistical study of eating out in Finland. Spending in three different settings – on fast food, on midday meals, and in restaurants at other times – indicates that the social determinants of each are significantly different. No social variable greatly affects the probability of purchasing lunch; presumably therefore very many people of varied position and situation, unable to return home during the day for whatever reason, eat commercially prepared meals. Eating lunch out is of no social significance. By contrast, those who spend most on fast foods are the young; and those who eat in restaurants on other occasions are predominantly from higher social classes. Different contexts are dominated by different sorts of people; unequal exposure to particular eating situations is socially determined.

If eating is the sum effect of many situated events, the sociologically appropriate question is whether there is a social logic to the situations in which people find themselves. Sociological inquiry then might identify a second-order logic, that of the chain of situations in which people eat, which would be affected either by socio-demographic variables like whether both partners have full-time jobs, household type and size, or by social forces associated with events, like frequency of attendance at celebrations or the habit of taking Sunday lunch. Thus regularity may exist behind the superficial patternlessness of the single and singular event. Ways of life comprise a chain of situations. Some chains are more regular, routine and predictable than others. People with routinized chains are likely to have more predictable consumption patterns and their planning will be comparatively easy. For other people consumption situations may be less predictable, thus social planning of diet will be more difficult and the nature of their search for food different. Those who are uncertain about their social plans are likely to need more versatile food items: those with more regular social habits may be more predictable in their food choice.

The situational logic governing food consumption tends to give an exaggerated impression of fragmented and patternless behaviour. To uncover principles of taste behind the apparent serendipitous or highly fragmented set of episodes of eating we need to examine the sequence of situations that people pass through. In addition, we need to analyse the 'bundles' of items selected over a number of events or period of time. Trends in consumption of single items are very hard to interpret; it is the combinations of items that is important. Which bundle is chosen depends upon economic circumstances, aesthetic sensibility, or social planning.

Social trends and structural antinomies

Situational logic operates within a wider orbit of social forces. Social scientists have several ways of trying to represent these grander processes. In this book I have tried to characterize the pressures and constraints that orient consumer behaviour both in terms of social trends, like informalization, and structural antinomies, like the ambivalence of modernity. None of these can be observed directly. They are ways of characterizing the broad forces impacting upon the selection of which items to purchase and which meals to prepare. The defining feature of such forces are contested and ways of identifying their operation for purposes of measurement even more hazardous. Nevertheless they offer some means of interpreting the environment in which people make their decisions about consumption. Though other structural oppositions could be deployed to characterize the vagaries of consumer behaviour, there is something reassuring about the way that those apparent in representations of food also apply readily to other fields of consumption.

9.6 In conclusion

The main innovations in the sociology of consumption in the last decade have resulted from a new preoccupation with identity value acquired through the purchase of commodities. Arguably this element has been emphasized unduly, thereby encouraging the view that consumer behaviour has primarily been driven by processes of individualization and stylization. It remains possible that personal, and even more so social, identity is still more readily achieved through non-commodified processes, the outcome of social learning from family, friends, occupational groups, religious associations and clubs for enthusiasts. This is not necessarily to deny that we have learned to manipulate commodities for purposes of appearance more effectively than before, probably as a result of guidance from the marketing industries and partly because the options are greater than before. But the identities thereby created are probably shallow, their significance being exaggerated by the strongest of postmodernist theses. There remains more to self and identity than can be derived exclusively from the spheres of mass media and commodities. Food is a good illustration. Though it does have some application, it is not much used in the playing of identity games. Food scares, anorexia nervosa, family meals and the like seem deeper rooted, in the structural anxieties associated with social membership and emotional security.

Since patterns in the field of food are not generalizable to all other areas it would be inappropriate to suggest that any theory of consumption be abandoned on the basis of the present analysis. It is more fitting to conclude with constructive suggestions about the desirable features of an adequate theory of consumption as disclosed by the case study of food. First, consumption cannot be reduced to the act of purchase, for much work is involved in adapting commodities for use. Much of the time routine domestic labour turns something not immediately edible or normatively acceptable into something that is socially appropriate, thereby achieving what Kopytoff calls 'singularization'. Consumption should not be reduced to shopping. Second, the power of mass rationalization should not be underemphasized when examining consumption practices. Despite evidence of niche consumption and of neo-tribal behaviours which set some groups of people visibly apart from others on the basis of their tastes, fast food, cook-chill dishes, concentration in the retailing sector, and the proliferation of expert practical and technical advice provide constant forces towards standardization. Commodity culture retains its inbuilt tendencies to encourage mass markets. Nevertheless, persistent group differentiation structures consumption patterns; income, class, gender and life-course stage all continue to constrain practice. Material constraints have not dissolved. Still, this fails to deliver an adequate sociological explanation of choice. Individual idiosyncrasies and purely personal tastes must remain forever beyond the limits of sociological explanation. But more attention to the situational logic of selection, put in the context of general institutional forces and collective action, can yet enhance sociological understanding of the field of consumption.

Notes

1 Consumption, Taste and Social Change

1. The implications of this for the conceptualization of class are profound, for a class condition becomes very hard to identify separately from the cultural manifestations of economic position. Yet this is precisely what some (e.g. Goldthorpe & Marshall, 1992) see as the task of class analysis. A historical perspective implies exploring precisely the extent to which lifestyle continues to map on to economic condition. Bourdieu pre-empts this inquiry by definition. What I seek to do is to see whether this definitional move has empirical validity.

2. Among proponents of such a position there is limited agreement about when the process became significant or effective and to what degree it has permeated contemporary societies. Some authors would see mass culture as having replaced class cultures earlier in the 20th century.

3. It is therefore initially reassuring that Sobel's (1981) technically sophisticated approach to examining the relationship between lifestyle variation and structural differentiation did uncover substantial evidence of 'stylistic unity' even from relatively unpromising data on household expenditure.

2 The New Manners of Food: Trends and their Sociological Interpretation

1. The conspicuous, and misplaced, exception is reduced seasonality, which is not a feature of socio-demographic structure and probably ought to be considered as counter-evidence to the push towards more variation.

2. The argument about increased diversity of motivation is obscure.

3. The nine causes of the diminishing contrasts identified are: 20th-century sensitivity to undernourishment; 17th-century pressures to self-control; developments in technology, for manufacturing and transporting food; printing; changes in social power ratios leading to democratization; mobilization of concern for health; the incorporation of peasant cuisine into the bourgeois repertoire; extension of the catering trade in the 20th century; and fashion and inverted snobbery. The causes of the four indicators of increased variation are: the collapse of a rigid style hierarchy; mass circulation of magazines dealing with domestic cookery; the reduced distance between domestic and commercial cookery; and greater diversity of motivation among those involved in food preparation Mennell, (1985: 322–31).

4. My translation of 'Or la situation moderne se caracterise de plus en plus par les manifestations de l'individualisme, de plus en plus par l'autonomie et l'anomie, et de moins en moins par l'hétéronomie (l'imposition au sujet de règles extérieures) . . . .'

5. My translation of '"Comment choisir?" devient une question obsédante, envahissante, parfois insurmontable.'

6. Featherstone's heroic consumer, who exhibits no stylistic unity, would be excluded on the basis of this definition.

7. Bell appears to have changed his mind by the time he wrote *The Cultural Contradictions of Capitalism* (1976).

8. The appropriate terminology for referring to middle-class strata is much disputed in contemporary sociology. One of the problems arises because of empirical uncertainty about the

degree of social homogeneity characterizing people in non-manual occupations. On the one hand, groups of people in non-manual occupations are sufficiently differentiated to make it seem inappropriate to talk of the middle class, since such a term implies a degree of unity. On the other hand, the differences between groups are not sufficiently clear, systematic and pronounced to permit their identification as separate classes. In the light of this genuine quandary, I adopt the convention of using the term 'fractions of the middle-class', which refers to putatively emergent systematic divisions among non-manual workers. Such fractions are identified in the text as amalgamations of different occupational groups (usually of the socio-economic groups used in British official statistics), these being the most informative type of empirical indicator of class position available in the statistical sources that I was examining. Hence I refer often to the middle class, but without seeking to imply that its members necessarily share the same economic or cultural resources.

3 Measuring Change in Taste

1. The data was made available by the Department of Employment through the Economic and Social Research Council's Data Archive and has been used by permission of the Controller of H.M. Stationery Office.

4 Novelty and Tradition

1. The first function explained 64 per cent of variance, the second 24 per cent.
2. This can be deduced from the relative size of the groups' means on the first canonical function, the difference between that of the youngest group in 1968 and the rest being larger than for any other model that was constructed.

Table 4.i *Differences by age in food expenditure by women in single person households, 1968 and 1988*

1968

Canonical discriminant functions evaluated at group means
(group centroids)

Group	Function 1
1	4.04
2	1.00
3	0.30
4	−0.26

Function 1 explained 58.54% of variance

1988

Canonical discriminant functions evaluated at group means
(group centroids)

Group	Function 1
1	2.66
2	1.21
3	0.34
4	-0.52

Function 1 explained 80.73% of variance

Groups: 1. < 30   2. 30–44   3. 45–59   4. 60+.

3. This statistical effect was much less pronounced, but still significant, among men in 1968; but the youngest men are primarily distinguished by eating out and potato products, and by their aversion to the mature diet.

4. Norman (1991) identified a generation of women who were influenced by the cookery books of Elizabeth David.

5. The distinctiveness of people over 60 arises partly because they take few meals at work.

5 Health and Indulgence

1. In the UK, state food policies created between 1930 and 1950 had encouraged expanded consumption of meat protein, dairy products and sugars which, while serving to provide cheap sources of concentrated energy and thus promoting growth in young people, had unforeseen detrimental long-term consequences for mature adults. Substantially increased proportions of food taken from sugar, hard fats and meat resulted in a diet 'whose composition was unlike that ever eaten before, at any time in history, anywhere in the world' (Cannon, 1993: 5). Since the 1960s, reports from various government agencies in North America and northern Europe, and medical reports from the UK and USA, as well as from the World Health Organization, have identified a causal link between dietary trends and the spread of new diseases and causes of death. But the UK government remained reluctant to introduce new policies or to issue dietary guidelines which might encourage altered eating habits.

2. Although it was not an initial reason for choosing 1967–8 as the baseline date for my study, it is fortuitous that this also allows some investigation of the effects of health messages, since 1969 saw the launch of the first government campaign directed towards more healthy eating.

3 More flexible weight-loss diets presumably carry some protection against failure and make the eating behaviour of the person dieting appear less exceptional to others than would have the strict versions proposed in the 1960s and 1970s.

4. See for example Synott, 1993; Shilling, 1993; Featherstone et al., 1991; Scott & Morgan, 1993.

6 Economy and Extravagance

1. There are, of course, other possible interpretations of *nouvelle cuisine*. Fischler (1980: 946) sees its simplicity as a response to scares about food. Wood (1991, 1994: 14) considers it as primarily a social purity movement in which individualist *petit bourgeois* producers collude with young, newly rich professional customers to construct a mythology of its healthfulness and its aesthetic superiority. Its promoters understand the cuisine of one such as Michel Guérard as 'a revolutionary method . . . for producing exquisite food for those people like himself, who passionately loved food but wanted to remain slim and healthy' (in Guérard, 1978: 9).

2. The Club's journal, which became the annual *Good Food Guide* published now by the Consumers' Association, was designed to locate, and thus support, better restaurants; to aid the spread of good taste; and to indicate a demand for fine food which was infrequently met by the British catering industry. The *Good Food Guide* has always exhorted its readers to complain to restaurateurs when meals are of an inadequate standard.

3. Though, once again, it might be pertinent that there is no possibility of gain for the magazines from the advertising of eating out, which may be one reason for its virtual absence.

4. In general, this parallels Heath et al.'s (1985) conclusions on the basis of studies of voting: that the working class itself has not changed much since the 1960s, except that it has decreased in size.

5. All the relationships mentioned in the following paragraphs were significant at a level of 0.05 or better using Kendall's tauB statistic.

6. This may be cause or effect of the magazines' sources of advertising revenue, for they carry very few ads for alcohol or public catering services.

7 Convenience and Care

1. *Woman's Weekly*, 19 Nov. 1991.
2. It is possible to read the Stork ad differently, for it does display a certain humour and it might have been read as giving reassurance about the impression that the short-cut route to pastry might offer. Indeed, why should the manufactured frozen pastry be in any way inferior to a home-made alternative? It could be an anxiety-reducing device (cf. Bauman, 1988). But one suspects that most would read it otherwise.
3. The main exception was *My Weekly*, which offered a recipe for duck instead. *Good Housekeeping* offered recipes for duckling and goose in addition to one for turkey.
4. Much of the material in this section is drawn from two papers written with Kevin Hetherington: see Warde and Hetherington, 1993, 1994.
5. Some 45 tasks or services were investigated, ranging from childcare to gardening, ironing to car maintenance.
6. The index of unconventionality was constructed as follows. In each household where a woman had last done painting, washing the car, cutting the grass or wallpapering, one point was added for each task. If a man did tidying up, hoovering, cleaning the lavatory, cooking the family meal, washing clothes or the main shopping one point was added for each. The maximum possible score was thus 10. These tasks were chosen as ones done by a person of the 'wrong' gender with some degree of regularity (in practice at a proportion of about 5:1) in the population sampled.
7. The level of men's involvement in food preparation is greater than that discovered by Charles and Kerr. In their sample of 200 households, only two men shared cooking equally and a further 23 men cooked regularly, but less often than every other day (1988: 40). This means that the proportion of households which would have a man cooking on any specified day would be about 5 per cent.

8 The Reconstruction of Taste

1. Moreover, 70 per cent said they collected recipes and 62 per cent said they read recipes for pleasure. McKie and Wood (1992: 16) argue that recipes have a moral tone. I don't agree: I think they are technical, with slight overtones of style-policing; I do agree with their endorsement of Barthes's observation that 'recipes set standards, standards which it is often impossible for the everyday cook to achieve'.
2. As Burnett (1989: 314) observes, no comparable data on the daily menus of a large sample of British households has been collected since Warren (1958).
3. Gregson and Lowe (1994) chart the re-emergence of domestic service in the 1980s. This did not entail demand for cooks, nor were many of the job advertisements examined for housekeepers. This is some indication that there are other acceptable alternative domestic or commercial means to manage any problems of food provisioning faced by dual-career households.
4. This criticism suggests the need to concentrate on how people learn and amend their tastes.
5. Ironically, the antinomy with which Bauman is primarily concerned, the ambivalence of modernity, the difficulties of managing the tension between personal adventure and social rootedness, is the one least likely to cause guilt.

9 Theories of Consumption and the Case of Food

1. This gives rise to what Simmel (1968: 44) described as 'the typically problematic situation of modern man . . . his sense of being surrounded by an innumerable number of cultural elements which are neither meaningless to him nor, in the final analysis, meaningful. In their mass they depress him, since he is not capable of assimilating them all, nor can he simply reject them, since after all, they do belong *potentially* within the sphere of his cultural development.'

Appendix: Technical
Details about Methodology

Magazines

The sample

The study involved detailed examination of a sample of women's magazines in each of two twelve-month periods in 1967–8 and 1991–2. The five most widely circulated women's weekly magazines and the five most widely read monthly magazines were consulted. The measure of 'most widely read' was the JICNARS *National Readership Survey*. The second tranche of data was collected before the publication of the relevant JICNARS survey so the magazines were selected on the basis of the circulation figures of the period July 1990–June 1991. The circulation figures are listed in Table A.1. Thus 80 issues were examined in depth, those current on the 15th day of the month, in November of 1967 and 1991, and in February, May and August of 1968 and 1992.

Age and class differentiation of the readerships are shown in Table A.2.

In each issue all articles and columns relating to food were examined. The number of recipes included, the amount of space devoted to food articles and to food advertisements were calculated (see Table A.3).

In addition a systematic sample of recipes was drawn. In 1967–8, every eighth recipe in the monthly magazines was examined, starting with the first recipe in the bestselling magazine and continuing through to the end of the fifth monthly magazine. For the weekly magazines, every fourth recipe was analysed. In the 1991–2 tranche, every fourth recipe in the weeklies was coded and every tenth one in the monthlies. This adjustment was necessary because there were proportionately slightly more recipes in the monthlies at the later date. This produced 114 recipes in the earlier year, 124 in the later period.

Content analysis of the recipes

A detailed examination of the magazines of November 1991, including adverts and pictures, produced a pilot coding frame for recipes, which were then coded. The attempt to apply the same frame to magazines from November 1967 indicated some problems of comparison. A substantially

Table A.1 *Size of circulation and readership of popular
magazines used for recipe sample, 1967 and 1991*

1967–8 (Jan.–June 1968)

	Circulation	Readership (thousands)
Woman	2,760,455	9.817
Woman's Own	2,109,925	9.027
Woman's Realm	1,263,704	5.729
Woman's Weekly	1,673,128	4.352
My Weekly	not available	2.238
Family Circle	1,112,028	4.237
Woman and Home	718,016	3.479
Good Housekeeping	187,126	3.035
Ideal Home	247,173	2.901
She	284,255	2.709

1991–2 (fieldwork period July 1990–June 1991)

	Circulation	Readership (thousands)
Woman's Own	826,320	4.445
Bella	not available	4.369
Woman	801,383	3.118
Woman's Weekly	981,001	2.946
Best	not available	2.945
Prima	655,925	2.651
Family Circle	415,195	2.177
Good Housekeeping	354,375	2.127
Woman and Home	458,403	2.089
Cosmopolitan	408,398	1.848

revised coding scheme was then created and applied to the systematic sample of recipes. Fifty-five categories were deployed. For each feature appearing in a selected recipe, the coding sheet would be marked. Some of the coding was simple: for instance where it was noted how many servings a dish would provide. For other features, it was the words used by the journalist in setting up and describing a sample recipe that were recorded. Text considered relevant included the instructions about preparation of the individual recipe, the preamble to that recipe, and where appropriate the preamble to a set of recipes to which the selected recipe belonged. For example, if the article was entitled 'Quick meals', or if the discussion at the beginning of the article said 'these are quick recipes to prepare', then every sampled recipe in the article would be marked as 'quick'. Thus recipes were examined in the context of the article in which they appeared. Synonyms for terms like 'quick' were, necessarily, also coded, though this of course created some danger of inaccurate recording. This, along with a comparatively small sample size, should be borne in mind when evaluating the results of the analysis.

Table A.2 *Readership profiles of magazines, by age and social grade, included in the sample, 1968 and 1991*

1967–8 (Jan.–June 1968)

	% ABC1*	% age 15–34
Woman	37	40
Woman's Own	37	41
Woman's Realm	36	36
Woman's Weekly	29	35
My Weekly	26	32
Family Circle	49	47
Woman and Home	49	27
Good Housekeeping	59	31
Ideal Home	55	41
She	57	46

1991–2 (fieldwork period July 1990–June 1991)

	% ABC1*	% age 15–34
Woman's Own	39	43
Bella	36	44
Woman	40	42
Woman's Weekly	39	22
Best	40	48
Prima	47	49
Family Circle	52	30
Good Housekeeping	68	27
Woman and Home	53	16
Cosmopolitan	65	64

* ABC1 Institute of Practitioners in Advertising classification of occupations comprising upper middle, middle and lower middle class.

There is a certain spurious accuracy in the results of most content analysis. Precision is compromised by sorting by hand, by employing more than one coder, by need for judgment when deciding what is to count as a synonym, and so forth. At the analysis stage, some categories were felt to be of dubious reliability: in particular, inter-coder reliability was poor with respect to the categories intended to indicate style and they have not been used in the analysis in the text. The categories used for analysis are listed in Table A.4 and the frequency with which each occurred is given.

For analytic purposes the categories were often collapsed to give measures of the frequency of appeal to more general concepts. Thus, the eight principles of recommendation were synthetic concepts, amalgamating subsidiary elements. The scores for the more general synthetic categories are presented in Table A.5, the frequency being given for each annual sample, for weekly and monthly magazines separately. The frequency with which different descriptive aspects occurred (like ethnic attribution, number of servings, etc.) has been referred to in the text, where appropriate.

Table A.3 *Number of recipes, number of pages and proportion of space devoted to articles about food and advertisements for food, 1967 and 1991 (pages and percentages)*

November 1967	Recipes n	Articles pp.	%	Adverts pp.	%	Total pp.
Woman	5	1	1	14	18	80
Woman's Own	8	3	2	7	6	104
Woman's Realm	7	4	6	8	13	64
Woman's Weekly	15	5	6	5	7	72
My Weekly	0	–	–	2	4	48
Family Circle	34	14	11	26	20	130
Woman and Home	15	8	5	12	7	168
Good Housekeeping	14	28	14	20	10	190
Ideal Home	25	29	11	5	2	238
She	60*	15	8	17	9	196

November 1991	Recipes n	Articles pp.	%	Adverts pp.	%	Total pp.
Woman's Own	7	4	6	8	12	68
Bella	12	5	8	9	14	64
Woman	5	3	5	8	13	60
Woman's Weekly	8	4	6	7	10	68
Best	36	11	16	8	13	68
Prima	39	39	21	25	13	188
Family Circle	42	26	20	21	16	132
Good Housekeeping	50	34	15	42	18	234
Woman and Home	31	25	15	21	13	164
Cosmopolitan	7	7	2	19	6	294

* Includes the annual cookery pull-out supplement.

The Family Expenditure Survey and discriminant analysis

The Family Expenditure Survey (FES)

The *FES* was collected in both 1968 and 1988 for the Department of Employment by the Office of Population Censuses and Surveys. It contains a multitude of data on household expenditure which is gathered from a diary in which all respondents record their expenditure for two weeks. This includes spending on housing, cars, clothing, etc. The derived database used in this study for 1988 contained only one week's expenditure, and for households rather than the individuals therein.

The data on food expenditure is broken down into food categories: different types of meat, milk products, etc. There were 65 food and 7 alcohol categories in 1968, 49 food and 9 alcohol categories in 1988.

A main advantage of the *FES* is that it contains substantial amounts of socio-demographic information on income, social class, region and so forth.

Table A.4   *Coding categories for recipes: frequency of reference to attributes of dishes in 1967–8 and 1991–2 (percentages)*

	1968	1992
TRADITION		
1. Traditional: explicit	1	3
2. Traditional: implicit	4	4
3. Authentic and traditional (old-fashioned)	5	3
4. Imaginative/creative and traditional	1	8
5. Explicitly traditional, but not UK	3	10
ETHNIC ORIGIN SPECIFIED		
7. Country/region: explicit	17	22
8. Country/region: implicit	9	5
NOVELTY		
14. Novel: explicit (foreign, fashionable, newly created, exotic)	17	12
15. Novel: implicit	22	5
16. Artistic (*nouvelle cuisine*, decorated celebration cakes)	4	5
HEALTHY		
20. Explicit (healthy, nutritious, balanced, etc.)	4	16
21. Implicitly healthy	1	4
22. Fat, fibre or carbohydrate content stated	–	15
23. Slimming: explicit	5	2
24. Calories estimated (number)	–	54
26. Vegetarian: explicit	1	6
27. Vegetarian: implicit (by ingredients)	–	6
INDULGENT		
28. Explicit (spoiling self, naughty, breaking rules)	2	7
29. Implicit (tempting, etc.)	6	10
CONVENIENT		
30. Convenience: explicit	6	3
31. Convenience: implicit	–	6
32. Quick	14	15
33. Easy	11	22
34. Preparation time given (minutes)	8	44
36. Unconscious (inc. storage & freezing)	6	30
37. Time-saving technology (microwave, pressure cooker, etc.)	4	5
HOME-MADE		
40. Family food: explicit (home-made, Mother's cooking)	20	8
41. Nostalgic	4	2
42. Emotion supporting (comforting)	3	–
43. Extensive time invested	5	–
47. Creative (using high skill)	4	3
48. Didactic (pictures, step-by-step instructions, information about ingredients)	19	62
ECONOMY		
50. Cost per head (£s)	14	23
51. Economical: explicit	15	12
52. Economical: implicit	1	2
53. Expensive/extravagant: explicit	8	1
54. Expensive/extravagant: implicit	2	–

Table A.4 *(cont.)*

FUNCTIONAL
55. Functional/useful (goodness, satisfying, filling, everyone/family/
    children like it)   12   15
56. Functional/sensual (tasty, appetizing, delicious)   46   65
58. Ingredients (quality explicitly mentioned)   7   10

STYLE
63. Advice on accompaniments (substantial foods, like vegetables
    dishes)   14   26
68. Seasonal: explicit (spring, winter, etc.)   8   6

MEALS AND OCCASIONS
70. Special occasion   27   31
71. Whole meal described (i.e. all courses)   8   15
74. Accompanying alcohol recommended   11   12

Table A.5 *References in recipes to aggregated attributes of dishes in 1967–8 and 1991–2, in samples of weekly and monthly magazines (percentages)*

	1968		1992	
	weekly	monthly	weekly	monthly
a) Eight principles of recommendation				
Tradition (1–5)*	23	8	20	30
Novelty (14–6)	18	56	10	33
Healthy (20–4)	20	3	58	72
Indulgent (28–9)	7	19	28	6
Convenient				
aware (30–4)	23	32	65	69
unconscious (36–7)	14	8	33	33
Home-made (40–3)	34	26	12	5
Economical (51–2)	25	11	18	3
Extravagant (53–4)	7	13	2	–
b) Other attributes				
Ethnic cuisine identified (7–8)	9	31	23	28
Vegetarian (26–7)	2	–	12	14
Skilled (47–8)	11	31	62	64
Functional (55–6)	59	50	73	66
Seasonal (68)	2	11	3	9
Special occasion (70)	23	29	18	44
Whole meal described (71)	14	4	5	20
Alcohol (74)	11	11	2	22
N =	44	72	60	64

* For numbered component categories see Table A.4.

In 1968 a sample of 7,184 households was achieved from an approach to 10,752 addresses chosen by a three-stage stratified rotating design in which the primary sampling units are the administrative areas of Great Britain and the local authority areas of Northern Ireland. The same design was used in 1988, when 7,265 households were involved after approaching 12,000. All individuals within the household keep a diary of expenditure for two weeks. A household is defined generally as a person or group of people living at the same address 'having meals prepared together and with common housekeeping' (*FES*, 1968) and only private households are involved.

The *FES* has some limitations for the analysis to which it was subjected. First, because of infrequency of purchase of certain items, a zero expenditure may be recorded by a respondent even though there is a positive average household expenditure on such products. Items like cooking oil or flour might fall into this category; milk and bread are unlikely to. Second, the food categories are broad, including a wide range of items with different functions and/or symbolic significance, The category 'dry cereals' includes muesli, semolina, spaghetti and blancmange powder. The category 'cheese' includes Cheddar and Roquefort. Third, if a considerable amount of money is spent on, say, beef, it will not be possible to determine whether this signifies the purchase of expensive cuts or large quantities. Fourth, personal consumption of food items is not separable in this data set. Although in principle access is available to individual expenditure on food, in practice most households have one or two members who are responsible for shopping, such that individual preferences, and personal consumption, are not directly deducible (except in the case of single person households). Given these limitations, however, it can be assumed that group differences in behaviour tend to be underestimated; social groups are probably more distinct in their food consumption than these data suggest.

Discriminant analysis

Discriminant analysis is a multivariate technique which can be used to create a system of equations (similar in some respects to regression equations) which are used to discriminate between different groups of cases within the sample. The groups have usually already been ascertained, as was the case here. The method can also be used to see which variables serve to discriminate most efficiently between the groups.

Two types of discriminant function were examined, Fisher's linear discriminant functions and canonical discriminant functions (see Norusis, 1986: B8–9 for details). The same classification results occur whichever system of equations is used. In addition, stepwise methods were used to reduce the number of variables in the analysis to allow easier interpretation.

There are many criteria available to distinguish between good and bad discriminatory variables and the method used was based on minimizing Wilks's Lambda (see Norusis, 1986: B17–21). One problem with stepwise methods is that they do not necessarily produce optimal results because they do not attempt to test every possible combination of variables.

As a final test of a discriminant equation's suitability for distinguishing between the groups, a table is produced of the percentages of correctly specified cases and the percentages of cases falling into the wrong categories. If there are patterns of expenditure associated with social groups then we should expect the number of correctly classified cases to be greater than would be expected by chance. So for a four-class system we would expect more than 25 per cent of cases to be correctly classified by the functions if the analysis is working.

The best summary expression of the results of a discriminant analysis is to show how effectively a model predicts the group to which an individual household belongs on the basis of its food purchasing pattern. The summary statistic shows the level to which the variables (food items) allocate households to the class group.

One problem concerns the presentation of the results from a discriminant analysis. The space required to produce detailed results is prohibitive. This particularly affects the linear discriminant and canonical discriminant functions, which register a value for every food item included in the analysis.

Greater Manchester survey, 1990

Questionnaires were completed in October and November 1990 in the Greater Manchester region. The sample is skewed towards a particular population as a consequence of instructing students following A-level courses, including sociology, to administer the schedule to one of their parents. Instructions to the interviewers were designed to obtain roughly even numbers of male and female respondents: it was asked that those with surnames A–H should where possible interview a female adult in their household (usually their mother) and the remainder a male adult household member. If this was not possible they should interview someone else; and if an interview was refused they should record the fact and again interview another person. Of the final effective sample, 62 per cent of respondents were female. Twelve per cent of households contained no resident male adult, so interviewers actually interviewed a male in 43 per cent of the households where that was possible. There were a small number of refusals, 25 in all, of which 26 per cent were mothers, 57 per cent fathers, 17 per cent 'others'.

Of the 334 questionnaires returned, 11 were unusable due to being poorly administered and were removed from the analysis. Thus 323 households were considered. The respondents, because they were almost all parents of an A-level student, clustered between the ages of 36 and 55 (see Table A.6).

People at the life-cycle stage of having teenage children are normally relatively affluent, because parents are still of working age, and in those

Table A.6   *Age of respondents*

	n	% (of valid responses)
30 or less	2	1
31–35	12	4
36–40	76	25
41–45	127	41
46–50	55	18
51–55	26	8
56–60	9	3
60+	3	1
unrecorded	13	–
Total	323	101

Table A.7   *Gender and marital status of respondents*

	%	n
Lone male adult	2	6
Male married or living as married	36	116
Lone female adult	12	39
Female married or living as married	50	162
Total	100	323

Table A.8   *Household size (including all children)*

Number of persons in household	n	%
2	9	3
3	73	23
4	144	45
5	69	21
6	19	6
7	8	3
8	1	0
Total	323	101

households with two adults present both are likely to be engaged in employment. The exception is households headed by lone parents, a group susceptible to poverty. The marital status of respondents is shown in Table A.7. Eighty-six per cent of households contained a couple living as married.

Household size was also large in our sample, due again to the life-cycle stage of our respondents. Table A.8 indicates that about half our sample of households contained four people, counting children.

In all, 46 per cent of households contained a child 15 years of age or less. Only 6 per cent contained a child under 5 years old.

Table A.9   *Occupational characteristics of respondents and their partners if they acknowledge being in employment, excluding inadequately specified*

	Men		Women	
	n	%	n	%
Managerial & professional	103	41	20	8
Intermediate white-collar	47	19	152	60
Personal services	7	3	47	19
Foreman	21	8	6	2
Manual	55	22	19	8
Self-employed	20	8	8	3
Total	253	101	252	100

The sample was an affluent one, as shown by measures of material well-being, housing type, car ownership, possession of consumer durables, etc. For instance, 86 per cent lived in owner-occupied property and 47 per cent of households had regular use of two cars. The affluence of the sample reflects its occupational and class characteristics. The occupational characteristics of the respondents and their partners (where applicable) is given in Table A.9. There were considerably greater proportions of household members in managerial and professional occupations than is typical of the British workforce as a whole. In effect 41 per cent of our households contained a male member of the salariat.

Men's and women's occupational positions were combined in terms of standard sociological classifications. We derived classifications for men separately, for women separately and for households.

Participation of women in the labour market is one of the key variables in standards of living, domestic divisions of labour, etc. Of all principal adult women in the sample 43 per cent were in full-time paid employment, 38 per cent in part-time paid work and a mere 14 per cent were engaged full-time in housework.

Two other features of the sample deserve notice. First, the sample lived in Greater Manchester and its environs, including Bury, Bolton, Blackburn, Salford and Stockport. Second, the households contained many more female than male members: there were 642 women over the age of 16 but only 450 men over 16. This presumably is the result both of young women being more likely to take A-level sociology, hence more of the interviewers (who are co-residents) are female, and of there being more female than male lone parents.

The sample contained neither one-person households nor couples living alone without any co-resident children. The proportion of households in the UK of the types in our sample is about 15 per cent. Hence our sample, on aggregate, contains households that are larger, include more couples, are of higher socio-economic status and are commensurately richer. It is worth pointing out that the sample is comparable with many other earlier sociological investigations, where households containing children and with heads aged between 20 and 65 have been very popular as samples for researching the family, stratification, etc.

Finally, the questionnaires were administered by students, not by a professional survey research organization. The research was partly designed to provide practical ways for students to learn about survey methods. It was not possible to check systematically for interviewer reliability. I was convinced, though, that interviews were undertaken in a responsible and committed fashion by students who were well briefed and conversant with technical aspects of interviewing. There are, in addition, some positive advantages in having household members as the interviewers, since they must be acknowledged experts regarding the content of the replies.

References

Abercrombie, N. & Warde, A. (eds) (1992) *Social Change in Contemporary Britain*. Cambridge: Polity.

Adorno, T. (1991) *The Culture Industry: selected essays on mass culture*. London: Routledge.

Aglietta, M. (1979) *A Theory of Capitalist Regulation*. London: Verso.

Anderson, B. (1983) *Imagined Communities*. London: Verso.

Appadurai, A. (1988) 'How to make a national cuisine: cookbooks in contemporary India', *Comparative Studies of Society and History*, 31(1): 3–24.

Atkinson, P. (1983) 'Eating virtue', in A. Murcott (ed.) *The Sociology of Food and Eating*. Aldershot: Gower. pp. 9–17.

Auty, S. (1992) 'Consumer choice and segmentation in the restaurant industry', *Services Industries Journal*, 12(3): 324–39.

Ballaster, R., Beetham, M., Frazer, E. and Hebron, S. (1991) *Women's Worlds: ideology, femininity and the woman's magazine*. London: Macmillan.

Bartlam, M. (1993) 'Healthy and light foods: understanding the consumer', *British Food Journal*, 95(3): 3–11.

Baudrillard, J. (1988) *Selected Writings*. Cambridge: Polity.

Bauman, Z. (1983) *Memories of Class: the pre-history and after-life of class*. London: Routledge & Kegan Paul.

Bauman, Z. (1988) *Freedom*. Milton Keynes: Open University Press.

Bauman, Z. (1990) *Thinking Sociologically*. Oxford: Blackwell.

Bauman, Z. (1991) *Modernity and Ambivalence*. Cambridge: Polity.

Beardsworth, A. & Keil, T. (1990) 'Putting the menu on the agenda: a review article', *Sociology*, 24(1): 139–52.

Beardsworth, A. & Keil, T. (1992) 'The vegetarian option: varieties, conversions, motives and careers', *Sociological Review*, 40(2): 253–93.

Beck, U. (1992) *Risk Society: towards a new modernity*. London: Sage.

Bell, D. (1976) *The Cultural Contradictions of Capitalism*. London: Heinemann.

Bell, D. (1988) *The End of Ideology: on the exhaustion of political ideas in the fifties*, 2nd edition. Cambridge, MA: Harvard University Press.

Benson, J. (1994) *The Rise of Consumer Society in Britain, 1880–1980*. London: Longman.

Berman, M. (1983) *All That is Solid Melts into Air*. London: Verso.

Bordo, S. (1992) 'Anorexia nervosa: psychopathology as the crystallization of culture', in D.W. Curtin & A.M. Heldke (eds) *Cooking, Eating, Thinking: transformative philosophies of food*. Indiana: Indiana University Press. pp. 28–55.

Bourdieu, P. (1984) *Distinction: a social critique of the judgment of taste*. London: Routledge & Kegan Paul.

Burnett, J. (1989) *Plenty and Want: a social history of food in England from 1815 to the present day*. London: Routledge.

Butler, T. & Savage, M. (eds) (1995) *Social Change and the Middle Classes*. London: UCL Press.

Calhoun, C., LiPuma, E. & Postone, M. (eds) (1993) *Bourdieu: critical perspectives*. Cambridge: Polity.

Calnan, M. (1990) 'Food and health: a comparison of beliefs and practices in middle-class and working-class households', in S. Cunningham-Burley & N.P. McKeganey (eds) *Readings in Medical Sociology*. London: Tavistock. pp. 9–36.

Campbell, C. (1987) *The Romantic Ethic and the Spirit of Modern Consumerism*. Oxford: Blackwell.

Cannon, G. (1993) 'The new public health', *British Food Journal*, 95(5): 4–11.

Charles, N. & Kerr, M. (1988) *Women, Food and Families*. Manchester: Manchester University Press.

Charsley, S. (1992) *Wedding Cakes and Cultural History*. London: Routledge.

Cowan, R.S. (1983) *More Work for Mother: the ironies of household technology from the open hearth to the microwave*. New York: Basic Books.

Coward, R. (1984) *Female Desire*. London: Granada.

Crawford, W. & Broadley, H. (1938) *The People's Food*. London: Heinemann.

Cronin, J. (1984) *Labour and Society in Britain, 1918–1974*. London: Batsford.

Cross, G. (1993) *Time and Money: the making of consumer culture*. London: Routledge

Department of Health, Committee on the Medical Aspects of Food Policy, (1991) *Dietary Reference Values for Food Energy and Nutrients for the United Kingdom*. June. London.

DeVault, M. (1991) *Feeding the Family: the social organization of caring as gendered work*. Chicago: University of Chicago Press.

Douglas, M. (1975) 'Deciphering a meal', in *Implicit Meanings: essays in anthropology*. London: Routledge & Kegan Paul. pp. 249–75.

Driver, C. (1983) *The British at Table, 1940–1980*. London: Chatto and Windus.

Durkheim, E. (1970) *Suicide: a study in sociology*. London: Routledge & Kegan Paul. First published 1895.

Ehrenreich, B. (1983) *The Hearts of Men: American dreams and the flight from commitment*. London: Pluto.

Elias, N. (1978) *The Civilizing Process: the history of manners*. Oxford: Blackwell.

Elias, N. (1982) *The Civilizing Process: state formation and civilization*. Oxford: Blackwell.

England, P. & Farkas, G. (1986), *Employment, Households and Gender: a social economic and demographic view*. Hawthorne, NY: Aldine de Gruyter.

Erickson, B. (1991) 'What is good taste for?', *Canadian Review of Sociology and Anthropology*, 28(2): 255–78.

Ewen, S. (1988) *All Consuming Images: the politics of style in contemporary culture*. New York: Basic Books.

Fantasia, R. (1995) 'Fast food in France', *Theory and Society*, 24: 201–43.

Featherstone, M. (1987) 'Lifestyle and consumer culture', *Theory Culture & Society*, 4(1): 55–70.

Featherstone, M. (1990) 'Perspectives on consumer culture', *Sociology*, 24(1): 5–22.

Featherstone, M. (1991) *Consumer Culture and Postmodernism*. London: Sage.

Featherstone, M., Hepworth, M. & Turner, B. (eds) (1991) *The Body: social process and cultural theory*. London: Sage.

Ferguson, M. (1982) *Forever Feminine: women's magazines and the cult of femininity*. London: Heinemann.

FES (Family Expenditure Survey) (various years), HMSO: Department of Employment; became *Family Spending*, Central Statistical Office, after 1992.

Fiddes, N. (1991) *Meat: a natural symbol*. London: Routledge.

Finch, J. & Mason, J. (1993) *Negotiating Family Responsibilities*. London: Routledge.

Fine, B. & Leopold, E. (1993) *The World of Consumption*. London: Routledge.

Finkelstein, J. (1989) *Dining Out: a sociology of modern manners*. Cambridge: Polity.

Fischler, C. (1980) 'Food habits, social change and the nature/culture dilemma', *Social Science Information*, 19: 937–53.

Fischler, C. (1993) *L'(h)omnivore: le goût, la cuisine et la corps*. n.p.: Editions Odile Jacob.

Furst, E. (1988) 'The cultural significance of food', in P. Otnes (ed.) *Sociology of Consumption: an anthology*. Oslo: Solum Forlag. pp. 89–100.

GBDE (Great Britain Department of Employment) (1976) *Family Expenditure Survey 1968* [computer file]. Colchester: ESRC Data Archive.

GBDE (Great Britain Department of Employment) (1990) *Family Expenditure Survey 1988* [computer file]. Colchester: ESRC Data Archive.

Gershuny, J. (1978) *After Industrial Society*. London: Macmillan.

Gershuny, J. (1988) 'Time, technology and the informal economy', in R. Pahl (ed.) *On Work: historical, comparative and theoretical approaches*. Oxford: Blackwell. pp. 579–97.

Gershuny, J. (1992) 'Change in the domestic division of labour in the UK: dependant labour versus adaptive partnership', in N. Abercrombie & A. Warde (eds) *Social Change in Contemporary Britain*. Cambridge: Polity. pp. 70–94.

GFG (*Good Food Guide*) (various years) London: Consumers' Association and Hodder & Stoughton.

Giddens, A. (1991) *Modernity and Self-Identity*. Cambridge: Polity.

Gofton, L. (1995) 'Convenience and the moral status of consumer practices', in D. Marshall (ed.) *Food Choice and the Consumer*. Glasgow: Blackie. pp. 152–81.

Gofton, L. and Ness, M. (1991) 'Twin trends: health and convenience in food change or who killed the lazy housewife?', *British Food Journal*, 93(7): 17–23.

Goldthorpe, J. (1982) 'On the service class, its formation and future', in A. Giddens & G. MacKenzie (eds) *Classes and the Division of Labour*. Cambridge: Cambridge University Press. pp. 162–85.

Goldthorpe, J. (1987) *Social Mobility and Class Structure in Britain*. 2nd edition. Oxford: Clarendon Press.

Goldthorpe, J. (1995) 'The service class revisited', in T. Butler & M. Savage (eds) *Social Change and the Middle Classes*. London: UCL Press. pp. 313–29.

Goldthorpe, J. & Marshall, G. (1992) 'The promising future of class analysis: a response to recent critiques', *Sociology*, 26: 381–400.

Goodman, D. & Redclift, M. (1991) *Refashioning Nature: food ecology and culture*. London: Routledge.

Gorz, A. (1985) *Paths to Paradise*. London: Pluto.

Graham, H. (1987) 'Being poor: perceptions and coping strategies of lone mothers', in J. Brannen & G. Wilson (eds) *Give and Take in Families: studies in resource distribution*. London: Allen & Unwin. pp. 56–76.

Gregson, N. & Lowe, M. (1994) *Servicing the Middle Classes: class, gender and waged domestic labour in contemporary Britain*. London: Routledge.

Gronow, J. (1991) 'Need, taste and pleasure: understanding food and consumption', mimeo, Dept of Sociology, University of Helsinki.

Gronow, J. (1997) *Sociology of Taste*. London: Routledge.

Guérard, M. (1978) *Michel Guérard's Cuisine Gourmande*. London: Macmillan.

Habermas, J. (1976) *Legitimation Crisis*. London: Heinemann.

Hamilton, M. (1993) 'The beliefs and values of followers of distinctive diets: whole, health and organic food consumption – alternative therapy or spiritual quest?' Paper delivered at Arbeitsgemeinschaft Ernährungsverhalten e.V. 16th Annual Scientific Meeting, Potsdam. October.

Harvey, D. (1989) *The Condition of Postmodernity*. Oxford: Blackwell.

Heath, A., Jowell, R. & Curtice J. (1985) *How Britain Votes*. Oxford: Pergamon.

Hebdige, D. (1988) *Hiding in the Light: on images and things*. London: Comedia.

Hermes, J. (1995) *Reading Women's Magazines*. Cambridge: Polity.

Hetherington, K. (1992) 'Stonehenge and its festival: spaces of consumption', in R. Shields (ed.) *Lifestyle Shopping: the subject of consumption*. London: Routledge. pp. 83–98.

Hirsch, F. (1978) *Social Limits to Growth*. London: Routledge & Kegan Paul.

Hirschman, A. (1982) *Shifting Involvements: private interest and public action*. Princeton, NJ: Princeton University Press.

Hobsbawm, E. (1978) 'The forward march of labour halted?', in E. Hobsbawm & M. Jacques (eds) *The Forward March of Labour Halted?* London: Verso. pp. 1–19.

Hobsbawm, E. & Ranger, T. (eds) (1983) *The Invention of Tradition*. Cambridge: Cambridge University Press.

Hochschild, A.R. (1983) *The Managed Heart: the commercialization of human feeling*. Berkeley, CA: California University Press.

Ilmonen, K. (1991) 'Change and stability in Finnish eating habits', in E. Furst, R. Prattala, M.

Eckstrom, L. Holm, & U. Kjaernes, (eds) *Palatable Worlds: sociocultural food studies*. Oslo: Solum Forlag. pp. 169–84.

Jenkins, R. (1992) *Pierre Bourdieu*. London: Routledge.

JICNARS (Joint Industry Committee for National Readership Surveys) (various years) *National Readership Survey*. London: Institute of Practitioners in Advertising.

Karisto, A., Prattala, R. & Berg, M.-A. (1993) 'The good the bad and the ugly: differences and changes in health related lifestyles', in U. Kjaernes, L. Holm, M. Ekstrom, E. Furst & R. Prattala (eds) *Regulating Markets, Regulating People: on food and nutrition policy*. Oslo: Novus Forlag. pp. 185–204.

Kopytoff, I. (1986) 'The cultural biography of things: commoditization as process', in A. Appadurai (ed.) *The Social Life of Things: commodities in cultural perspective*. Cambridge: Cambridge University Press. pp. 64–94.

Lasch, C. (1978) *The Culture of Narcissism: American life in an age of diminishing expectations*. New York: Norton.

Leborgne, D. & Lipietz, A. (1988) 'New technologies, new modes of regulation', *Environment and Planning D: society and space*, 6(3): 263–80.

Lee, M.J. (1993) *Consumer Culture Reborn: the cultural politics of consumption*. London: Routledge.

Levenstein, H. (1988) *Revolution at the Table: the transformation of the American diet*. Oxford: Oxford University Press.

Levenstein, H. (1993) *Paradox of Plenty: a social history of eating in modern America*. Oxford: Oxford University Press.

Lien, M. (1995) 'Fuel for the body – nourishment for dreams: contradictory roles of food in contemporary Norwegian advertising', *Journal of Consumer Policy*, 18: 157–86.

Linder, S.B. (1970) *The Harried Leisure Class*. New York: Columbia University Press.

Lukes, S. (1975) *Emile Durkheim: his life and work*. Harmondsworth: Penguin.

Lury, C. (1996) *Consumer Culture*. Cambridge: Polity.

Lury, C. & Warde, A. (1997) 'Expert knowledge and change in the advertising industry', in M. Nava, A. Blake, I. MacRury & B. Richards (eds) *Buy This Book: studies in advertising and consumption*. London: Routledge.

McCracken, E. (1993) *Decoding Women's Magazines: from Mademoiselle to Ms*. London: Macmillan.

Mack, J. & Lansley, S. (1985) *Poor Britain*. London: Allen & Unwin.

McKie, L. & Wood, R. (1992) 'People's sources of recipes: some implications for an understanding of food-related behaviour', *British Food Journal*, 94(2): 12–17.

McRae, S. (1990) 'Women and class analysis', in J. Clark, C. Modgil & S. Modgil (eds) *John H. Goldthorpe: consensus and controversy*. Brighton: Falmer. pp. 117–34.

Maffesoli, M. (1988) 'Jeux de masques: postmodern tribalism', *Design Issues*, 4(1–2): 141–51.

Martens, L. & Warde, A. (1995) 'The future of eating out'. Paper presented at ESRC/Flora Nation's Diet conference, London, November.

Martin, B. (1981) *A Sociology of Contemporary Cultural Change*. Oxford: Blackwell.

Mennell, S. (1985) *All Manners of Food: eating and taste in England and France from the Middle Ages to the present*. Oxford: Blackwell.

Mennell, S., Murcott, A. & van Otterloo, A. (1992) *The Sociology of Food: eating, diet and culture*. London: Sage.

Metcalfe, A. (1992) 'The curriculum vitae: confessions of a wage labourer', *Work, Employment and Society*, 6(4): 619–41.

Miller, D. (1987) *Material Culture and Mass Consumption*. Oxford: Blackwell.

Mingione, E. (1991) *Fragmented Societies: a sociology of economic life beyond the market paradigm*. Oxford: Blackwell.

Moorhouse, H. (1983) 'American automobiles and workers' dreams', *Sociological Review*, 31(3): 403–26.

Murcott, A. (1982) 'On the social significance of the "cooked dinner" in South Wales', *Social Science Information*, 21: 677–95.

Murcott, A. (1990) 'From "government orange" to "no milk, unless it's skimmed": nutrition and health in post-war Britain'. Paper delivered to Institute of Contemporary British History conference 'Understanding Post-War British Society', London School of Economics.

NFS, National Food Survey Committee, MAFF (various years) *Household Food Consumption and Expenditure*, London: HMSO.

Norman, J. (1991) 'Cooking by the book: the influence of cookery books on eating habits in Britain'. Paper delivered to the British Association annual conference, Plymouth. August.

Norusis, M. (1986) *The SPSS Guide to Data Analysis for SPSSX*. Chicago, IL: SPSS Inc.

Oakley, A. (1974) *The Sociology of Housework*. Oxford: Martin Robertson.

Pahl, J. (1989) *Money and Marriage*. London: Macmillan.

Pahl, R. (1984) *Divisions of Labour*. Oxford: Blackwell.

Pahl, R. (1988) *On Work: historical, comparative and theoretical approaches*. Oxford: Blackwell.

Pahl, R. (1989) 'Is the emperor naked? Some questions on the adequacy of sociological theory in urban and regional research', *International Journal of Urban and Regional Research*, 13(4): 709–20.

Parents for Safe Food (1990) *Safe Food Handbook*. London: Ebury Press.

Payne, M. & Payne, B. (1993) *Eating Out in the UK: market structure, consumer attitudes and prospects for the 1990s* (Economist Intelligence Unit Special Report 2169). London: Economist Intelligence Unit and Business International.

Pinch, S. (1986) *Cities and Services: the geography of collective consumption*. London: Routledge.

Piore, M. & Sabel, C. (1984) *The Second Industrial Divide*. New York: Basic Books.

Riley, M. (1994) 'Marketing eating out', *British Food Journal*, 96(10): 15–18.

Ritson, C. & Hutchins, R. (1990) 'The consumption revolution', in J.M. Slater (ed.) *Fifty Years of the National Food Survey, 1940–90*. London: HMSO. pp. 35–46.

Ritzer, G. (1993) *The McDonaldization of Society*. Thousand Oaks, CA: Pine Forge Press.

Savage, M. (1989) 'Spatial differences in modern Britain', in C. Hamnett, L. McDowell & P. Sarre (eds) *The Changing Social Structure*. London: Sage. pp. 244–68.

Savage, M., Barlow, J., Dickens, P. & Fielding, T. (1992) *Property, Bureaucracy and Culture: middle-class formation in contemporary Britain*. London: Routledge.

Schulze, G. (1992) *Die Erlebnisgesellschaft: Kultursoziologie der Gegenwart*. Frankfurt am Main: Suhrkamp.

Scott, S. & Morgan, D. (1993) (eds) *Body Matters: essays on the sociology of the body*. Brighton: Falmer.

Sheihan, A., Marmot, M., Taylor, B. & Brown, R. (1990) 'Recipes for health', *British Social Attitudes*, 7: 145–60.

Shilling, C. (1993) *The Body and Social Theory*. London: Sage.

Silver, H. (1987) 'Only so many hours in a day: time constraints, labour pools and demand for consumer services', *Service Industries Journal*, 7(4): 26–45.

Simmel, G. (1968) 'On the concept and the tragedy of culture', in *Georg Simmel: the conflict in modern culture and other essays*. New York: Teachers' College Press. pp. 27–46. First published 1911.

Simmel, G. (1991) 'The problem of style', *Theory Culture & Society*, 8(3): 63–71. First published 1908.

Simmonds, D. (1990) 'What's next?: fashion, foodies and the illusion of freedom', in A. Tomlinson (ed.) *Consumption, Identity and Style: marketing, meanings and the packaging of pleasure*. London: Routledge. pp. 121–38.

Simms, C. (1994) 'A study of the social relations involved in vegetarianism'. MA dissertation, Lancaster University.

Smith, C., Child, J. & Rowlinson, M. (1989) *Reshaping Work: the Cadbury experience*. Cambridge: Cambridge University Press.

Sobel, M. (1981) *Lifestyle and Social Structure: concepts, definitions, analyses*. New York: Academic Press.

Social Trends (various years). London: HMSO.

226 *References*

Synott, A. (1993) *The Body Social: symbolism, self and society*. London: Routledge.
Toivonen, T. (1994) 'Does consumption determine social class?: on the changing pattern of consumption determination', *Journal of Consumer Studies and Home Economics*, 18: 45–63.
Tomlinson, G. (1986) 'Thought for food: a study of written instructions', *Symbolic Interaction*, 9(2): 201–16.
Tomlinson, M. & Warde, A. (1993) 'Social class and change in the eating habits of British households', *British Food Journal*, 95(1): 3–11.
Townsend, P., Phillimore, P. & Beattie, A. (1988) *Health and Deprivation; inequality and the North*. London: Croom Helm.
Turner, B. (1982) 'The government of the body: medical regimens and the rationalization of diet', *British Journal of Sociology*, 33(2): 254–69.
Urry, J. (1990) *The Tourist Gaze: leisure and travel in contemporary societies*. London: Sage.
Veblen, T. (1925) *The Theory of the Leisure Class: an economic study of institutions*. London: Allen & Unwin. First published 1899.
Wandel, M. (1994) 'Understanding consumer concern about food-related health risks', *British Food Journal*, 96(7): 35–40.
Warde, A. (1991) 'Gentrification as consumption: issues of class and gender', *Environment and Planning D: society and space*, 9(2): 223–32.
Warde, A. (1993) 'Producers, profits and pictures: an analysis of advertisements for manufactured food', in U. Kjaernes, L. Holm, M. Ekstrom, E. Furst & R. Prattala (eds) *Regulating Markets, Regulating People: on food and nutrition policy*. Oslo, Novus Forlag. pp. 137–52.
Warde, A. (1994a) 'Consumers, consumption and post-Fordism', in R. Burrows and B. Loader (eds) *Towards a post-Fordist Welfare State?* London: Routledge. pp. 223–38.
Warde, A. (1994b) 'Consumers, identity and belonging: reflections on some theses of Zygmunt Bauman', in N. Abercrombie, R. Keat & N. Whiteley (eds) *The Authority of the Consumer*. London: Routledge. pp. 58–74.
Warde, A. & Hetherington, K. (1993) 'A changing domestic division of labour?: issues of measurement and interpretation', *Work Employment and Society*, 7(1): 23–45.
Warde, A. & Hetherington, K. (1994) 'English households and routine food practices: a research note', *Sociological Review*, 42(4): 758–78.
Warde, A., Hetherington, K. & Soothill, K. (1991) *Divisions of Labour Revisited: Greater Manchester, 1990*. Lancaster: Lancaster Regionalism Group Working Paper 44.
Warde, A., Soothill, K., Shapiro, D. & Papantonakou, A. (1989) *Divisions of labour in NorthWest England*. Lancaster: Lancaster Regionalism Group Working Paper 38.
Warde, A. & Tomlinson, M. (1995) 'Taste among the middle classes, 1968–88', in T. Butler & M. Savage (eds) *Social Change and the Middle Classes*. London: UCL Press. pp. 241–56.
Warren, G. (ed.) (1958) *The Foods We Eat*. London: Cassell.
Wernick, A. (1991) *Promotional Culture: advertising, ideology and symbolic expression*. London: Sage.
Wilson, G. (1989) 'Family food systems, preventive health and dietary change: a policy to increase the health divide', *Journal of Social Policy*, 18: 167–85.
Winship, J. (1987) *Inside Women's Magazines*. London: Pandora.
Wood, R. (1991) 'The shock of the new: a sociology of nouvelle cuisine', *Journal of Consumer Studies and Home Economics*, 15(4): 327–38.
Wood, R. (1994) 'Dining out on sociological neglect', *British Food Journal*, 96(10): 10–14.
Wood, R. (1995) *The Sociology of the Meal*. Edinburgh: Edinburgh University Press.
Wouters, C. (1986) 'Formalization and informalization: changing tension balances in civilizing processes', *Theory Culture & Society*, 3(1): 1–18.
Young, M. and Willmott, P. (1973) *The Symmetrical Family: a study of work and leisure in the London region*. Harmondsworth: Penguin.

Index